Sustaining Linguistic Diversity

Georgetown University Round Table on Languages and Linguistics series
Selected Titles

Crosslinguistic Research in Syntax and Semantics: Negation Tense and Clausal Architecture
RAFFAELLA ZANUTTINI, HÉCTOR CAMPOS, ELENA HERBURGER, PAUL H. PORTNER, EDITORS

Discourse and Technology: Multimodal Discourse Analysis
PHILIP LEVINE AND RON SCOLLON, EDITORS

Educating for Advanced Foreign Language Capacities
HEIDI BYRNES, HEATHER D. WEGER-GUNTHARP, KATHERINE SPRANG, EDITORS

Language in Our Time: Bilingual Education and Official English, Ebonics and Standard English, Immigration and Unz Initiative
JAMES E. ALATIS AND AI-HUI TAN, EDITORS

Language in Use: Cognitive and Discourse Perspectives on Language and Language Learning
ANDREA E. TYLER, MARI TAKADA, YIYOUNG KIM, AND DIANA MARINOVA, EDITORS

Linguistics, Language, and the Professions: Education, Journalism, Law, Medicine, and Technology
JAMES E. ALATIS, HEIDI E. HAMILTON, AND AI-HUI TAN, EDITORS

Linguistics, Language, and the Real World: Discourse and Beyond
DEBORAH TANNEN AND JAMES E. ALATIS, EDITORS

SUSTAINING LINGUISTIC DIVERSITY
Endangered and Minority Languages and Language Varieties

Kendall A. King, Natalie Schilling-Estes, Jia Jackie Lou,
Lyn Fogle, and Barbara Soukup, *Editors*

GEORGETOWN UNIVERSITY PRESS
Washington, D.C.

Georgetown University Press, Washington, D.C. www.press.georgetown.edu
© 2008 by Georgetown University Press. All rights reserved. No part of this
book may be reproduced or utilized in any form or by any means, electronic
or mechanical, including photocopying and recording, or by any information
storage and retrieval system, without permission in writing from the publisher.

Library of Congress Cataloging-in-Publication Data

Sustaining linguistic diversity : endangered and minority languages and language
varieties / Kendall A. King . . . [et al.], editors.
    p. cm.—(Georgetown university round table on languages and linguistics series)
    Includes bibliographical references.
    ISBN 978-1-58901-192-2 (alk. paper)
1. Language attrition. 2. Linguistic minorities. 3. Language revival. 4. Language policy.
I. King, Kendall A., 1969–
    P40.5.L28S87 2008
    306.44—dc22   2007019460

♾ This book is printed on acid-free paper meeting the requirements of the American
National Standard for Permanence in Paper for Printed Library Materials.

15 14 13 12 11 10 09 08   9 8 7 6 5 4 3 2
First printing

Printed in the United States of America

Contents

PART III: DEVELOPING

AFTERWORD

▨ Illustrations

Introduction

KENDALL A. KING, NATALIE SCHILLING-ESTES, LYN FOGLE, JIA JACKIE LOU, AND BARBARA SOUKUP

IN THE LAST THREE DECADES, what might be called the field of endangered and minority languages has evolved rapidly. In short order we've moved from the initial dire warnings of linguists such as Michael Krauss in the 1980s and early 1990s (Krauss 1992), to the explosion of media attention on "last speakers" throughout the 1990s, to, in more recent years, the development and refinement of theoretical frameworks for assessing linguistic health and endangerment as well as critiques of some of the assumptions underlying those models (e.g., UNESCO Ad Hoc Expert Group on Endangered Languages 2003; Fishman 1991, 2001; King 2001; Nettle and Romaine 2000; Romaine 2006). Further, we have seen the rapid development of organizations, funding programs, and community-based efforts to document, maintain, and develop receding languages and language varieties (Grenoble and Whaley 1998, 2006; Hinton and Hale 2001; UNESCO Endangered Languages Programme 2007).

A wide range of individuals has participated in these developments, with members of endangered language communities rightly playing an increasingly vocal role. Yet while general interest, scientific investigation, and practical work have exploded over the last decades, efforts have also become more differentiated and diffuse and, in turn, more embedded in academic subareas and in particular local endangerment situations. As a result, the connections and comparisons—across different research paradigms but also across different communities—have become more difficult to make. Concomitantly, as more descriptive work from a wide range of world regions and perspectives has been conducted, there is growing recognition that some of our current terminology, frameworks, and research approaches are inadequate. As more and more data are gathered, even seemingly basic questions become increasingly complicated: How do we determine which languages count as "endangered"—or even "minority," for that matter? Who makes such classifications, and what's at stake? Moreover, what are the different meanings and functions of "language revitalization" in linguistic, political, and ideological terms? There are pressing practical questions as well. For instance, how do we make sure that language data are widely accessible while also preserving confidentiality? How do we maintain the trust of the speakers whose generosity we depend on as we seek to further our knowledge of the full scope of human language variety? More broadly, should we focus solely on the most highly endangered and smallest languages, or can we also learn about the linguistic and

1

social underpinnings of the recession of linguistic diversity by studying endangered dialects of majority languages? And, finally, how far and in what ways should linguists and other researchers move beyond academic circles in working with language and dialect endangerment? What are the best modes and models of collaboration in defining, documenting, and developing minority and endangered languages and language varieties?

This book seeks to address these and related questions. Our aim for this volume is to bring together a diverse group of papers written by active researchers and practitioners involved in different types of work with minority and endangered languages and language varieties around the globe. These papers were initially presented at the Georgetown University Round Table conference in Washington, D.C., March 3–5, 2006. We have organized these into three complementary strands: defining, documenting, and developing, each representing a major area of recent work.

By "defining," we refer to efforts that address how languages and language varieties are best classified, for instance, as "endangered" or "moribund," and equally important, what the implications of such classifications are, and who should have the final say in making them. In the first part of the book, Suzanne Romaine examines responses to different endangerment situations, ranging from noninterference, to documentation, to active involvement in maintenance and revitalization efforts, arguing that revitalizing an endangered language is integrally linked to maintaining the community who speaks it. Wesley Y. Leonard questions the very notion of an extinct language and, from a first-person perspective, discusses the implications of different metaphors for describing the status of the Miami language. M. Paul Lewis, in turn, proposes a general system for establishing parameters of language vitality in view of standardizing data collection.

The second part of the book centers on the documentation and description of endangered languages and focuses both on best practices, methods, and goals in documentation and on up-to-the-minute reports from the field. Gregory R. Guy and Ana M. S. Zilles provide exacting documentation of the continuing loss of diversity in vernacular Brazilian Portuguese and convincingly demonstrate that such loss is a grave blow to linguistic science because it diminishes our resources for exploring how and why intralanguage diversity arises, develops, and patterns. Christine Mallinson also explores diversity in a minority language variety, though her focus is on a minority within a minority (African Americans in predominately white Appalachia) and on individuals' agentive use of linguistic resources from a variety of dialects in shaping and reshaping personal and group identity. Emily McEwan-Fujita, through an ethnographic study of a Gaelic language-planning organization in Scotland, analyzes the negotiation of language ideologies in the everyday practices of language revitalization professionals. Finally, Nancy H. Hornberger draws on Bakhtinian theory to discuss the role of voice in forming identities for young biliterate children.

The third part of the book analyzes current practices in developing endangered languages and dialects, and in particular language revitalization efforts and outcomes. Tadhg Ó hIfearnáin offers new data describing the language situation in the Gaeltacht region of Ireland and tackles the complicated issue of how promoting standardization may actually hinder language revitalization efforts. Leena Huss outlines the mostly positive impact of the ratification of the European Charter for Regional or Minority Languages in Norway and Sweden while cautioning that policies must be tailored to suit the needs of individual minority language communities as well as regularly evaluated and revised to ensure optimal outcomes. Paul D. Fallon presents the case of the Blin language of Eritrea and focuses on five areas of corpus planning (determination, codification, elaboration, implementation, and cultivation), suggesting a need for more materials in the language. And Teresa L. McCarty, Mary Eunice Romero-Little, and Ofelia Zepeda draw from a major ethnographic project to describe the current ideological and social practices surrounding Navajo loss and revitalization.

The last two chapters in this part consider language diversity in the United States overall. Joy Kreeft Peyton, Maria Carreira, Shuhan Wang, and Terrence G. Wiley emphasize language preservation and revitalization through nurturing rather than discouraging existing linguistic diversity, for example, through strengthening heritage language education efforts. Similarly, Walt Wolfram stresses the importance of educating the public on the value of linguistic and cultural diversity not only in schools but also via informal and entertaining educational venues including museum displays and video documentaries.

Finally, the two chapters in our afterword focus on the human lives at stake. Elana Shohamy, drawing from historical analysis of one of the most well-known cases of revitalization, that of Hebrew in Israel, forces us to consider the human costs and personal sacrifices that are often part of language revitalization efforts. William Labov concludes with an eloquent reminder of the human value of the speakers of minority languages and language varieties and echoes back to the first chapter in our volume in his assertion that linguistic diversity must never be purchased at the price of minority speakers' autonomy and quality of life but can only be sustained in a world where diversity in all its forms is embraced and treasured.

We warmly thank all of the contributors as well as the hundreds of participants of GURT 2006. Our hope is that the efforts presented here help to advance our collective understanding of the best models, approaches, and practices for sustaining linguistic diversity, one of the most important challenges of our generation and for those to come.

REFERENCES

Fishman, Joshua A. 1991. *Reversing language shift: Theoretical and empirical foundations of assistance to threatened languages.* Clevedon, UK: Multilingual Matters.
———, ed. 2001. *Can threatened languages be saved? Reversing language shift, revisited: A 21st century perspective.* Clevedon, UK: Multilingual Matters.
Grenoble, Lenore A., and Lindsay J. Whaley, eds. 1998. *Endangered languages: Language loss and community response.* Cambridge, UK: Cambridge University Press.
———. 2006. *Saving languages: An introduction to language revitalization.* Cambridge, UK: Cambridge University Press.
Hinton, Leanne, and Ken Hale, eds. 2001. *The green book of language revitalization in practice.* New York: Academic Press.
King, Kendall A. 2001. *Language revitalization processes and prospects: Quichua in the Ecuadorian Andes.* Clevedon, UK: Multilingual Matters.

Krauss, Michael E. 1992. The world's languages in crisis. *Language* 68:4–10.

Nettle, Daniel, and Suzanne Romaine. 2000. *Vanishing voices: The extinction of the world's languages.* Oxford, UK: Oxford University Press.

Romaine, Suzanne. 2006. Planning for the survival of linguistic diversity. *Language Policy* 5:443–75.

UNESCO Ad Hoc Expert Group on Endangered Languages. 2003. Language vitality and endangerment. UNESCO. www.unesco.org/culture/en/endangeredlanguages (accessed October 1, 2007).

UNESCO Endangered Languages Programme. 2007 UNESCO. www.unesco.org/culture/en/endangered languages (accessed October 1, 2007).

I

Defining

1

Linguistic Diversity, Sustainability, and the Future of the Past

Merton College, University of Oxford

ONE OF THE MOST STRIKING FEATURES of our world is its astonishing diversity. This diversity is reflected not only in the rich variety of plant and animal species and ecosystems in nature but also in the variety of cultures and languages in human societies. In his inimitable fashion Woody Allen once quipped, "I am [at] two with nature."[1] Allen, of course, is the quintessential urbanite, and it is perhaps hard to imagine anyone further removed from nature than modern city dwellers in industrialized nations, where human activities appear to take place largely outside nature. Living in buildings constructed from artificial materials, buying our food in supermarkets rather than growing it ourselves, perhaps driving occasionally to the woods so that we can take weekend hikes into "nature," nature gets pushed further to the margins of our existence and extremes of our consciousness. It does seem that we and nature are two. Indeed, Cajete (1994, 26) attributes what he calls the "crisis of modern man's identity" to our "cosmological disconnection from the natural world."

Although our efforts to distance ourselves from nature, and to contain and control it through technological innovations, may temporarily obscure the coevolution and interdependency of life, human history is written in the same book as natural history. Every plant and animal owes its existence to a single-celled ancestor that evolved some 3.9 billion years ago. As Lakota belief has it, "Mitakuye oyasin" (We are all related; Ross 1989). Diversity has been with us since life began, and we humans have inherited a world of difference. The tendency of evolution to this point has played out toward more life forms and greater cultural diversity. Although we are still in the early stages of understanding the ramifications of diversity in ecosystems, species, cultures, and languages, there is a growing body of factual evidence and supporting theory pointing to an impending extinction crisis in the realms of both biological and cultural-linguistic diversity. We are crossing a threshold of irreversible loss of species and languages into a fundamentally changed and less diverse world. What is being destroyed is the fundamental process that generated the very conditions of life that we are at home in. The continuation of large-scale speciation and language genesis is threatened by the elimination of the conditions that historically made them possible.

A new wave of interdisciplinary studies is yielding a holistic view of diversity and consideration of how these two worlds of difference, biological and cultural/ linguistic, are related and what common factors are at work to diminish them, or conversely, to sustain them (see, e.g., Harmon 2002). I hesitate to use the term "sustainability" at all because it has become such a fashionable, but all too often vacuous, buzzword. Nevertheless, to talk about the notion of sustainability in rela- tion to linguistic diversity is really to ask how communities around the world can sustain continued use of their languages in the future in the face of the spread of global languages such as English. In a world where the forces of globalization are creating technology and social conditions for achieving widespread homogeneity, the future will not be like the past.

Three Responses to the Loss of Linguistic Diversity

I want to examine three responses to the threats posed to linguistic diversity.

1. Do nothing.
2. Document endangered languages.
3. Sustain/revitalize threatened languages.

The first and second positions are not logically incompatible; that is, one may feel we should do nothing to stop language loss but that documentation is worth- while. Likewise the second and third positions may go hand in hand. Many revital- ization projects have documentation as a goal and a necessity. Both kinds of effort, documenting and revitalizing activities, can help sustain and preserve a language. Nevertheless, the various assumptions underlying these three approaches articulate different conceptions about the values of linguistic diversity and what I have called the "future of the past" (with acknowledgment to Alexander Stille 2002, from whom I have borrowed the phrase).

Position 1: Do Nothing

Although the linguistic community became aware of the problem of language death as more than an academic concern during the 1990s, and a few books aimed at the general public have heightened awareness, I suspect Fishman (1994, 60) is unfortunately right when he says that "very few people (including most of their own speakers) care about the impending demise of small languages." Some of the most prominent pieces in the media have actually been quite negative, if not downright celebratory, at the prospect of the disappearance of languages. Malik (2000, 16) writes, for example, "What if half the world's languages are on the verge of extinction? Let them die in peace."

A variety of justifications are used in support of this position, sometimes re- ferred to as benign neglect or laissez-faire. Its advocates include not only many pop- ular commentators but also some linguists such as Edwards (1985, 86). One argu- ment rests on the view that we should accept changes in language use as "normal." Extinction is just a fact of life. Journalist David Berreby (2003, F3) writes: "Every day, English, Spanish, Russian and French, along with almost all other living lan- guages are being altered by speakers to suit changing times. . . . Language evolution is taking place every day; why interfere with it?" He attempts to naturalize change by failing to distinguish change in general from language shift and death. In doing so, he obscures the sense of loss that accompanies the process when change takes the form of language shift.

Another variant of this argument is rooted in the ideology and rhetoric of free market capitalism, which argues that a free, competitive market in any activity should produce an optimal distribution of that activity for all concerned. Language death occurs because people make a free choice to shift to another language. As people are rational beings who may reasonably be expected to know where their self-interest lies, we, as outside observers, cannot condemn such choices nor should we intervene in the linguistic market. The decline of some languages is just a side effect of countless individual choices and thus is no more or no less morally significant than a change in the price of fish. Malik (2000, 16), for instance, claims that the reason why most languages die is "not because they are suppressed, but because native speakers yearn for a better life. Speaking a language such as English, French, or Spanish, and discarding traditional habits, can open up new worlds and is often a ticket to modernity."

Although some of these critics acknowledge that the rapid decrease in the number of languages over the past few centuries is connected with European colonization of the world and Western economic expansion, they tend to downplay the power imbalances underlying the material, political, and economic domination of most of the world's small language communities. This imbalance has allowed a few metropolitan groups a virtual stranglehold upon global resources and global power. Language death does not happen in privileged communities; it happens to the dispossessed and disempowered—a point I return to later.

Still another argument underpinning the laissez-faire position has been articulated by linguists as well as popular critics. I paraphrase it crudely with the slogan "Keep politics out of science." Berreby (2003) states bluntly: "The study of languages is a scientific enterprise, the effort to preserve them is not. It is a political question." Ladefoged (1992, 810) responded similarly to a set of papers arguing for the preservation of languages that we must be "wary" of arguments for preserving languages "based on political considerations." Linguists should behave with "professional detachment." Speaking as a linguist who had conducted fieldwork in Tanzania, where Swahili is replacing a number of smaller languages, he observed that "tribalism is seen as a threat to the development of the nation, and it would not be acting responsibly to do anything which might seem, at least superficially, to aid in its preservation" (809). Like Berreby and others, Ladefoged pointed to the continual change leading to new varieties of language. Berreby, for instance, says that we are in no danger of running out of languages and that maybe we have all the languages we deserve and need. When we need a new one, we just invent it. Ladefoged (1992, 811) also opines that "the world is remarkably resilient in its preservation of linguistic diversity." Whether the forces creating linguistic diversification are ahead of those destroying it is actually questionable, but that does not mean we can dismiss current and future losses as insignificant. Dorian (1993, 577–78), for example, observes that if a fifth of the world's buildings were threatened with destruction, architects still might well speak of imminent catastrophic destruction, even though more buildings could be built in the future.

The job of linguists in Ladefoged's (1992, 811) view is "to lay out the facts concerning a given linguistic situation." Similarly, Berreby (2003, F3) writes that "the elucidation of language in all its complexity is an enthralling scientific enterprise" but that "saving endangered languages" is not a part of it. Berreby thus wonders "where science ends and politics begins." Posing the question in this way presupposes that science exists in a social and political vacuum. Unfortunately there is no politically neutral lens through which one can view what Ladefoged calls "the facts." It is an indisputable fact that Eyak, a native Alaskan language, may disappear very soon after its one remaining speaker, Marie Smith Jones, dies, but this fact is viewed quite differently by Malik than it is by others such as myself. However, I will postpone considering my views until after I have looked at the second position.

Position 2: Documentation
The arguments supporting documentation include the safeguarding of linguistic diversity, contributing to a knowledge base for language universals, and the Western idea that knowledge in and of itself is valuable. I think most linguists would agree on the value of documenting endangered languages. A substantial literature is emerging on the topic of documentary linguistics in an effort to establish a set of best practices (Lehmann 2001; Himmelmann 1998). Some linguists, however, also regard documentation as a safer, more scientific, and more politically neutral act as well. For some, this belief is based on an acceptance of the view that linguists cannot or should not do anything to intervene in the various larger forces that fuel language shift. Newman (1998), for instance, characterizes endangered languages as a "hopeless cause" even though he regards documentation as an urgent scientific task. Ladefoged is clearly among the linguists supporting this position as are Robins and Uhlenbeck (1991) in their respective capacities as president and secretary-general of the Comité International Permanent de Linguistes (CIPL) and as editors of a volume titled *Endangered Languages*. They explain in the preface to the book that the linguist's task is largely one of recording languages, writing grammars and dictionaries, and so on and that the most urgent priority is certainly for documentation. Thus Robins and Uhlenbeck (1991, xiii) declare, "The Comité International Permanent de Linguistes (CIPL) is fully aware that as an apolitical organisation it is unable to reverse this process of gradual decline of many languages, because this process is largely determined by social and political factors beyond our influence. Nevertheless, CIPL cannot remain idle. . . . We have to make an effort at least to record languages threatened by extinction, to encourage and enable linguists to do fieldwork, to write grammars, to compose dictionaries, and to preserve and make accessible their oral and written literature."

A number of national funding bodies such as the U.S. National Science Foundation, the German Volkswagen Stiftung, and international agencies such as UNESCO have undertaken documentation projects and set up archives to serve as repositories for data. The recent Rausing bequest to the University of London's School of Oriental and African Studies (SOAS) to support academic research on endangered languages has placed its emphasis on documentation. The Hans Rausing Endangered Languages Project (HRELP) aims to give some £15 million in research grants over a ten-year period in support of documentation projects because they believe that "this is the surest way of helping the endangered language communities we're working with" (www.hrelp.org/grants/). They propose to "support the documentation of as many threatened languages as possible, focused on where the danger of extinction is greatest, facilitating the preservation of culture and knowledge, and creating repositories of data for the linguistic and social sciences and for indigenous communities. . . . Projects aimed primarily at language revitalisation will not be supported." The guidelines for grant applicants explain further: "Whilst the link between documentation and revitalisation is appreciated (and desirable), the prime focus of the funding is documentation. Applicants are encouraged to structure the documentation in ways which assist the local communities to perceive and foster language and also increase the potential for ELDP (Endangered Languages Documentation Project) funds to be combined with revitalisation funds from other sources." Thus the guidelines already suggest that the "facts" to be recorded should explicitly be structured in a particular way.

In her reply to Ladefoged, Dorian (1993, 576) points out that "linguistic salvage work that consists solely of recording for posterity certain structural features of a threatened small language is inevitably a political act, just as any other act touching that language would be. . . . Fieldwork, however antiseptic it may try to be, inevitably has political overtones." Moreover, a presumption of value underlies the documenting enterprise. Dorian is right to stress that linguists "cannot enter the threatened language equation without becoming a factor in it."

Even if we could put politics aside, there are considerable problems with putting all our eggs in the documentation basket. Although technological innovations have provided us with better and more sophisticated tools than ever before for studying and preserving linguistic data in the form of tape and video recording, digital databases, and so on, there is a distinction to be made between documenting language data and preserving or sustaining a language. What is being saved or preserved? Nora and Richard Dauenhauer put it best when they say, "Preservation . . . is what we do to berries in jam jars and salmon in cans. . . . Books and recordings can preserve languages, but only people and communities can keep them alive" (quoted in Lord 1996, 68).

For some like Berreby, documentation holds out the prospect of revival at a later stage. He writes, "If the information and political will are present, Ubykh can be revived 500 years from now. Hebrew, after all, was brought back from ancient texts into daily use after 2,000 years" (Berreby 2003, F3). The last known speaker of Ubykh was Tevfik Esenc, who died in 1992. Berreby's claim rests on a misunderstanding of the circumstances surrounding the so-called revival of Hebrew and the extent to which it provides a suitable model for the majority of the world's endangered languages. If Berreby is right, there's not a lot to worry about, except perhaps the question of how to proceed to document as much as possible from as many languages as possible before they die.

As scholars work to record endangered languages, relying on ever more advanced forms of technology in their efforts, the enormity of the task as well as the rate of technological change pose formidable challenges. Some of the new information technologies that we think of as "advanced" are actually proving to be far less durable than the older technologies of print and stone that technology gurus assured us they would replace. I am not, of course, suggesting that we should abandon documentation projects or carve phonetic transcriptions on stone tablets but rather that we should not be naïve either about what documentation can achieve. Thanks to technological advances, we can record and archive massive amounts of information onto smaller and smaller storage devices at the same time as we can access seemingly infinite amounts of information on the Internet. A CD or DVD-ROM on which I save the file for this chapter is, for all its advances and massive amount of storage space, far more fragile and vulnerable than the Gutenberg Bible produced in Mainz circa 1450. The appearance of the Gutenberg Bible heralded a new era in the distribution of information, one that has only been matched in recent times by the impact of computing technologies. The Bodleian library at the University of Oxford recently displayed its copy of the Gutenberg Bible, which was believed to be one of the best preserved. Naturally a lot of effort was involved in preserving the book for centuries and will need to be continued if the book is to endure. No one knows how many books and printed manuscripts from the past have been lost, but there may be no reason to be more optimistic about the amount of information from today's documentation projects that will survive even fifty years in the future. "One of the great ironies of the information age," writes Alexander Stille (2002, 300), "is that while the late twentieth century will undoubtedly have recorded more data than any other period in history, it will also almost certainly have lost more information than any previous era."

Data recorded on CD-ROM and other digital storage devices are not necessarily any more secure than words on medieval manuscripts copied and recopied down through the ages by monks and scribes. As old storage mechanisms become obsolete, information must be continuously moved to the latest medium or the data will be lost. A vast amount of data is for all intents and purposes lost because we have lost the technology required for viewing/hearing it. E-mail records from the Reagan White House, fewer than twenty years old, languish in unreadable computer formats. Moreover, Stille underlines the dizzying pace with which archives are filling up: the U.S. National Archives and Record Administration opened a new storage facility in 1994 that was intended to last several decades, but despite the fact that it is the third-largest government building, it is already approaching its storage capacity.

The fragility of all recording and preservation technologies is satirized in a story relevant to my concern with endangered languages, Epeli Hau'ofa's (1993) story "The Glorious Pacific Way." On a tiny island in the Pacific, Ole Pasifikiwei, who records oral traditions in his spare time from his job as chief eradicator of pests and weeds, comes to the attention of a Mr. Harold Minte, a visiting diplomat on a mission to identify projects aimed at preserving the Pacific way of life that are worthy of funding. After much negotiation about how to tailor his work in such a way so as to meet Minte's eligibility criteria, Ole manages to get a grant of two thousand dollars to buy a typewriter and a filing cabinet to record and store the material that he has been writing down by hand in exercise books. As Ole becomes ever more proficient in manipulating international development organizations, he receives more and more money. Mr. Minte also obtains an invitation for him to attend an international work-shop in Manila funded by an international organization on the correct method of col-lecting and recording oral traditions. On his return from the training course, however, Ole finds that his aunt, who has been taking care of his house in his absence, has used all his exercise books for toilet paper or sold them cheaply to her needy neighbors. All the information he spent seven years gathering goes literally "down the bloody drain" (Hau'ofa 1993, 92). Although the main point of Hau'ofa's story is to satirize international funding agencies, it highlights the paradox in the fact that our forms of preservation may themselves destroy what they seek to preserve. Folk traditions and other forms of knowledge passed down orally for generations are always only a gen-eration away from extinction, but they become vulnerable to other dangers once writ-ten down. So it is with all technologies. Probably every field-worker has lost some precious piece of data. I still recall the one occasion in Papua New Guinea when one of the oldest men I interviewed spoke in the only piece of connected discourse he ever uttered in Tok Pisin. He was a bush pidgin speaker. However, I did not manage to record it on tape because not only one tape recorder but also a backup recorder failed to work properly.

Another risk of accumulating increasing data is the difficulty in distinguishing the essential from the ephemeral. I applaud those who are engaged in developing much needed standards of documentation, but inevitably today's concerns may not be those of the future. As Dorian (1993, 578) suggests, records that satisfy a phoneti-cian are likely to disappoint an ethnographer of speaking. What is salvaged will inev-itably be small compared to what will be lost. Even working for forty years with a dwindling community of Scottish Gaelic speakers in three East Sutherland villages, Dorian has increasingly come to realize many of the interesting things she was un-aware of until it was too late to record them. She is now one of a few remaining mem-bers of a group of speakers whom as a young woman she called older and younger fluent speakers.

Position 3: Sustain/Revitalize
A number of linguists, myself included, have worked at broadening the public per-ception of the link between the survival of linguistic diversity and environmental is-sues. Nettle and Romaine (2000) argue that the greatest linguistic diversity is found in areas that are also high in biodiversity. These regions are inhabited by indigenous peoples who represent around 4 percent of the world's population but who speak at least 60 percent of its languages and control or manage some of the ecosystems rich-est in biodiversity. Not only do biodiversity and linguistic diversity share the same geographic locations, but also they face common threats. Whether or not one accepts a coevolution of biological and linguistic diversity on theoretical grounds, it is hard to ignore the similarities in the practical forces driving biological extinctions and cul-tural/linguistic homogenization. The dangers facing small communities are greater than ever before. This is reflected in the increasing number of languages that die each year, as the homelands of indigenous peoples are being destroyed, or they are assimi-lated into larger nation-states, some of which are actively seeking to exterminate them.

Because the historical causes of the threats facing the earth's languages, cultures, and biodiversity are the same, the solutions are also likely to come from the same place: empowering local people. The idea that linguistic diversity should be sustained is not a sentimental attachment to some idealized past as critics suggest but is part of the promotion of sustainable, appropriate, empowering development. At this point we must come back to some of my earlier remarks about how some of the supporters of the benign neglect position have glossed over undeniable disparities in power underlying the history of language shift.

In many cases shift occurred not because of an increase in the available choices but because of a decrease in choice brought about by the exercise of undemocratic power. Such power is almost always wielded by denying access to resources from which communities make their living. Languages can only exist where there is a community to speak and transmit them. A community of people can exist only where there is a viable environment for them to live in and a means of making a living. Where communities cannot thrive, their languages are in danger. When languages lose their speakers, they die. Extinctions in general, whether of languages or species, are part of a more general pattern of human activities contributing to radical alterations in our ecosystem. In the past these extinctions took place largely without human intervention. Now they are taking place on an unprecedented scale through our intervention—in particular, through our alteration of the environment. The extinction of languages can be seen as part of the larger picture of worldwide near-total ecosystem collapse.

Buruma's (2001) attempt to rebut Nettle and Romaine's (2000) claim concerning the intimate connections between environmental disruption and language loss actually supports their position when one looks more closely at the details in the context of the larger picture. "Deaths are always sad events," Buruma (2001, 24) writes, but he is "not sure the ecolinguists always deplore these losses for the right reason. When languages die because their speakers are massacred or forced to change, this is indeed deplorable, but the ecolinguists think diversity is a good thing per se, and the loss of any language, no matter how small, and whatever the circumstances of its demise, a loss to humanity." Although Buruma (23) agrees that ecolinguists "sometimes with good reason" link the ruin of native habitats with waves of Europeans/Americans crashing through what he calls the "fragile world of small peoples and tribes," he seems conveniently unaware of the magnitude of the losses and their consequences.

Yes, there is that "little matter of genocide," as Churchill (1997) called it, and just as importantly its continuing denial. Although many of those individually affected by what Crosby (1993) has called "ecological imperialism" were small peoples and tribes, many populations, especially in Mesoamerica, were substantial. Collectively, the population of native North and South America comprised somewhere between 100 and 150 million people around 1500. By 1890 the sustained impact of European conquest and newly introduced diseases such as smallpox and measles to which the native inhabitants had no immunity obliterated as much as 97–99 percent of the population.

It has been said of Margaret Thatcher that she "owed a lot to a lack of knowledge of history" (Anderson 2004, 22). So too does Buruma's misrepresentation of the extent of threat and loss suffered by one indigenous people in particular, namely, the Inuit in Nunavut. Although he acknowledges that the Inuit are a threatened community, Buruma (2001, 26) maintains that they are threatened not by the Canadian government but "because they are a dwindling group on the edge of the world." He notes that their suicide rate is "horrendous," but he adds, "They do still speak their language. Another expression of their identity is shooting rare Bowhead whales with .50 caliber hunting rifles. The point here is not to be facetious. The hunts are not just for the meat. They are defended on cultural grounds: shooting whales is deemed essential for the preservation of identity. This, surely, is not what the ecolinguists have in mind" (Buruma 2001, 26).

No, indeed it is not. Here is an interesting case that illustrates nicely my earlier point about the impossibility of laying out "the facts of the linguistic situation," to use Ladefoged's (1992, 811) phrasing, without engaging in politics. Buruma's statement is also a good example of a style of pseudoscientific argumentation that Gould (1981, 117) has described as typical of those whom he calls intellectual charlatans: "They begin with conclusions, peered through their facts, and came back in a circle to the same conclusions."

The idea that there is a correlation between horrendous rates of suicide, hunting endangered species, and maintaining the Inuit language is, to say the least, spurious. To imply by juxtaposition of these facts that there is a causal connection that contradicts the links that Nettle and Romaine (2000) make between the linguistic diversity and the need for sustainable habitats is a distortion of our arguments. We certainly did not suggest that maintaining indigenous languages would guarantee preservation of biodiversity, especially in the absence of policies of sustainable development. Sen (1999) has argued that freedom of choice is both a principal means and end of development. Good development involves local community involvement, control, and accountability. It is not about setting indigenous peoples aside in isolated reservations or expecting them to go on completely unchanged. It is merely about giving them real choice about what happens in the places where they live. This is precisely what many people have lacked.

Although the Inuit have now had control over their territory for five years, it is naïve to suppose that the people are no longer threatened by the Canadian government, as if all will suddenly be well after centuries of resource depletion through outside commercial activities and misguided missionary and government policies aimed at the destruction of much of native language and culture. These continue to have a profound and far-reaching impact on all aspects of native life, culture, and well-being. Unfortunately, it is far easier and quicker to destroy resource bases than to rebuild them. To suggest that the Inuit are deliberately pursuing policies leading to the extinction of bowhead whales in order to preserve their identity is to misunderstand the grounds for native self-determination and the compromised conditions under which it has often been achieved or continually denied. Let us consider some of the facts that Buruma ignores.

The new territory of Nunavut (which means "our land" in the Inuktitut language) came into being on April 1, 1999, granting the Inuit people self-rule and control over their own institutions. The creation of Nunavut was the result of the largest land claim agreement in Canadian history and turned a dream into reality for the twenty-seven thousand some residents who make their homes in twenty-six small communities spread out over an area about one-fifth the size of Canada. Although Nunavut has been home to the Inuit for millennia, it was part of Canada for more than a century. During that time, and even centuries before it, from the time explorers, traders, whalers, and missionaries entered the Arctic beginning in the 1600s, the people's traditional ways of managing their land and resources according to their own needs and customs were progressively undermined (Brody 1975).

About fifty years ago the Canadian government attempted to end their customary seminomadic existence on the land by moving traditional Inuit extended family camps to settlements, where they would rely on southern imported goods instead of hunting. Under Canadian rule they had no legal rights over the use of the natural resources and the land they had lived on for centuries. Construction of Canadian and U.S. military bases and radar stations intended to serve as the primary line of air defense against a possible invasion of North America disrupted caribou migration patterns. Now superseded by more modern surveillance technology and the demise of the Cold War, these abandoned stations stretching three thousand miles along the 69th Parallel on the Arctic coastline from the Yukon Territory to Baffin Island pose the biggest cleanup operation in North America to rid the environment of toxic waste and the remaining facilities. A particular problem is contamination caused by the leeching of polychlorinated biphenyls (PCBs), a mixture of chemicals widely used in the 1950s in paint and transformers. Inuit women have levels of PCB in their breast milk five to ten times greater than those found among women in southern Canada. PCBs, pesticides, and other pollutants from the south and from other parts of the world have been discovered in the ice and soil as well as in the fat of seals and other animals the Inuit have traditionally relied on for subsistence (Rasmussen 2002, 87).

The Inuit also killed whales as a vital part of their traditional hunting economy. In addition to the meat, the blubber from the whale was also valued as a source of food as well as heat and light. Commercial whalers discovered the bowhead whale as early as 1611 in the eastern Arctic. During the nineteenth and twentieth centuries commercial whalers reduced the bowhead whale populations to the point of extinction and then abandoned arctic waters when the remaining whales were too few to make the expeditions profitable. Since 1946 bowhead whales have been completely protected from commercial whaling. As part of their signing of a 1993 land-claims settlement with the Canadian government that led to the creation of Nunavut, the Inuit demanded the right to resume bowhead hunting on a regulated basis. Between 1991 and 2002 they killed only five bowheads, under a strict quota from the Canadian government. Although some experts believe that a harvest of this scale is sustainable, environmental pressure groups along with industrialized nations, whose exploitative commercial whaling brought the bowhead to the brink of extinction, are attempting through the International Whaling Commission to curtail the Inuit's historic right to subsistence whaling.

The territory's suicide rate is indeed horrendous, as Buruma states. It is nearly six times the national Canadian average. During Nunavut's first year as a territory, twenty people committed suicide, and dozens of others tried. Yet this depressing fact, which not coincidentally is mirrored in many other indigenous communities around the world, also needs to be examined in the historical and cultural context of the colonialism that produced a collective sense of shame about native languages and identities.

In Canada, the federal government and churches entered into a formal partnership to run a residential school system for Indian and Inuit children as part of the government's assimilation policy. Education in such church-run, government-funded residential schools was supposed to prepare children for life in white society by denying them their native identity and forcing them to learn in an alien cultural and linguistic environment where their own languages were forbidden. The residential school system was in operation for nearly 150 years. In some parts of Canada as many as five generations of children attended, and some communities were depopulated of children between the ages of five and twenty. In the 1950s and 1960s Inuit children attended residential schools in Inuvik, Chesterfield Inlet, Churchill, and various other communities, where they were separated from their families and communities. In this way missionaries undermined traditional social structures and the transmission of cultural and linguistic knowledge from one generation to the next. They replaced the children's Inuit names given by elders with Christian ones. In the 1940s, the federal government added a number to this name. One woman's name was Annie E7-121. Some Inuit children sent to Toronto schools wore a string with a disc indicating their number (*Report of the Royal Commission on Aboriginal Peoples* 1996).

The hearings of the Royal Commission on Aboriginal Peoples (1996) uncovered the tragic legacy that the residential school system has left with many former students. The Inuit attribute high suicide rates to past assimilation attempts and lack of self-determination. Research supports their belief and indicates that a variety of risk factors may be systemic to the life experience of many Inuit communities, among them unemployment, poverty, poor education, lack of opportunity, and loss of cultural identity. Suicides rates are highest among young people, particularly young men. Many young people are weakly integrated into traditional culture and disconnected from their elders and family support networks.

At the same time, the education system does not offer them opportunities, so they lack skills that would allow integration into Western society. The traditional role of men as hunters has been disrupted by the introduction of the Western economy. The inability to meet the burden of providing for their families has damaged self-esteem. Communities where the market for sealskins has collapsed have been among the hardest hit by high suicide rates (Kral 2003). The Inuit hope that self-government will help them reclaim their identity and confidence. Research has shown that a high level of cultural spirituality and cultural orientation and strong social identity may be protective factors against low self-esteem, stress, and hopelessness (Chandler and Lalonde 1998; Garroutte et al. 2003; Kral et al. 1998).

Given huge upheavals such as these, the surprise is not that indigenous languages have declined but that some such as Inuktitut have survived at all. Buruma (2001, 26), however, argues that the Inuit are threatened because they are a "dwindling group on the edge of the world." This observation betrays a fairly typical schizoid way of thinking about indigenous peoples as living on the edge, stuck in a traditional society and a primitive way of life doomed to extinction by the inexorable march of progress. Buruma espouses an irreconcilably contradictory view of indigenous peoples, demonizing them and romanticizing them. He denies them the right to exist in modernity with his remark about hunting whales with .50 caliber rifles. The survival of indigenous peoples is now often dependent on modern means of production and transport that they pay for with money acquired from wage labor. But rather than being swallowed up by homogenizing forces, many recast their dependencies on modern modes of production in order to reconstitute their own cultural ideas and practices and themselves as traditional communities. During the nineteenth and twentieth centuries, as the Inuit became increasingly dependent on a market economy, they adopted new technology to earn income from industries centered on seal netting, fox trapping, and cod, char, and salmon fishing.

Again, the issue of choice is important. The Inuit would prefer to adopt only those outside elements that facilitate their own practices. They have chosen the rifle and snowmobiles but prefer to use their own language among themselves. Yet government policies have aimed at imposing a whole package deal of capitalism intended to displace rather than supplement the Inuit way of life. In doing so, they force a choice between tradition and modernity by denying the people the right to continue living on their own land and resources in ways that they choose (Brody 1975). From another part of the Arctic, Kawagley (1995, 105–6) articulates a perspective of the Yupiaq people of southwestern Alaska, which demands that native people be allowed to consider technology before it is introduced to their villages. What he calls "soft technology" provides a means to temper and adapt Western technology to local culture and ecology so that it does not make excessive nonsustainable demands on the environment. Soft technology does not replace indigenous technologies but seeks to update or fine tune them. The task for the Yupiaq is to reconstruct and redefine a new native identity built around native traditions, because at the moment their youth are like round pegs in square holes, emotionally and mentally exhausted from the inability to succeed in the native world as traditionally defined or in the modern world as defined and controlled by others (Kawagley 1995, 111–12).

Policies narrowly focused on economic development defined in Western terms have narrowed people's options and are then used to justify more economic development, usually in the form of mining natural resources such as gas and oil that the rest of Canada urgently needs, as the solution to problems that were caused by the imposition of a Western economy in the first place. Cajete (1994, 79) argues that every time a deeply rooted culture is dispossessed and forced from the land in the name of progress, the viability of humans living in that environment is affected. Supplanting indigenous knowledge and stewardship of a local ecology with Western technology rarely succeeds because these new alien technologies fail to respect the intimate relationships between people and the environment. More often than not, a human and ecological wasteland is left in the wake of Western economic and resource development schemes. Ultimately, what the Inuit and other indigenous peoples are being told by Buruma and others is to stop being themselves, move south and assimilate, and they will be all right. Widdowson and Howard (2002, 32), for instance, dismiss traditional knowledge as "nothing more than a blend of traditional survival skills and superstition." Widdowson (2005, 18n) claims that making Inuktitut the official language of the newly created territory of Nunavut "creates tremendous problems because it is a pre-literate language not suited for use in complex legal and bureaucratic procedures." In her view Nunavut is unviable: "The only sensible policy in the long run appears to be . . . depopulation of Nunavut and the gradual integration of the Inuit into more productive processes" (Widdowson 2005, 23).

Many other critics of the campaign supporting linguistic diversity think in a similar dichotomizing fashion about language, namely, that preserving native languages entails abandoning modernity. Malik (2000, 17), for instance, sees such efforts as having

> much . . . in common with reactionary, backward-looking visions [that] seek to preserve the unpreservable, and all are possessed of an impossibly nostalgic view of what constitutes a culture or a "way of life." It is modernity itself of which Nettle and Romaine (2000) disapprove. They want the peoples of the Third World, and minority groups in the West, to follow "local ways of life" and pursue "traditional knowledge" rather than receive a "Western education." This is tantamount to saying that such people should live a marginal life, excluded from the modern mainstream to which the rest of us belong. There is nothing noble or authentic about local ways of life; they are often simply degrading and backbreaking.

Needless to say, Nettle and I don't endorse the view Malik attributes to us. We don't think "sulking on your own rock is a state worth preserving," as he puts it. The preservation of a language in its fullest sense ultimately entails the maintenance of the community who speaks it, and therefore the arguments in favor of doing something to reverse language death are ultimately about sustaining cultures and habitats. In discussions of language maintenance, revitalization, and so on there is a tendency to reify languages, when it is communities and language ecologies we should be talking about. As Cajete (1994, 81) puts it, we need to revitalize our ecological relationships. When we lose sight of people and the communities that sustain languages, it becomes easy to argue, as a number of critics have, that there is no reason to preserve languages for their own sake. Maintaining cultural and linguistic diversity is a matter of social justice because distinctiveness in culture and language has formed the basis for defining human identities. We should think instead about languages in the same way as we do other natural resources that need careful planning: they are vital parts of complex local ecologies that must be supported if global biodiversity is to be sustained.

ACKNOWLEDGMENTS

I dedicate this chapter to the memory of Father Royden B. Davis, dean of the College of Arts and Sciences at Georgetown University from 1966 to 1989. This chapter is a revised version of a lecture I gave in November 2004 while I held the Royden B. Davis Chair of Interdisciplinary Studies. I thank Kendall King and Natalie Schilling-Estes for giving me the opportunity to publish the chapter in this volume, where I hope it may serve as a public acknowledgment of my gratitude to the benefactors of the chair for their generosity in funding this position, as well as to Dean Jane McAuliffe of Georgetown College and my colleagues in the Department of Linguistics for hosting me.

NOTE

1. Reportedly Allen's first published joke, this quote exists in several versions: "I am at two with nature." http://en.wikipedia.org/wiki/Woody_Allen (accessed May 3, 2006). "I am two with nature." www.brainyquote.com/quotes/authors/w/woody_allen.html (accessed May 3, 2006).

REFERENCES

Anderson, Bruce. 2004. Here's to you Mrs. Thatcher. *FT [Financial Times] Magazine,* May 8, 22.
Berreby, David. (2003). Fading species and dying tongues: When the two part ways. *New York Times,* May 27, F3.
Brody, Hugh. 1975. *The people's land: Eskimos and whites in the eastern arctic.* Harmondsworth: Penguin.
Buruma, Ian. 2001. Road to Babel. *New York Review of Books,* May 31, 23–26.
Cajete, Gregory. 1994. *Look to the mountain: An ecology of indigenous education.* Durango, CO: Kivaki Press.
Chandler, Michael J., and Christopher E. Lalonde. 1998. Cultural continuity as a hedge against suicide in Canada's First Nations. *Transcultural Psychiatry* 35:193–211.
Churchill, Ward. 1997. *A little matter of genocide: Holocaust and denial in the Americas, 1492 to the present.* San Francisco: City Lights.
Crosby, Alfred W. 1993. *Ecological imperialism: The biological expansion of Europe, 900–1900.* Cambridge: Cambridge University Press.
Dorian, Nancy C. 1993. A response to Ladefoged's other view of endangered languages. *Language* 69:575–79.
Edwards, John. 1985. *Language, society and identity.* Oxford: Basil Blackwell.
Fishman, Joshua A. 1994. On the limits of ethnolinguistic democracy. In *Linguistic human rights: Overcoming linguistic discrimination,* ed. Tove Skutnabb-Kangas and Robert Phillipson, 49–61. Berlin: Mouton de Gruyter.
Garroutte, Eva Marie, Jack Goldberg, Janette Beals, Richard Herrell, Spero M. Manson, and the AI-SUPERPFP Team. 2003. Spirituality and attempted suicide among American Indians. *Social Science and Medicine* 56:1571–79.
Gould, Stephen Jay. 1981. *The mismeasure of man.* New York: W. W. Norton and Co.
The Hans Rausing Endangered Languages Project, www.hrelp.org (accessed October 19, 2004).
Harmon, David. 2002. *In light of our differences: How diversity in nature and culture makes us human.* Washington, DC: Smithsonian Institution Press.
Hau'ofa, Epeli. 1993. *Tales of the Tikongs.* Suva, Fiji: Beake House.
Himmelmann, Nikolaus P. 1998. Documentary and descriptive linguistics. *Linguistics* 36:161–95.
Kawagley, A. Oscar. 1995. *A Yupiaq worldview: A pathway to ecology and spirit.* Prospect Heights, IL: Waveland Press.
Kral, Michael J. 2003. *Unikkaartuit: Meanings of well-being, sadness, suicide and change in two Inuit communities.* Final Report to the National Health Service.
Kral, Michael J., Meeka Arnakaq, Naki Ekho, Okee Kunuk, Elisapee Ootoova, Malaya Papatsie, and Lucien Taparti. 1998. Stories of distress and healing: Inuit elders on suicide. In *Suicide in Canada,* ed. Antoon A. Leenaars, Susanne Wenckstern, Isaac Sakinofsky, Ronald J. Dyck, Michael J. Kral, and Roger C. Bland, 179–88. Toronto: University of Toronto Press.
Ladefoged, Peter. 1992. Another view of endangered languages. *Language* 68:809–11.
Lehmann, Christian. 2001. Language documentation: A program. In *Aspects of typology and universals,* ed. Walter Bisang, 83–97. Berlin: Akademie.
Lord, Nancy. 1996. Native tongues. *Sierra Magazine* 81(6): 46–69.
Malik, Kenan. 2000. Let them die. *Prospect* 57 (November): 16–17.

Nettle, Daniel, and Suzanne Romaine. 2000. *Vanishing voices: The extinction of the world's languages.* Oxford: Oxford University Press.

Newman, Paul. 1998. "We has seen the enemy and it is us": The endangered language issue as a hopeless cause. *Studies in the Linguistic Sciences* 28:11–20.

Rasmussen, Derek. 2002. Qallunology: A pedagogy for the oppressor. *Philosophy of Education* 2002: 85–94.

Report of the Royal Commission on Aboriginal Peoples. 1996. Ottawa: Government of Canada.

Robins, Robert H., and Eugenius M. Uhlenbeck, eds. 1991. *Endangered languages.* Oxford: Berg.

Ross, Allen C. 1989. *Mitakuye oyasin, "We are all related."* Fort Yates, ND: Bear Press.

Sen, Amartya. 1999. *Development as freedom.* New York: Alfred Knopf.

Stille, Alexander. 2002. *The future of the past: How the information age threatens to destroy our cultural heritage.* New York: Farrar, Straus and Giroux.

Widdowson, Frances. 2005. The political economy of Nunavut: Internal colony or rentier territory? Paper prepared for annual meeting of Canadian Political Science Association, University of Western Ontario, June.

Widdowson, Frances, and Albert Howard. 2002. The aboriginal industry's new clothes. *Policy Options,* March: 30–34.

2

▩ When Is an "Extinct Language" Not Extinct?
Miami, a Formerly Sleeping Language

WESLEY Y. LEONARD
University of California, Berkeley

▩ **MANY MIAMI PEOPLE,** myself included, experience a paradox when we speak our heritage language, which is said to be "extinct." But what does it mean to be extinct? While members of the Miami nation have a number of ways of viewing the world, I believe it is fair to assume that we all know extinct species are those where the last living example has died and where there will never be living examples of that species again. The problem occurs when this idea gets extended to languages such as Miami, as the paradox of speaking an extinct language is not imaginary. This chapter first resolves that paradox by situating the story of how Miami was reclaimed from extinction within a proposed category of "sleeping languages," which I define as those that are not currently known but that are documented, claimed as part of one's heritage, and thus may be used again.[1] Second, it offers a formal means of integrating these sleeping languages into endangered language theory and discusses what some of the larger implications and challenges of doing so might be.

This story reflects my perspectives and experiences as a linguist with an interest in indigenous language reclamation, a member of the Miami Tribe of Oklahoma, and chair of the Miami Language Committee. The motivation for the chapter comes from my belief that a more accurate classificatory system will contribute to better language policy and a better understanding of indigenous peoples, many of whom claim heritage to a sleeping language. Except where noted otherwise, "we" refers to myself and others who have been active in Miami language reclamation programs under the belief that our language and culture are important for community well-being, but the opinions expressed in this chapter should not be taken to represent the entire Miami community.

A Brief History of Language Shift in the Miami Community

Miami is one of the major dialects of Miami-Peoria (also called Miami-Illinois), a language of the Algonquian language family that is classified as extinct by well-known sources such as the *Ethnologue* (Gordon 2005).[2] However, as detailed later, it is not and never was extinct; it was merely sleeping. Due to reclamation efforts that began in the 1990s, it might now be said to have been awakened.

23

With the passing of the "last" fluent speaker in the early 1960s, Miami really was a sleeping language for about thirty years. The key criterion for being a sleeping language is the existence of documentation and of people with heritage to the language but no individuals with substantial knowledge of the language. That shift from Miami to (only) English had been occurring since the nineteenth century and was driven by the forced division of the Miami community in 1846 and English-only practices in the federal Indian boarding school system, among other reasons (see Baldwin 2003 and Rinehart 2006 for further discussion).

Documentation of Miami-Illinois occurred in the late seventeenth to mid-eighteenth centuries by French missionaries, and substantial work continued into the nineteenth and twentieth centuries by many others, including linguists Albert Gatschet and Truman Michelson (Costa 2003). Although the historically spoken language is thought to be undocumented in audio form (aside from a short 1949 recording), the written documentation is vast and includes dictionaries, texts, overt grammatical information such as verb paradigms, and information about sociolinguistic norms. However, wide awareness of the existence and interpretability of those materials is a recent phenomenon. Richard Rhodes noted (personal communication 2004) that Algonquianists had viewed Miami as a puzzle that couldn't be solved until David Costa found and collected the historical documents and then pieced the structure of the language into a useable form in his dissertation (Costa 1994; updated as Costa 2003). Furthermore, valuable documentation of the language is still surfacing. For example, a seventeenth-century dictionary discovered in 1999 contains information not attested in any other known records (Costa 2005). This anecdote shows that even when a language's documentation appears to be insufficient for reclamation purposes, new investigation and scholarship may prove otherwise.

Beyond the seemingly spotty documentation, there is the additional point that Miami was spoken and known by no one. In this way, it was unlike any of the well-recognized classical or liturgical languages that are called "dead" but are in fact known and actively used in certain domains. Furthermore, while reclamation of some languages without speakers may be aided by "language rememberers"—those who don't speak the language but were exposed to it enough earlier in their lives to have some residual knowledge—there are no elderly semispeakers of Miami, and "remembering" of this type is highly limited. Our elders are instrumental in sharing cultural knowledge and supporting the language reclamation efforts, but none can understand a novel sentence or serve as language informants. This relatively small group of elders with memory of the language collectively remember only a few words and names, fixed phrases, and songs; some can speak in general terms about how the language sounded and the social contexts of its use. As recently as 1990, the aforementioned was the most substantial language knowledge held in the Miami community. Thus, while Miami may not have been the best prototype of "sleeping" given that a few people always knew a few words, by any practical assessment, it was a sleeping language.

With respect to knowledge by younger Miamis around that same period, the scope was even more limited. Fragments of Miami came up only in the aforementioned songs and in naming practices—and only in a minority of Miami families. My own experience as a child in the 1980s serves as an example of what a Miami youth might be expected to have known. I come from a family highly involved in our tribe, with my grandfather having served as chief for most of my life, and I grew up participating in many Miami cultural activities. That high level of connection noted, my entire Miami language knowledge as a child was comprised of my own Miami name alongside a few other names; *bezon,* a word for "hello" that happens to be a borrowed term; and finally, that there was a language called "Miami." (I didn't know *myaamia,* the name of the language in the language, until much later.) To the best of my knowledge, many Miami children in the 1980s did not know a single Miami word.

Particularly around the mid-twentieth century, the period in which the use of the Miami language was declining—eventually to a state of sleep—the Miami Tribe of Oklahoma as a political and cultural entity was likewise undergoing hardship. Elders today talk about how the future of the tribe at the time looked bleak, and how attendance at official meetings of the General Council (the people) was sometimes so low that they struggled to meet the quorum requirements established in the tribal constitution. Furthermore, there was no obvious place to hold those meetings as the nation had no land base. This was an especially problematic factor given that much of Miami cultural practice revolves around interacting with the land.

That was then. After an economic expansion facilitated by gaming revenues in the late 1990s to early 2000s and the creation of a formal language program following an Administration for Native Americans grant to create workshops for training tribal members to teach our language, the present situation is greatly different. Despite the history of two forced removals in the nineteenth century, the era of federal boarding schools, and other kinds of marginalization, the Miami Tribe of Oklahoma exists today as a growing nation with well over three thousand enrolled members and strong support from the General Council and the elected leadership to promote language reclamation efforts.[3] The overall vitality and future prospects of the Miami nation have made a significant shift from a lack of even a common building as recently as the mid-1970s to having tribally owned and operated administrative and community spaces, several successful business ventures, a growing land base, and many social and educational programs today.

Like the economic situation, the scope of language reclamation efforts has moved from "ground zero" (Baldwin 2003) to becoming a significant program. Although there had been a growing sentiment in the 1980s among tribal members that language and culture were missing in their lives, it wasn't until after David Costa's dissertation and funding became available that major efforts at the tribal level began. The teacher-training workshops that began in the mid-1990s continue (now as general language workshops) and have been supplemented by cultural immersion camps for Miami youth, language CDs, lesson books, games, other language-learning tools, and some (classroom-style) classes. Importantly, these efforts are now primarily funded directly by our tribal government and hence are guided by tribal priorities rather than those of outside agencies. Other programs focus more on teaching and experiencing our unique culture and supplement the language-focused activities, thus creating a natural balance in which language and culture are intertwined and build off each other. After ten years of these efforts, there are now hundreds of Miami people with some knowledge of the language and perhaps about fifteen people with conversational proficiency. Many Miami families have incorporated the language into their daily communication, and a few children are being raised with the language.

Furthermore, the Myaamia Project, an initiative at Miami University whose mission is "to facilitate and encourage the preservation, promotion, and research of Miami Nation history, culture and language" (Baldwin 2003, 20), began in 2001 and has been a successful impetus for promoting scholarship that is beneficial both to the Miami community and to Miami University.[4] Major products resulting from that initiative include the first modern Miami dictionary (Baldwin and Costa 2005).

This history is of great significance. Both in terms of the existence and usability of the language documentation and in terms of the economic and cultural stability that facilitates seeking out and using that documentation, Miami might have appeared once to have been essentially an irretrievably lost language. At best, it looked to be in a deep stage of sleep. Despite those challenges it has nonetheless undergone substantial reclamation, thus offering real hope to other communities whose language situations appear bleak.

Classifying Language Vitality: Integrating Sleeping Languages

While not normally explicitly acknowledged, most existing classifications of what is often termed "language vitality" are based primarily on (perceived) patterns of current use and not around the potential of future use—except, ironically enough, in predictions that the use of the language in question will decline or stop. The widely used Graded Intergenerational Disruption Scale (Fishman 1991, 2001), for example, is largely framed around whether children acquire the language in the home and whether the language currently is being used in domains such as education, work, and government; it does not include languages that have gone out of use. This is not, however, meant to imply that issues related to the possibility of increased or new future use have not been included in endangered language classification systems. Rather, the issue is that sleeping languages have not been given a formal place. It is true that some recent scholarship (e.g., UNESCO 2003; Lewis 2006) has incorporated the quality and quantity of documentation as a criterion to assess endangerment, but it does not extend to recognition of sleeping languages or any similarly framed category. Likewise, the term "sleeping" has been introduced in the literature (e.g., Amery 1995; Hinton 2001), but its definition and intended scope are not made explicit. I offer an extension of the linguistic notion of "competence" as a way to make that next step and formally include sleeping languages in endangered language theory.

Long used in linguistics, "competence" has been taken to refer to the cognitive capacity that allows an individual human to speak or comprehend a language, and its counterpart, "performance," refers to the actual use or comprehension stemming from that capacity (see Chomsky 1965). I suggest that the notion of competence should be extended outside of the individual and into the community. Again, it refers to the capacity that allows a language to be spoken and comprehended, but under the revised definition it can include *any* kind of capacity—whether it be knowledge held by a living person or that which exists in documentation (either of the language itself or of closely related varieties that could be consulted to reconstruct it). Thus the key question might be phrased, "Does the language as a system exist in some usable form?" For sleeping languages, the answer is "yes." Schematically they can thus be represented as [+competence, –performance] and differ from truly extinct languages, which are [–competence, –performance].

Unlike the view where the death of the "last" speaker represents a language having become extinct and hence outside the scope of what is called "language endangerment," I further propose that levels of this endangerment can be characterized as falling into a continuum that includes sleeping languages, as shown in figure 2.1.

The idea of the continuum is that there are an infinite number of points, and one could add or delineate any number of categories as appropriate to the specific issue at hand; those presented here are intended only to be examples. Certainly, any given language variety does not have a specific point at which it becomes 100 percent "safe"—hence the arrow at the left edge of figure 2.1. The other extreme on the right, conversely, *is* a specific point and represents either the death of the last person with knowledge of an undocumented language or the loss of all existing documentation of a language without speakers (e.g., in a fire). Languages that are irretrievably lost are by definition no longer "in danger of being lost" and are thus strange to conceptualize under a frame of endangerment. Therefore truly extinct languages are placed outside of the continuum altogether.

Under this view, the transition of a language from one with living knowers to one that is sleeping is not the endpoint that it has traditionally been deemed. Instead, it is a change of state that can be represented schematically as [+competence, +performance] → [+competence, –performance]. This change may correspond to a higher level of endangerment, but it hardly corresponds to one of irretrievable loss. Sleeping languages thus fall on the continuum somewhere around the "more endangered" area, with individual languages falling at different points, depending on the level to which they are documented, how much the community wants to learn and use them, and details of various socioeconomic factors that can facilitate or hinder the reclamation process. Miami was once near the rightmost point of the continuum but is slowly moving to the left.

Having established why sleeping languages are different from truly extinct languages, the question remains why they should be classified as "endangered

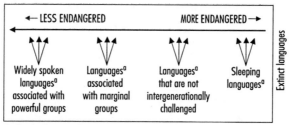

ᵃTechnically, the status refers to specific language *varieties*—not whole languages—because individual dialects will always have different levels of prestige and socioeconomic support.

Figure 2.1 A Revised View of the Language Endangerment Continuum

languages." One answer is that the definition of "endangered"—in danger of being lost—basically applies; the competence of the people who claim heritage to sleeping languages may never be realized. A related answer is that the guiding principles driving endangered language theory and practices of reversing language shift (Fishman 1991, 2001) apply to sleeping languages and their reclamation; a number of well-recognized indirect factors figure into both sleeping and nonsleeping languages alike. These include educational policies that promote or prohibit language teaching and use in schools; immigration and other demographic trends; and issues of social desirability, perceived economic value, and how members of the academic community (especially linguists) view the importance of the language in question with respect to documentation, revitalization, and other priorities. Such social factors are fully relevant for sleeping languages in that the potential for their reclamation—that is, the competence held by the people who claim heritage to it—is not stagnant but instead changes based on a variety of trends and pressures.

In particular, the factor of priorities within academia has special relevance for sleeping languages and warrants additional discussion. One of the main differences between sleeping and (endangered) languages with speakers is that formal tools of linguistics—and hence linguists—may be more necessary for the reclamation of the former because the language will usually need to be reconstituted. Conversely, for endangered languages that are fluently known, immersion exists as an option for creating new speakers. Fortunately for Miami people, Algonquianist David Costa continues his research on our language, the findings of which have been indispensable to the reclamation effort. Our competence as current and potential future speakers has increased because he and others have gathered, analyzed, and collated information about our language into a more useable form.

Equally important as the research itself may be the guidance that comes from the people who do it. Specialists in linguistics and related fields are often consulted for advice and direction. That advice should be realistic but inspiring, but we must also question its reliability. (Here, "we" includes everybody—whether a community member, a trained specialist, or both, as in my case.) The following anecdote offers an example of why this is so.

In the 1990s, linguist and Miami tribal member Daryl Baldwin spoke to other specialists at language conferences and elsewhere and told them of how he was learning the Miami language so that he could raise his children with the language. All but one of those he spoke to told him that it was a noble idea, but that it wouldn't work. Today, however, the six members of the Baldwin family speak Miami on a daily basis, and the youngest two have been acquiring it in the home. Intergenerational transmission has started again, albeit on a small scale. Of course, language reclamation is a multigenerational process and will likely involve levels of proficiency lower than "fluent" for quite some time, but we can at least say that the language is not extinct and that many specialists' predictions were wrong.

The question then arises as to why languages like Miami are still called extinct, which is an issue that involves far more than just a formal recognition of competence and sleeping languages. The first and simpler problem is that people are just misinformed about Miami. The bigger and more complicated problem is that of "linguistic purism," the ideology that a language has a given "correct" form and that its transmission and use should follow certain established patterns. As argued by Dorian (1994), purist ideologies can hurt the new generation of speakers. Similarly, in a study that examines why Kwak'wala (Kwakiutl) language revitalization efforts are thought to be failing despite an increase in younger people who know the language, Goodfellow (2003) argues that a lack of recognition of the legitimacy of the way young people speak explains this paradox. She concludes that "the greatest obstacle to keeping Native American languages thriving is a prevalent belief of linguists, language planners, teachers, and the general public that a language must somehow be maintained in its 'pure' form, which usually means the oldest form of the language now spoken by elderly people" (2003, 53).

Calling the purist attitude the greatest obstacle may be a stretch, but it is certainly among the largest problems. In the extreme view within this ideology, a reclaimed language will *never* be a legitimate representation of the historically spoken language, which therefore really may be thought of as extinct. I suspect that this is why Miami's reclamation is only partially recognized as legitimate in the larger community and why Daryl got the responses that he did when he related his desire for his children to know their language and culture. Anybody can recognize the hypothetical possibility of learning a language from written documentation and communicating with it, but unfortunately, some don't recognize the legitimacy of doing so.

Within the Miami community itself we have dealt with the potential challenges of purism by being up front about the fact that our language learners will speak an anglicized version of Miami and that this change is okay. Furthermore, it has been noted (e.g., Spolsky 2002) that the absence of native speakers can provide an ironic benefit in that there won't be anybody to criticize the language being spoken differently, and this may be true for us. Still, I would hesitate to conclude that our elders would be less supportive if they were themselves speakers. While it's true that some of them have questioned the importance of language reclamation, how realistic it is, and whether writing the language is appropriate (Rinehart 2006, 227), as noted earlier, they are generally supportive of the reclamation efforts.

Fortunately, purist ideology from the younger members of the Miami community has also not been a significant obstacle. While the question of authenticity occasionally gets posed, it's not a recurrent theme. Likewise, although participants in our summer language workshops do express concern about speaking Miami "correctly" and sometimes get discouraged about speaking lest they say something "wrong," I have never heard an adult learner chastise somebody else for saying something in a nonstandard way. Those of us who teach language workshops acknowledge that there is a standard form to the language that we try to use as a basis of instruction, but we de-emphasize the importance of maintaining this standard relative to the ideas that we should just speak, not be afraid to make mistakes, and that we are asserting our linguistic rights as Miami people when we speak our language.

Conversely, I have heard non-Miamis use purist rhetoric in reference to our modern language and people many times. The following examples (and the sorts of answers I have offered) are not exact quotations but are representative of the sort of commentary I have heard: "How can you be sure what Miami used to sound like?"

(We can't be sure, as is the case for most languages.) "But how can you talk about modern concepts?" (When we need to create a word, we do—in a Miami way; the lexicon is not a frozen entity.) "I met some Miamis and thought they didn't seem Indian."

The last point, while seemingly unrelated to language reclamation, is perhaps the most important. There is an added burden to indigenous communities in that the competence held by the community members involves not just the knowledge of the language (or the ability to acquire it from documentation) but also the strength to reject colonialist views—extensions of the purism referred to earlier—that the only real Indian languages and cultural ways are those that existed far in the past. I reject those views. Historical Miami culture is historical Miami culture, and modern Miami culture is modern Miami culture; both are legitimate. The core values and traditions are the same and need to be maintained, but the details of daily life have changed, and like all peoples, we Miamis are a very diverse group. The grammar of the language and the ways in which it is used follow the same pattern. While the modern version of Miami seems similar enough to the variety described in the documentation that they would be mutually intelligible, of course they are different; *all* currently spoken languages have changed from how they used to be spoken. Are they all extinct?

The existence of these changes in itself is hardly remarkable, but given that Miami still gets labeled "extinct," some discussion of those changes is warranted to substantiate the claim that the language really is in use. One such example involves recent lexical innovation. Often, we have dealt with lexical gaps by semantically broadening existing words. For example, *aahteeleentanto* (extinguish it [the flame]) now also means "turn it off" in reference to items powered by electricity. Elsewhere we have created words using existing Miami roots. Examples include *kiinteelintaakani*—literally "the fast-thinking thing"—to mean "computer" and *aacimwaakani*—literally "the narrating thing"—to mean "telephone." *Hohowa* is a sort of hybrid, combining the English *ho ho* with the Miami animate suffix to mean "Santa Claus." Loan-translations include *nintaya keetoopiita*—literally "my pet is thirsty"—which generally means "my car needs gasoline" (calqued from Kickapoo, a related language). These words are now common.

More telling to demonstrate the language's active use is the existence of recent "naturally evolved" adages—new sayings that occurred in spontaneous conversation and that have been adopted by some segment of the Miami speech community as a fixed collocation. An example that was proverbialized early in our language reclamation efforts is *piici wiihsa eehtooki waapimotaya* (she must have many blankets), a phrase that refers to the Miami cultural practice of gifting people with blankets and means that somebody must be an important person (as evidenced by their having received many gifts). A less exalting example is *amahkisena noontiahtoonki* (his moccasins were set outside), which describes a man in certain unfortunate circumstances and is framed around the historical practice of a woman being able to divorce her husband by placing his personal belongings outside the *wiikiaami* (wigwam).

Using Metaphors to Talk about Languages:
The Miami "Awakening"

From the arguments made in this chapter, one may be led to the assumption that the use of death and extinction metaphors for languages is never appropriate, but they do have their place. Even I occasionally use them, but only in situations where I have made a conscious decision to do so for a sound political, social, pedagogical, or descriptive reason. The rationale comes down to how different metaphors have different social effects and also how they differ in their levels of accessibility to the wide range of audiences that one might need to speak to.

Indeed, the biological metaphor of death or extinction is strong in that it not only emphasizes that languages are intimately connected with humans (Nettle and Romaine 2002, 7) but also frames the issue of the recent unprecedented rate of language "loss" as a crisis. There is nothing inherently wrong with using these terms to describe languages or even adopting them as category names. Rather, the problem lies in using such "final" terms blindly or because they are the only known option. The use of any metaphor can be a speech act (see Searle 1969)—in other words, the metaphor may superficially look like only a description but in fact is often used as a call for action. That said, a suggestion of impending "language extinction" may be very strong in a context where a language has not yet ceased to be known. Conversely, it can be a disservice to a community whose language is sleeping. We need a different metaphor.

However, while I maintain that [+competence, –performance] languages should be categorically differentiated from those that are [–competence, –performance] for several social and descriptive reasons, I acknowledge that there is no single correct way to describe and incorporate this differentiation. Nobody can predict exactly how others will understand their metaphor (or even a literal description), but the key to being effective is to really consider the choices. The second part of using a metaphor successfully might be to state explicitly why it was chosen in the first place.

On that note, it is with an ongoing personal reflection and after extended discussion with others that I have chosen to refer to the state of the Miami language from the 1960s to the early 1990s as "sleeping"—using an accessible metaphor that is not only more accurate than "extinct" but also that, importantly, comes from the Miami community. As argued in Hill (2002) the discourse of experts has a large influence in framing the issues around endangered languages and can be problematic when it doesn't capture the points of view of people with heritage to those languages. "Sleeping" is notable in that it does reflect a Miami point of view; our cultural reclamation efforts are named *myaamiaki eemamwiciki* (the Miami Awakening)—literally, "the Miamis awaken"—and sleeping is the counterpart to that awakening. This metaphor revolves around the idea that the knowledge that allowed our community to remain strong historically has not disappeared but that some of it must be actively sought and taught because it has been hidden for some time. As an extension of the metaphor, our annual cultural immersion youth camps, which are among the most important of the reclamation programs, are called the *eewansaapita* (he [the sun] rises) camps.

In conclusion, there are many ways to talk about language, all with political and social implications. The specific terms used and the ideas they imply guide policy, research, and even how people view their own heritage languages—or, for that matter, how they view their heritages, period. Formerly sleeping languages such as Miami serve communicative and social functions, and among other factors, I believe that our recognition of the fallacy of extinction has facilitated our coming as far as we have in awakening *myaamia*—both the language and the culture. Perhaps a wider recognition of this fallacy will facilitate other sleeping languages' coming back into use and being recognized as the legitimate codes that they are. May the *myaamiaki* (the Miami people) and members of other communities no longer have to experience the paradox of communicating and fostering an identity through an extinct language.

ACKNOWLEDGMENTS

I cannot list all of the people whose ideas and encouragement have led to my writing this chapter, but I owe a particular thanks to Daryl Baldwin and family, Miami Cultural Preservation Officer Julie Olds, and others who participate in Miami language efforts and show that *myaamia* is not extinct! I also owe a special thanks to Lisa Bennett, Leanne Hinton, Kendall King, Suzanne Romaine, an anonymous reviewer, and to multiple participants at GURT 2006 who provided valuable feedback on earlier versions of this chapter. Finally, *mihši neewe* (big thanks) to the leaders of the Miami Tribe of Oklahoma—particularly my grandfather, Chief Floyd Leonard—for believing in the future of our people and in our linguistic competence.

NOTES

1. This chapter focuses on smaller, indigenous communities such as the Miami whose languages went out of use recently and completely (see Amery 1995 for a discussion of Nunga reclamation, another representative example). Due to space limitations, this chapter does not explicitly address other languages such as the obvious example of Hebrew that have parallels (but important historical and social differences) with my proposed category of sleeping languages.

2. Here I refer to the lay usage of the term "extinct," adopting the point of view that a nonspecialist looking up information on his or her heritage language would likely have. In the *Ethnologue* itself, this term is defined as referring to a language with no living, first-language speakers and hence would have accurately described Miami from the 1960s to the 1990s. Furthermore, the 2005 edition acknowledges that "some linguists would not consider a language extinct if there are revitalization efforts and the language is being used as a second language even though there are no longer first-language speakers," and the *Ethnologue*'s editorial staff is discussing better ways to categorize languages like Miami in future editions (M. Paul Lewis, editor, personal communication, 2005).

3. Members of the Miami Indians of Indiana (primarily descended from Miamis who were not part of the 1846 removal from the ancestral homelands) and of the Peoria Tribe of Oklahoma (primarily descended from bands historically known as "Illinois") also have the same heritage language. Thus the total number of people with heritage to the Miami-Peoria language is more than ten thousand. As my enrollment, professional relationship, and most of my direct experience are with the Miami Tribe of Oklahoma specifically, I do not have the background to fully comment on the scope of language reclamation by members of these other groups except to say that it exists and that some families have come a long way in their language reclamation efforts.

4. Miami University (Oxford, Ohio) is a state institution that takes its name from the Miami people and that now has a special relationship with the Miami Tribe of Oklahoma. The Myaamia Project grew out of that relationship and exists to promote and oversee research on Miami tribal issues (particularly language). It is unique in that the research is directed by Miami tribal community needs but occurs in a major academic institution and thus serves the larger academic community as well. See www.myaamiaproject.org, Baldwin (2003), and Baldwin and Olds (2007) for further discussion of the Myaamia Project's history, goals, and impact.

REFERENCES

Amery, Rob. 1995. It's ours to keep and call our own: Reclamation of the Nunga languages in the Adelaide region, South Australia. *International Journal of the Sociology of Language* 113:63–82.

Baldwin, Daryl. 2003. Miami language reclamation: From ground zero. Available online at http://writing.umn.edu/docs/speakerseries_pubs/baldwin.pdf (accessed November 16, 2004).

Baldwin, Daryl, and David J. Costa. 2005. *myaamia neehi peewaalia kaloosioni mahsinaakani: A Miami-Peoria dictionary.* 1st ed. Oxford, OH: Myaamia Project.

Baldwin, Daryl, and Julie Olds. 2007. Miami Indian language and cultural research at Miami University. In *Beyond red power: New perspectives on American Indian politics and activism since 1900,* ed. Daniel M. Cobb and Loretta Fowler, 280–90. Santa Fe: School for Advanced Research Press.

Chomsky, Noam. 1965. *Aspects of the theory of syntax.* Cambridge, MA: MIT Press.

Costa, David J. 1994. The Miami-Illinois language. PhD diss., University of California, Berkeley.

———. 2003. *The Miami-Illinois language.* Lincoln: University of Nebraska Press.

———. 2005. The St-Jérôme dictionary of Miami-Illinois. In *Papers of the Thirty-Sixth Algonquian Conference,* ed. H. C. Wolfart, 107–33. Winnipeg: University of Manitoba Press.

Dorian, Nancy C. 1994. Purism vs. compromise in language revitalization and language revival. *Language in Society* 23:479–94.

Fishman, Joshua A. 1991. How threatened is "threatened"? A typology of disadvantaged languages and ameliorative priorities. In *Reversing language shift: Theoretical and empirical foundations of assistance to threatened languages,* ed. Joshua A. Fishman, 81–121. Clevedon: Multilingual Matters.

———, ed. 2001. *Can threatened languages be saved? Reversing language shift revisited.* Clevedon: Multilingual Matters.

Goodfellow, Anne. 2003. The development of "new" languages in Native American communities. *American Indian Culture and Research Journal* 27:41–59.

Gordon, Raymond G., Jr., ed. 2005. *Ethnologue: Languages of the world* (15th edition). Dallas, TX: SIL International. Also available online at www.ethnologue.org

Hill, Jane. H. 2002. "Expert Rhetorics" in advocacy for endangered languages: Who is listening, and what do they hear? *Journal of Linguistic Anthropology* 12:119–33.

Hinton, Leanne. 2001. Sleeping languages: Can they be awakened? In *The green book of language revitalization in practice,* ed. Leanne Hinton and Ken Hale, 413–17. San Diego: Academic Press.

Lewis, M. Paul. 2006. Evaluating endangerment: Proposed metadata and implementation. Paper presented at GURT 2006, Washington, DC, March 3.

Nettle, Daniel, and Suzanne Romaine. 2002. *Vanishing voices: The extinction of the world's languages.* New York: Oxford University Press.

Rinehart, Melissa A. 2006. Miami Indian language shift and recovery. PhD diss., Michigan State University.

Searle, John R. 1969. *Speech acts: An essay in the philosophy of language.* Cambridge: Cambridge University Press.

Spolsky, Bernard. 2002. Norms, native speaker and reversing language shift. In *Pedagogical norms for second and foreign language learning and teaching,* ed. Susan Gass, Kathleen Bardovi-Harlig, Sally Sieloff Magnan, and Joel Walz, 41–58. Philadelphia: John Benjamins.

UNESCO Ad Hoc Expert Group on Endangered Languages. 2003. *Language vitality and endangerment.* Paris: UNESCO Expert Meeting on Safeguarding Endangered Languages.

3

▨ Evaluating Endangerment: Proposed Metadata and Implementation

M. PAUL LEWIS
SIL International

▨ **AS AWARENESS OF** and concern for the loss of linguistic and cultural diversity has grown in the last two decades (e.g., Craig 1992; Fishman 1988, 1990, 1991, 2000, 2001; Hale 1992a, 1992b; Jeanne 1992; Krauss 1992; Nettle and Romaine 2000; Watahomigie and Yamamoto 1992), so too has interest in finding a way to evaluate the level of endangerment of the world's languages. A desire for a comprehensive description of the state of the linguistic world has developed from research on how many languages there are and where they are located to investigation of their transmission, use, and preservation (Brenzinger et al. 2003; Dorian 1989; Fishman 1991). The *World Languages Review* describes this agenda as follows: "How can we describe the sociolinguistic situation of the languages of the world in a way that lets us assess the situation of each language and at the same time put forward recommendations or patterns of action to help preserve the linguistic and cultural heritage of humanity?" (Martí et al. 2005, 1).

Categorization of the level of endangerment of a language is not a simple conceptual task, as it represents the intersection and interplay of many individual, group, and societal factors (Hyltenstam and Stroud 1996). Thus labels such as "endangered" or "highly endangered" entail constellations of factors relating to language use, language attitudes, language proficiency, population, location, socioeconomic status, and level of education among others. Theoretical formulations of how these factors relate to and affect each other are still developing. At the same time, more programmatic plans of action for preservation and revival (e.g., Crystal 2000; Fishman 1990, 1991; Grenoble and Whaley 1998; King 2001; Nettle and Romaine 2000) are also being proposed and implemented. Fishman's Graded Intergenerational Disruption Scale (GIDS) (Fishman 1991) provides the best known summation of the interplay of language transmission, language attitudes, and language use in language maintenance or shift to date; however, it doesn't provide a detailed set of factors to be evaluated or a well-defined way to measure progress in efforts to reverse language shift. UNESCO (Brenzinger et al. 2003) has more recently developed another comprehensive framework that is designed to provide evaluative measures, outlining nine factors in evaluating the level of endangerment of a language (intergenerational language transmission, absolute numbers of speakers, proportion of speakers within the total population, shifts in domains of language use, response to new domains and media, materials for language education and literacy, (governmental and institutional) language attitudes and policies, community members' attitudes toward their own language, type and quality of documentation. However, our ability to make use of such existing taxonomies is hampered by the fact that actual data from the field have been collected and compiled using a variety of classificatory schemes, which often renders analysis across different frameworks difficult and confusing. Further, for many languages the needed data are either not readily available or have not been collected at all (Lewis 2006). There appears, therefore, to be an immediate need for "standardization" in the collection of data for the evaluation of language endangerment.

This chapter represents an approach to such standardization, in a way that it is hoped will contribute to our knowledge of the situation of each language as well as to the identification of the most appropriate remedial steps to be taken in each case. I suggest parameters of vitality/endangerment and develop a generalizable set of situational factors to be tracked for the purpose of getting a better understanding of those parameters and, ultimately, evaluating the level of language endangerment in any given case. This proposal is intended to serve both researchers and activists of endangerment and revitalization, without prematurely binding them to any particular analytical framework.

Desiderata of a System for Evaluating Endangerment

There are some basic desiderata to be considered in the design of a system for evaluating language endangerment:

Comprehensiveness and universality. The kinds of data we ask for should be collectable from all regions of the world, from all language families, and from any and all situations.

Consistency and reliability. The kinds of data we collect must be operationalized in such a way that data can be compared across all languages and regions of the world. A common set of categories must be agreed on so that labels are understandable and ambiguities are reduced.

Validity. The data we collect must above all be valid indicators of characteristics that are demonstrably related to endangerment, as evidenced in ongoing research. Frameworks such as those developed by Fishman (1991, 2001), Hyltenstam and Stroud (1996), King (2001), and Brenzinger et al. (2003), among others, provide the essential elements for such a system.

Feasibility. The data must be collectable, maintainable, and manipulable in a relatively straightforward way.

Proposed Metadata

As outlined earlier, this chapter proposes a system for standardized collection of specific data that will contribute to our knowledge of the situation of each language. These data are categorized within seven parameters of vitality/endangerment and consist of situational factors.

The parameters amount to a set of metadata, a description of the general categories of data that are needed in order to be able to assist analysts in describing each language situation. The situational factors correspond to specific data items that should be collected within each general category. To designate the situational factors (tagged SF), an identifier that consists of a three-letter parameter designator, for example, AGE or DEM for demographics, STA for status, and so on, has been assigned to each situational factor, followed by a number. Numbering reinitializes for each parameter.

In large measure these data are already being collected in various forms. This proposal makes explicit the rationale for their collection and proposes a standardized format for reporting them.

Parameter 1: Age

Fishman (1991) declared that the loss of intergenerational language transmission is the most significant factor in language endangerment and identified the home domain as one of the most important regarding the retention of an endangered language and the reversal of language shift. Thus parents and immediate family appear to have the most important role in passing on a language from one generation to the next, although there is also evidence that communities play a significant role in language transmission (and perhaps more crucially in its revitalization; see King 2001, 209–11).

Proposal.   The following situational factors related to the age of speakers are proposed:

- The clearest and most feasible situational factor in support of an analysis of intergenerational language transmission is *the number of users by age group* (AGE-SF1).
- In addition, it may be quite helpful to identify for each language *the age of the youngest known user* (AGE-SF2). This number (the age) could then be used as a kind of index of language transmission, with higher age numbers indicating lower levels of language transmission and lower numbers indicating more robust transmission of the language from parent to child.

Complexities

- Issues related to age grading and apparent time (Hockett 1950; Labov 1972) must be taken into consideration. Fasold (1984, 215) observes that "it is often the case that different language behavior is expected of people in a society at different ages." Evaluation of the age cohort data needs to take such localized expectations into account.
- Researchers and data collectors will need to arrive at a consensus regarding the operationalization of AGE-SF1 by identifying a standard set of age cohorts. Use of different age thresholds between cohorts will diminish the comparability of the data. However, Eckert (1989) has noted that dividing the age continuum into equal chunks without reference to the actual life stages that are significant in a community can sometimes mask significant language-use patterns. Perhaps the identification of generational cohorts (i.e., children, parents,

grandparents) following Fishman (1991) would be sufficient for most
purposes.

▥ Researchers and data collectors will need to arrive at a consensus definition of
a "user." Will this include first-language (L1) users only? Children learning
the language as their second language (L2)? What level of proficiency in the
language constitutes one as a "user"? Inconsistencies in these definitions will
diminish the comparability of the data.

Parameter 2: Demographics
While the absolute number of speakers is an important datum to record, there are additional demographic factors that are helpful in evaluating the endangerment level of
a language.

Proposal.   The following situational factors are thus deemed particularly important in
this context:

▥ The *number of L1 users* (DEM-SF1) should be recorded, providing a way to
evaluate the size of the group in relation to other groups around it and in relation to the general norms of group size for the region (see DEM-SF5 next).

▥ The *number of users of the language as their L2* (DEM-SF2) gives an additional perspective on the language maintenance dynamics. In some cases, a
large number of L2 users in relation to the total ethnic population may indicate that the language is not being adequately transmitted to children but is being learned later in the community or through more formal means. Conversely, where there are a large number of people who use a language as their
second language who are not members of the ethnic group associated with the
language, there is a great likelihood that the vitality of the language in question is relatively strong or at least that the community in general finds some
benefit from acquiring the language, which could contribute to maintenance.

▥ The *number of L1 users who also use a (particular) L2* (DEM-SF3) gives a
view into the multilingualism situation and provides a way to begin to account
for the pressures from other languages that may be affecting ongoing language
maintenance. This situational factor identifies second languages being used
and provides a count of users for each. The total of these counts subtracted
from the count for the number of L1 users renders a count for the number of
users who are monolingual in L1.

▥ The *number of people who report their ethnic identity as that associated with
the language* (DEM-SF4; both users and nonusers) provides a way to compare
actual language use with perceived identity.

▥ The calculation of the *regional population norm of L1 users* provides a way to
contextualize population size (DEM-SF5). Grimes (1986) proposed a method-
ology for calculating the norms for language group size for the five regions of
the world used by the *Ethnologue* (Grimes 1984): Africa, the Americas, Asia,
Europe, and the Pacific. He noted that the absolute number of users varies

considerably from one part of the world to another and that what may constitute a very large language group in one region could conceivably be quite
small in another. Moreover, Grimes (1986) observed that the distribution of
languages by population in each of the five regions followed a log-normal distribution. That is, the language population totals for any given region when
expressed as logarithms and plotted on a graph form a bell curve (a "normal"
distribution), though the overall shape of the bell curves differ from region to
region. This, he asserted, indicates that there are regional norms of language
size that can be determined through statistical methods. Absolute numbers for
populations tell us little if they are not considered in comparison with the
norms for the region in which they are found.

I am proposing that these norms be recalculated periodically based on the most
current data available and that these norms be used as a means of evaluating the
absolute population numbers provided by DEM-SF1, DEM-SF2, DEM-SF3, and
DEM-SF4.

- The *absolute proportion* (DEM-SF6), represented by DEM-SF1 (L1 users
  only) divided by the total population of a reference group (e.g., total population of a country), is proposed as an additional demographic situational factor
  that can be used to evaluate the level of endangerment. This statistic shows
  the size of a group relative to the overall population (i.e., the percentage of the
  total population) and gives some sense of its visibility on the national (or regional) level.
- In addition, it is proposed that *patterns of residence* (DEM-SF7) also be taken
  into consideration and recorded. Communities that are in different residential
  patterns (e.g., traditional villages, displaced, widely scattered, urban enclaves,
  rural only, etc.) are likely to have different responses to contact and different
  outcomes in terms of threat and endangerment.

Complexities

- As described earlier (see Parameter 1), a consensus on the definition of a
  "user" is needed. This will determine whether semispeakers and others with
  limited proficiency will be counted in DEM-SF1, DEM-SF2, or only in
  DEM-SF4.
- Researchers will need to resolve how overlapping and nested identities will be
  handled. Individuals often identify themselves with more than one ethnic or
  social grouping. Depending on the situation, one of those identities may be
  more salient, making it difficult to come up with reliable data for DEM-SF4.
- A related issue is how discontinuous populations, displaced peoples,
  cross-border groups, and so on identify themselves. While they may share a
  common linguistic affiliation they may not share a common ethnic or cultural
  identity.
- In most cases, it is likely that the reference group used to calculate DEM-SF6
  will be the total population of a country, though there may be other ways of

specifying the demographic context against which the previously discussed population numbers will be analyzed. For example, on the one hand, a language group that resides in more than one country might actually be larger than the population of any one of the countries in which it is found. On the other hand, it may be found that the proportion of the language group population to the population of a specific region within a country may be more significant than its proportion to that of the country as a whole.

■ A set of common residence pattern categories needs to be identified and agreed upon as the values for DEM-SF7.

Additional Supporting Data.   Dates and sources for all of these statistics are needed in order to ensure the collection of comparable data within a reasonable time frame. It is impossible to collect all of the data for all of the languages of the world on a single day or month or even in a single year. This variation in the moment of collection will result in variability in the data, which can be controlled for to a certain extent by tracking both source and collection date.

Parameter 3: Language Use

Gal (1996, 586) describes language shift as a process "in which ever more speakers refrain from using language X and instead use language Y in ever more social functions and situations." Thus data about the social functions and situations, the domains of use, of a language, as well as ongoing changes in the assignment of those domains, contribute significantly to our understanding of the level of endangerment. In-depth research in each situation would ideally provide a more detailed analysis of language use patterns.

While there is general agreement that loss of domains of use indicates an erosion of the vitality of a language, the identification of what domains to track and the nature of any hierarchical organization of such domains is somewhat more tenuous and varied. An extensive list of possible domain categories is proposed in the following paragraphs, with the caveat that it may not be entirely practicable on a global scale within the desiderata listed earlier.

Proposal.   A variety of domain categories should be tracked, ranked from most informal and intimate (e.g., the Home domain) to most public and formal (e.g., a domain such as Government Functions). The configuration of the domains in which the language is predominantly used can provide a reasonable profile for each language. In addition, longitudinal comparisons of these domain configurations can provide insights into the direction and pace of language shift if it is occurring.

■ The *predominant use of the language in the home* (USE-SF1) records data that supports both an analysis of daily use patterns as well as providing an additional indicator of ongoing intergenerational language transmission.

■ The *predominant use of the language in Public Encounters* (USE-SF2) provides data on in-group public use of the language in locations such as the street, at community gatherings, and so on. These are likely to be informal encounters and provide a window into the community use of the language outside of the home.

- The *predominant use of the language in Recreation* (USE-SF3) provides data on the in-group public use of the language in recreational settings such as children playing together or informal team or sports activities. (Formally organized sports events may be better analyzed as Public Functions [USE-SF10] as they may, at least in some cases, represent out-group activities; see Lewis 2001, 62.)

- The *predominant use of the language in the public market* (USE-SF4) provides data on public commercial interactions that are primarily in-group oriented but may involve some interaction with outsiders as well.

- The *predominant use of the language at work* (USE-SF5) provides data on the language most closely associated with income generation. Language use in this setting may well be a strong indicator of where the community is finding its economic benefits and rewards, which could be a strong motivator for either language maintenance or language shift (Palmer 1996).

- The *predominant use of the language in religious gatherings* (USE-SF6) provides data on the use of language for worship, prayer, and religious ritual. If more than one religion or more than one kind of religious gathering is present in a community, this factor might be tracked separately for each. (Public, formal, religious gatherings may well pattern in the same way as formal public functions [USE-SF10, described later], so there would be no need to distinguish them.)

- The *predominant use of the language in stores and commercial establishments* (USE-SF7) provides data on language use in more formal commercial settings. In some situations, buying and selling may be done in a public market but also in more public, more formal, and perhaps more out-group-oriented settings than is captured in USE-SF4, such as stores and commercial establishments. If the patterns of language use here are different from those relating to the market, recognizing stores and commercial establishments as a different domain of use may be helpful.

- The *predominant use of the language in mass media* (USE-SF8) such as audio, video, film, or print (newspapers, signage, advertising, etc.) provides data on "new" domains of use for many minoritized languages.

- The *predominant use of the language in formal education* (USE-SF9) provides data on another potentially "new" domain of use and also implies a certain amount of development activity (which is tracked in DEV-SF7, DEV-SF 8, and DEV-SF 9).

- The *predominant use of the language in formal public functions* (USE-SF10) provides data on (potentially) mixed-group events and gives some insight into language attitudes: while the level of formality of an event very likely lies on a formal-informal continuum, some events can be clearly identified as ceremonial and formal: for example, inaugurations of institutional cycles (new governments, school terms, etc.) and similar civic events and nonreligious gatherings. The patterns of language use at such events may well provide some indication of which language(s) would be appropriate for public display and which would be considered inappropriate for such uses.

For each situational factor/domain described earlier, it is suggested that the data to be recorded could be one of three possible responses to the question "Is the language used predominantly in this domain?" The proposed response options are "yes," indicating clear predominant use of the language in this domain; "no," indicating clear lack of use in this domain; and "new," indicating that the language is gaining use or being introduced in this domain, though it may not yet be predominantly used. While much more detailed description of language use patterns is possible and even desirable, for the sake of feasibility the proposal is that the presence or absence of predominant use in each domain and the indication of growing use in a domain may be a minimum requirement.

Complexities

- Researchers will need to arrive at a consensus regarding the most appropriate inventory of domains to be tracked and how those domains are to be defined. Ten domains to track and evaluate represent a significant effort that may not be feasible on a wide scale. Other domain categorizations might be more widely applicable than those proposed here. Fishman (1991, 55) provides an example from Basque where only six domains were identified. Fishman's comment on the complexity of measurement of language use is that "sometimes there is simply no alternative to minimalism on the evaluation front" (54). Perhaps a less fine-grained but more generalizable set of domain categories would also meet the desiderata of comprehensiveness and feasibility.
- Researchers need to agree that simply recording "yes," "no," or "new" are appropriate responses. They may also want to add a response that indicates that a language is losing ground in a domain.

Parameter 4: Language Cultivation/Development, Literacy, and Education

It is useful to categorize the state of cultivation or development of each language. While the effects of cultivation efforts are variable, in general, development (graphization, standardization, elaboration, etc.) tends to increase prestige and subjective ethnolinguistic vitality.

Proposal.   Development might be categorized in terms of the following:

- The *existence and ongoing transmission of oral literature* (DEV-SF1), either through live practice and presentation or through audiovisual media.
- The *existence of a practical orthography* (DEV-SF2), which can be used for reading and writing and the production of literature.
- The *existence of standardization materials* (DEV-SF3) such as alphabet books, word books, glossaries, lexicons, and dictionaries in the language (for

users of the language), pedagogical and prescriptive grammars, usage and style manuals, and so on.

▨ The *existence of literacy instruction materials* (DEV-SF4) for use by beginning and intermediate readers and writers. This would include teachers' manuals and instructional helps. Other easy or early reading materials would also be recorded here.

▨ The *existence of a significant body of print literature* (DEV-SF5) beyond easy reading materials in the language.

▨ The *existence of mass media materials* (DEV-SF6) such as audio, visual, or print media for mass distribution.

▨ The *existence of elementary education materials* (DEV-SF7) in the language either as the medium of instruction or as a subject.

▨ The *existence of secondary education materials* (DEV-SF8) in the language either as a medium of instruction or as a subject.

▨ The *existence of tertiary education materials* (DEV-SF9) in the language either as a medium of instruction or as a subject.

Complexities

▨ In addition to the existence of an orthography, it may also be helpful to indicate whether or not there are multiple (perhaps competing) orthographies and the level of acceptance of each by the community. Background information on the history and rationale behind the various orthographic options can also be very helpful in evaluating the ethnolinguistic vitality and ideological currents within a language community.

▨ It is also clear that even though materials of the various types exist, they may not be used or accepted. Some may be outdated or have such a limited distribution that few potential users of the materials may be aware of them. In some situations, materials may have been produced but never published or distributed due to lack of resources. In addition, the report of the existence of such materials does not say anything regarding their quality or usability.

Additional Supporting Data

▨ It may also be helpful to track the script(s) in use or available to the community.

▨ For all of the situational factors that relate to the existence of particular kinds of materials (standardization, literacy, pedagogical, literature), it may be helpful to also track whether those materials are accessible to the communities where the language is spoken and whether they are in use.

▨ For the three situational factors that relate to the use of the language in education (elementary, secondary, and tertiary), it may also be important to track whether there exists a policy of such use and to what degree that policy is actually implemented and carried out in practice. See Parameter 5, Status and Recognition.

Parameter 5: Status and Recognition

While official recognition and language policy often are not reflected in usage, the creation of "space" for a language can be an important environmental variable that supports the ethnolinguistic vitality of a minoritized group of users.

Proposal.   Status and recognition might be recorded in terms of the following:

- Any and all kinds of *official and semi-official recognitions* (STA-SF1) of a language should be identified. Official recognition would include legislated designations as an official or national language, a medium of education, or some other functional assignment. Unofficial recognition might be a similar sort of functional assignment by a nongovernmental body such as an organization, union, or association. The information tracked would be the status assigned to the language, the agency assigning that status or giving it that level of recognition, and the date on which that status was granted.

Complexities

- Different kinds of recognition may bear more influence on the trajectory of a language than others. It might be useful to identify categories of status-assigning agencies in order to distinguish between recognitions that are highly significant and those that are less so. It is likely, however, that such categorizations of significance would be subjective and not universally accepted.
- The granting of status or recognition may be no more than rhetorical in some cases. The level to which a granted status is actually implemented and worked out in practical ways would also be of interest.

Parameter 6: Language Attitudes

Language attitudes have always been difficult to quantify and evaluate. There is an extensive literature dealing with both the theoretical construct and the methodologies for the assessment of attitudes (e.g., Agheyisi and Fishman 1970; Allard and Landry 1986; Bourhis 1983; Brudner and White 1979; El-Dash and Tucker 1975; Garrett, Coupland, and Williams 1999; Henerson, Morris, and Fitz-Gibbon 1987; Hewstone and Giles 1986; Lewis 1975; Ryan and Giles 1982; Shuy and Fasold 1973; Webber 1979; Wolff 1959). The two situational factors proposed here are no more than very general categorizations—a very blunt instrument for gauging language attitudes—that may nevertheless prove useful in providing a "rough cut" regarding attitudes in view of the desiderata of comprehensiveness and feasibility.

This parameter merits considerably more thought and development, and researchers are asked to generalize in their responses recognizing that much more could (and should) be said.

Proposal.   The situational factors for the evaluation of attitudes are the following:

- Attitude assessment should include an evaluation of the *number of community members who positively value their own language* (ATT-SF1), using the scale proposed in the UNESCO framework (Brenzinger et al. 2003): none, few, some, many, most, all. This provides a general sense of community support for the language (subjective ethnolinguistic vitality) without attempting to reduce that evaluation to a quantitative value that may give the impression of an indefensible level of precision.

■ This should be accompanied by a similar evaluation of the *number of members of the most significant outside group who positively value the language in question* (ATT-SF2). The same values proposed in the UNESCO framework (Brenzinger et al. 2003) could be used: none, few, some, many, most, all. This outsiders' evaluation of the language may represent merely sentimental or symbolic attitudes without implications for actual usage. (Note that the number of L2 users of the language is already tracked by the previously discussed DEM-SF2.)

Complexities

■ A consensus is needed on how to operationalize the response options (none, few, some, many, most, all) in order to maximize comparability between different reporting situations.

■ A consensus is also needed as to what the indicators of a positive evaluation are. Actual use of the language, the most concrete and readily observable indicator, is tracked in the demographic situational factors (DEM-SF1, DEM-SF2), but other behavioral and attitudinal indicators may be relevant as well. Possibilities include summary statistics regarding statements by users of the language, either positive or negative, that reveal their "sentimental" or "instrumental" (cf. Kelman 1971) attachment to the language, commitment measures such as those used by Fishman (1968), or other measures of behavioral outcomes (cf. Bourhis and Giles 1976; Giles and Bourhis 1976).

Parameter 7: Amount and Quality of Documentation

The amount and quality of documentation has no direct causative connection to the state of endangerment of a language. A language doesn't remain in use simply because a word list has been recorded or a grammatical description has been produced. However, the degree to which a language has been documented does contribute to the overall study of endangerment and to preservation and revitalization efforts. Descriptive materials help us better understand the process of language loss: What actually happens to the language's forms and structures as usage changes and transmission falters? Documentation also serves a vital archival function, preserving forms and structures that are disappearing and maintaining the potential for their retrieval and reintroduction.

Proposal.   Amount and quality of documentation may be categorized in terms of the following:

■ The *existence of a word list* (DOC-SF1). This should be accompanied by a description of the word list itself. Is it a standard list that is widely used for comparative purposes? How many words? Has it been modified? Added to? Any obvious anomalies in the list should be noted.

- The *existence of audio or video recordings* (DOC-SF2). Are there any audio or video recordings of the language? Of particular value are recordings of conversational data from which pragmatic techniques and strategies can be deduced. More scripted and polished recorded materials are also valuable, but conversational data provide important clues into the "social life of the language," as well as giving examples of linguistic structures (Penfield 2006).

While all documentary evidence should be clearly described and attributed, this is even more important with audio and video materials. Both a written record and an audio record should provide on the media itself the source(s), date, time, location, and researcher(s) involved. Additional metadata would include the nature of the recorded event (location, participants, description of the event), as well as information about the recording itself: the media format and recording equipment and technologies used and its archival quality and suitability for analysis or repurposing for language (re-)learning or revitalization.

- The *existence of phonological descriptions* (DOC-SF3). Useful additional data might include the extensiveness of the description, the theoretical model used, and the amount and source of the data used.
- The *existence of grammatical descriptions* (DOC-SF4). Useful additional data might include the extensiveness of the description, the theoretical model used, and the amount and source of the data used.
- The *existence of bilingual dictionaries* (DOC-SF5). The presence or absence of a descriptive bilingual dictionary (in contrast to a glossary or dictionary intended for native users—tracked separately under the previously discussed DEV-SF3) is a factor that can contribute significantly to revitalization efforts, in addition to enhancing the understanding of the lexicon and semantics of a language. Additional descriptive data regarding the size, thoroughness, and coverage of the lexicon as well as all languages used in the dictionary are helpful.
- The *existence of text collections* (DOC-SF6). Collections of texts provide a potentially rich set of resources both for study of the language and for reconstruction and revitalization. Additional data on such text corpora that should be recorded include dates of collection, participants/researchers involved, format of the archive, accessibility and availability, topics covered, discourse genre, and so forth.

Complexities.   The characterization of the quality of materials will inevitably be subjective. Linguistic adequacy of a data set is often determined by one's theoretical perspective. Data collected and analyzed by one linguist using one theoretical framework may not be considered very useful by another linguist working in a different theoretical framework. Nevertheless, the data used and the insights gained, no matter the theory that has been applied, are worth noting.

Additional Supporting Data. These situational factors cover a variety of documentary elements. For each, metadata about the documentation is also needed: who produced the documentation, when, some evaluation of quality (was it collected by a trained linguist?), does it describe a particular dialect or variant, who was it collected from and what was that person's proficiency in the language, and so on. The location and accessibility of the original documentation and any copies should also be noted.

Conclusion

This proposal calls for the organization and compilation of data regarding language endangerment in a standardized way that is intended to maximize its usefulness both for researchers of language vitality, maintenance, shift, obsolescence, and death and for language users, planners, and revitalizers.

The proposal organizes the data within seven parameters that are operationalized in terms of thirty-six situational factors. The parameters range in their scope to include primarily, but only partially, societal and group factors (cf. Hyltenstam and Stroud 1996), because at the level of global comprehensiveness being proposed, more individual factors would challenge the feasibility of the proposal. The Age and Demographics parameters contribute to a description of intergenerational transmission. The Use, Status, Attitudes, and Development parameters explore the contraction (or expansion) of the sociopolitical space available to the language. The Documentation parameter provides a basis for revitalizers and language-shift reversal practitioners to assess the resources they have at their disposal.

While Fishman's GIDS and the UNESCO framework (Brenzinger et al. 2003) inform this proposal, the intent is to provide for the collection of raw data for those working within any framework regarding the evaluation of the level of language endangerment and to contribute to the ongoing development of theoretical models via an expanded and validated system for collecting empirical evidence.

Although significantly elaborated at this point, this proposal is as yet far from complete. It is hoped that the descriptions of the complexities related to each of the parameters and situational factors provide an agenda for ongoing conversation and consensus building among theorists and practitioners.

REFERENCES

Agheyisi, Rebecca, and Joshua A. Fishman. 1970. Language attitude studies: A brief survey of methodological approaches. *Anthropological Linguistics* 12 (5): 137–57.

Allard, Real, and Rodrigue Landry. 1986. Subjective ethnolinguistic vitality viewed as a belief system. *Journal of Multilingual and Multicultural Development* 7 (1): 1–12.

Bourhis, Richard Y. 1983. Language attitudes and self-reports of French-English usage in Quebec. *Journal of Multilingual and Multicultural Development* 4:163–80.

Bourhis, Richard Y., and Howard Giles. 1976. The language of cooperation in Wales: A field study. *Language Sciences* 42:13–16.

Brenzinger, Matthias, Akira Yamamoto, Noriko Aikawa, Dimitri Koundiouba, Anahit Minasyan, Arienne Dwyer, Colette Grinevald, Michael Krauss, Osahito Miyaoka, Osamu Sakiyama et al. 2003. Language vitality and endangerment. www.unesco.org/culture/en/endangeredlanguages (accessed February 15, 2006).

Brudner, Lilyan A., and Douglas R. White. 1979. Language attitudes, behavior and intervening variables. *Trends in Linguistics, Studies and Monographs* 6:51–68.

Craig, Colette. 1992. A constitutional response to language endangerment: The case of Nicaragua. *Language* 68 (1): 17–24.

Crystal, David. 2000. *Language death.* Cambridge: Cambridge University Press.

Dorian, Nancy C., ed. 1989. *Investigating obsolescence: Studies in language contraction and death.* Cambridge: Cambridge University Press.

Eckert, Penelope. 1989. The whole woman: Sex and gender differences in variation. *Language Variation and Change* 1:245–67.

El-Dash, Linda, and G. Richard Tucker. 1975. Subjective reactions to various speech styles in Egypt. *International Journal of the Sociology of Language* 6:33–54.

Fasold, Ralph. 1984. *The sociolinguistics of society.* Ed. Peter Trudgill. Vol. 5, *Language in society.* Oxford: Blackwell.

Fishman, Joshua A. 1968. Sociolinguistics and the language problems of the developing countries. In *Language problems of developing nations,* ed. Joshua. A. Fishman, Charles. A. Ferguson, and Jyotirindra Das Gupta, 3–16. New York: Wiley & Sons.

———. 1988. Language spread and language policy for endangered languages. In *Proceedings of the Georgetown University Roundtable on Languages and Linguistics 1987,* ed. Peter. H. Lowenberg, 1–15. Washington, DC: Georgetown University Press.

———. 1990. What is reversing language shift (RLS) and how can it succeed? *Journal of Multilingual and Multicultural Development* 11 (1 & 2): 5–36.

———. 1991. *Reversing language shift.* Clevedon, UK: Multilingual Matters.

———. 2000. Reversing language shift: RLS theory and practice revisited. In *Assessing ethnolinguistic vitality: Theory and practice,* ed. Gloria E. Kindell and M. Paul Lewis, 1–26. Dallas: SIL International.

———, ed. 2001. *Can threatened languages be saved? Reversing language shift, revisited: A 21st century perspective, Multilingual Matters 116.* Clevedon, UK: Multilingual Matters.

Gal, Susan. 1996. Language shift. In *Kontaktlinguistik. Contact linguistics. Linguistique de contact,* ed. Hans Goebl, Peter H. Nelde, Zdenek Stary, and Wolfgang Wölck, 586–93. Berlin: Walter de Gruyter.

Garrett, Peter, Nicholas Coupland, and Angie Williams. 1999. Evaluating dialect in discourse: Teachers' and teenagers' responses to young English speakers in Wales. *Language in Society* 28:321–54.

Giles, Howard, and Richard Yvon Bourhis. 1976. Methodological issues in dialect perception: Some social psychological perspectives. *Anthropological Linguistics* 15:87–105.

Grenoble, Lenore A., and Lindsay J. Whaley. 1998. *Endangered languages: Language loss and community response.* Cambridge: Cambridge University Press.

Grimes, Barbara F., ed. 1984. *Ethnologue: Languages of the world.* 13th ed. Huntington Beach, CA: Wycliffe Bible Translators.

Grimes, Joseph E. 1986. Area norms of language size. In *Language in global perspective: Papers in honor of the 50th anniversary of the Summer Institute of Linguistics, 1935–1985,* ed. Benjamin F. Elson, 5–20. Dallas: Summer Institute of Linguistics.

Hale, Ken. 1992a. Endangered languages: On endangered languages and the safeguarding of diversity. *Language* 68 (1): 1–3.

———. 1992b. Language endangerment and the human value of linguistic diversity. *Language* 68 (1): 35–41.

Henerson, Marlene E., Lynn Lyons Morris, and Carol Taylor Fitz-Gibbon. 1987. *How to measure attitudes.* Newbury Park, CA: Sage Publications.

Hewstone, Miles, and Howard Giles. 1986. Social groups and social stereotypes in intergroup communication: A review and model of intergroup communication breakdown. In *Intergroup communication,* ed. William B. Gudykunst, 10–26. London: Edward Arnold.

Hockett, Charles F. 1950. Age-grading and linguistic continuity. *Language* 26:449–57.

Hyltenstam, Kenneth, and Christopher Stroud. 1996. Language maintenance. In *Kontaktlinguistik. Contact linguistics. Linguistique de contact,* ed. Hans Goebl, Peter H. Nelde, Zdenek Stary, and Wolfgang Wölck, 567–78. Berlin: Walter de Gruyter.

Jeanne, Laverne Masayesva. 1992. An institutional response to language endangerment: A proposal for a Native American Language Center. *Language* 68 (1): 24–28.

Kelman, Herbert C. 1971. Language as an aid and barrier to involvement in the national system. The motivation and rationalization for language policy. In *Can language be planned? Sociolinguistic theory and practice for developing nations,* ed. Joan Rubin and Björn Jernudd, 21–51. Honolulu: University of Hawaii Press.

King, Kendall A. 2001. *Language revitalization processes and prospects: Quichua in the Ecuadorian Andes.* Clevedon, UK: Multilingual Matters Press.

Krauss, Michael. 1992. The world's languages in crisis. *Language* 68 (1): 4–10.

Labov, William. 1972. *Sociolinguistic patterns.* Philadelphia: University of Pennsylvania Press.

Lewis, E. Glyn. 1975. Attitude to language among bilingual children and adults in Wales. *International Journal of the Sociology of Language* 4:103–25.

Lewis, M. Paul. 2001. *K'iche': A study in the sociology of language.* Dallas: SIL International.

———. 2006. *Towards a categorization of endangerment of the world's languages.* SIL Electronic Working Papers, 2006-002. Dallas: SIL International. Available from www.sil.org/silewp/abstract.asp?ref=2006-002

Martí, Félix, Paul Ortega, Itziar Idiazabal, Andoni Barreña, Patxi Juaristi, Carme Junyent, Belen Uranga, and Estibaliz Amorrortu, eds. 2005. *Words and worlds: World languages review.* Clevedon, UK: Multilingual Matters.

Nettle, Daniel, and Suzanne Romaine. 2000. *Vanishing voices: The extinction of the world's languages.* Oxford: Oxford University Press.

Palmer, Scott. 1996. The language of work and the decline of North American languages. *Notes on Literature in Use and Language Programs* 49:42–63.

Penfield, Susan B. 2006. Summary and Response to Panel Discussion on Community Involvement in Language Revitalization. Linguistic Society of America Annual Meeting. Albuquerque, NM.

Ryan, Ellen Bouchard, and Howard Giles, eds. 1982. *Attitudes toward language variation: Social and applied contexts.* London: Edward Arnold.

Shuy, Roger W., and Ralph W. Fasold, eds. 1973. *Language attitudes: Current trends and prospects.* Washington, DC: Georgetown University Press.

Watahomigie, Lucille, and Akira Yamamoto. 1992. Local reaction to perceived language decline. *Language* 68 (1): 10–17.

Webber, Richard. 1979. An overview of language attitude studies with special reference to teachers' language attitudes. *Educational Review* 31:217–32.

Wolff, Hans. 1959. Intelligibility and inter-ethnic attitudes. *Anthropological Linguistics* 1 (3): 34–41.

Documenting

4

Endangered Language Varieties
Vernacular Speech and Linguistic Standardization in Brazilian Portuguese

GREGORY R. GUY
New York University

ANA M. S. ZILLES
Unisinos

THE CENTRAL MOTIVATIONS for the attention paid to endangered languages by linguists and social scientists are twofold: above all there is concern for language as the embodiment or manifestation of the culture and history of the speakers and for the risk to that social and cultural heritage of a people that language loss entails. In addition, there is the professional concern of linguists at the loss of typological evidence about human linguistic capacity and specific evidence about the nature of the endangered language. And the preferred resolution for both of these concerns is to promote the preservation—or failing that, the documentation—of languages at risk.

Implicit in both of these motivations is some concept of just what are the social and linguistic characteristics that define a language variety as endangered. The most common conception is of some distinct language (typically bearing a language name) associated with a particular group of speakers—a people or ethnic group—which is threatened by absorption or replacement by some hegemonic language with which the endangered speakers are in contact. But the same issues—of vernacular response to contact with a hegemonic variety—also arise in connection with less distinctive, unnamed language varieties that are defined mainly by the social status of their speakers, that is, nonstandard, popular, or vernacular varieties. This includes low-status regional and local dialects, nonstandard varieties defined by social class or exclusion, and varieties associated with ethnic minorities. Indeed, any language variety that constitutes the verbal heritage of some speech community and experiences assimilatory contact with a dominant or standard language is potentially at risk; we will call such cases "endangered dialects." Of course, it is a truism to linguists that the difference between "language" and "dialect" is one of degree. These categories are really regions on a continuum of linguistic difference that has no natural dividing points. Hence there is no natural distinction between endangered language and endangered dialect. We use the term simply to focus attention on one end of this continuum.

What we wish to emphasize is that for many endangered dialects all the issues of endangerment are especially acute. These varieties may be especially valuable to linguistic science for their lack of prescriptive editing and for their potential to shed light on historical processes such as prior language contact, creolization, and popular linguistic developments that go unrecorded or devalued in the standard tradition. And they may be especially at risk because they lack names and popular recognition and may have no association with an identifiable "people." Such dialects lack social power, and in the modern world, many are faced with standardizing, assimilatory pressures under the impact of accelerating globalization, mass education, and mass communication. Varieties that are labeled according to the prevailing social wisdom as substandard, incorrect, uneducated, bad, sloppy, or whatever pejorative is attached, are often the deliberate targets of efforts at assimilation or eradication. And if their speakers believe these negative evaluations, they will often be willing participants, even advocates, for assimilation.

Popular Brazilian Portuguese

As a case in point we focus on the nonstandard or popular varieties of Brazilian Portuguese (PBP), which have been the subject of intensive sociolinguistic research for the past thirty years. As has been amply documented, a majority of Brazilians speak popular varieties that differ from the prescriptive standard and from the usage of the social elite, with respect to numerous features of phonology, morphology, syntax, and lexicon. Brazil is, in short, sociolinguistically highly diverse, and Brazilian Portuguese (BP) is a veritable tropical rainforest of linguistic variety. This variety has been of great interest to linguists and has provided evidence for numerous theoretical and historical claims, such as the parametric nature of syntactic change (Duarte 1995, 2000; Kato 2000; Tarallo 1995, working within Chomsky's Principles and Parameters model of grammar), the effect of saliency on syntactic change (Naro 1981; Naro and Lemle 1976), and notably the historical question of the source (Castilho 1992) and significance of this diversity. This is the issue we will focus on here.

The origins of PBP have been the subject of considerable debate. One common scholarly tradition attributes popular characteristics to the internal history of Portuguese, either seeking European sources or inferring spontaneous innovation within Brazil. But other approaches appeal to language contact. There is a current of scholarly opinion that has attributed PBP characteristics to contact with the indigenous languages of Brazil (cf. Schmidt-Riese 2000) including the *língua geral,* a Tupi-based lingua franca widely spoken in colonial times (Rodrigues 1993, 1996). For reasons of space, we will not explore this issue here. The other contact-based account of the origins of PBP appeals to the presence of the Africans who were brought to Brazil in great numbers during the period of the slave trade. Because Brazil has a huge population of African descent, and because the economies of colonial and Imperial Brazil were largely founded on a system of slave-based agriculture, one logically possible source of sociolinguistic diversity is prior language contact and creolization. This position has been advanced by a number of linguists from Mendonça (1935) and Mattoso Camara (1972) to Guy (1981), Holm (1992), and Lucchesi (2001). Crucially, it is the linguistic characteristics of the popular varieties that form the evidence for this reconstruction of historical events. As Mattoso Camara rightly notes, there's no good basis for claiming that standard BP was much influenced by contact with African languages or creolization. But popular varieties across Brazil, often spoken by people of African descent, show substantial evidence of such a history, a fact of considerable interest to Afro-Brazilians, other speakers of PBP, and linguists.

Importantly, the evidence of three decades of sociolinguistic research shows that the distinctive characteristics of PBP are receding on a broad front under standardizing pressures. Features of the contemporary social world, including urbanization, industrialization, mass advances in literacy and education, internal migration within Brazil, and improved transportation and communication, are all facilitating the rapid assimilation of nonstandard speakers to the socially dominant standard and the concomitant reduction in the use of popular features, the very features that provide evidence of the social heritage of the language. In this chapter we focus on one of the most distinctive characteristics of PBP, the high level of variability in agreement processes, and present evidence of how it is assimilating toward the standard language.

This evidence is drawn from both real-time and apparent time data. We will cite data from three different points in real time in Rio de Janeiro, covering the twenty-four-year span from 1976 to 2000, and apparent time data collected in 2000 in a very different location socially, the small community of São Miguel dos Pretos, founded by ex-slaves in the nineteenth century, in the southern state of Rio Grande do Sul. The corpora from which these data are drawn are the following: the 1976 corpus collected for the *Competências Básicas* project (Lemle and Naro 1977), which comprised interviews with twenty illiterate speakers in Rio de Janeiro; two sets of interviews (the first set recorded in the 1980s and the second in 2000) with a group of sixteen speakers from Rio of varying educational levels (Naro and Scherre 2003); and data from a stratified sample of twenty-four speakers from São Miguel dos Pretos, a small southern Afro-Brazilian community founded by ex-slaves in the nineteenth century (Almeida 2005).

The evidence of all of these data sets is consistent, showing a rise in the rate of use of standard features across real time and across age cohorts. In addition, panel data in Rio show a direct effect of education as a standardizing factor, in that speakers who increased their level of education between the initial and follow-up studies showed the highest increase in the use of standard forms. The São Miguel data also confirm the effect of increased education—the youngest speakers, who have a higher level of education than the older age groups, use the most agreement; São Miguel also illustrates the effect of other social pressures promoting the spread of standard features.

Variable Agreement

A very distinctive characteristic of PBP is variability in agreement marking. Standard Portuguese, dating from the time of Latin (and probably even from Proto-Indo-European), has always had obligatory, categorical agreement—in number and person between subject and verb, and agreement in number and gender within a noun phrase. But PBP, apparently from its earliest days, has had variable agreement marking in all of these processes. This variability can be seen in the text in (1) from George, an illiterate forty-eight-year-old male speaker from Rio interviewed in 1976 for the Competências Básicas project (cf. Guy 1981; Lemle and Naro 1977).

(1) **Os**   **pai**   *dela* FORU   *escravo*, *que eles*   ERAM   <u>**os**</u>
The(pl) parent(Ø) of her were(pl) slave(Ø), for they(pl) were(pl) the(pl)
<u>***negros.***</u>
blacks(pl).

      Os preto   *na época de cativeiro* ERA <u>*escravo.*</u>   ***Os***   ***branco*** *que*
The(pl) black(Ø) in time of slavery was(sg) slave(Ø). The(pl) white(Ø) who
ERA   <u>*senhor.*</u>
was(sg) master(Ø).
"Her parents were slaves, because they were the blacks. The blacks in slavery-days were slaves, it was the whites who were masters." (George, tape 17-7A:130f)

In this short text, George utters four two-word noun phrases (NP) (shown as bold in [1] above), of which one shows full standard agreement (*os negros*), while three (*os pai, os preto, os branco*) have one plural marker omitted (always the second one) but are all still clearly and overtly plural because of the plural morpheme –*s* appearing in the accompanying definite article *os*. There are also four tensed verbs with overt plural subjects (indicated by small caps in [1]), of which the first two are plural marked (*foru, eram*), whereas the last two are produced in third singular form. There are also four NP complements of copular sentences that in the standard language would arguably require plural markers (underlined in [1]): of these only *os negros* is plural marked; none of the other three complement NPs shows any plural marking (*escravo, escravo,* and *senhor*). This is variability of a high order, and the rapid alternation between presence and absence of number agreement marking is typical not only of this speaker but of popular Brazilian speech in general.

The sociohistorical question that arises in connection with data like this is "How does variability replace a categorical process, or, in other words, where does the absence of plural marking come from?" Naro, Lemle, Scherre, and others have argued that this is a spontaneous, internal development in BP (Naro 1981; Naro and Lemle 1976; Naro and Scherre 2003). But other scholars, such as Guy (1981), Holm (1992), and Lucchesi (2001), argue that absent or variable agreement arose from a creolized or creole-influenced history. They note that absence of agreement is typical of virtually all creole languages and that in Brazil this phenomenon appears at the same historical period as the arrival there of massive numbers of enslaved Africans. Elsewhere in the Portuguese-speaking world, similar phenomena are found in varieties involving contact with African languages (cf. Gärtner 2002); even in the classical (sixteenth century) Portuguese drama of Gil Vicente, the speech of black Africans is represented as lacking agreement.

The scholarly debate on this point has hinged crucially on the investigation of a number of well-documented morphosyntactic constraints on variable agreement, which provide vital evidence bearing on the origins and social history of PBP. We cite three of the constraints on number agreement by way of illustration. First are two constraints on subject-verb agreement: subject position, and morphological saliency of the plural marking. For subject position, preposed subjects (e.g., *As meninas chegaram* "the(pl) girls(pl) arrived(pl)") immediately adjacent to the verb trigger the highest rate of plural marking, while postposed (e.g., *chegaram as meninas* "arrived(pl) the(pl) girls(pl)") or distant (e.g., *as meninas que te contei finalmente chegaram* "the(pl) girls(pl) that I told you about finally arrived(pl)") subjects evoke much less verbal marking. The morphological saliency constraint works as follows: verb forms with highly distinctive number desinences (e.g., *ele cantou* "he sang" vs. *eles cantaram* "they sang") are much more likely to show plural marking than those forms where the singular and plural are only slightly or subtly different (e.g., *ele canta* "he sings" vs. *eles cantam* "they sing").

The creolist position on these constraints argues that they reflect natural constraints on acquisition of plural marking by speakers of a creole-influenced variety; the plural marking rule is acquired more readily in contexts where its operation is most evident or salient. Positionally, this means when the morphosyntactic relationship between subject and verb is most evident, that is, when they are adjacent in the canonical order SV; morphologically, acquisition of agreement is facilitated when the markers of plurality are especially distinctive.

The third constraint considered here affects nominal agreement. This involves another unusual positional constraint. Words at the beginning of a noun phrase, including both prenominal modifiers and head nouns that occur in first position, are extremely likely to bear a plural marker (at rates above 90 percent), while later positions, especially postnominal modifiers, are marked at much lower rates. Guy's creolist explanation of these facts is that they reflect a substratum effect, in that most of the West African languages that contributed speakers to the founding African population of Brazil had NP-initial number marking patterns (Guy 1981).

However, the crucial point that we wish to emphasize here is not the question of prior creolization but the erosion of the evidence. For all of these constraints on both of the agreement processes the popular patterns are succumbing to standard language influence, the rate of plural marking is climbing rapidly, and the distribution of plural markers across contexts is evening out. The spread of standardization is happening so fast that, in another few generations, it seems unlikely that there will be any evidence to discuss, and the sociolinguistic history that the popular varieties embody will be lost both to their speakers and to science.

The Advance of Plural Marking
First let us consider the overall rate of plural marking across all contexts. Table 4.1 summarizes the gross rates for the four samples of PBP speech cited earlier.

The Rio de Janeiro data show a fairly dramatic rise in the rate of plural marking in the twenty-four years from 1976 to 2000. In the earliest studies, the popular variety of working-class speakers showed a high level of absence of plural marking in both NPs and verbs; in Guy's (1981) analysis of Naro and Lemle's (1976) sample of illiterate speakers, nominal plurals were marked less than two-thirds of the time (64

▦ Table 4.1
Overall Rates of Plural Marking (percent)

Study/Place-Date	Nominal Plural Marking	Verbal Plural Marking (3p)
Ga /Rio-1976 (illiterates)	64	44
N&Sb/Rio-1980s	68	65
N&Sb/Rio-2000	81	81
Ac/São Miguel-2000	n.d.	80

aGuy 1981, twenty illiterate speakers in Rio, recorded in 1976.
bNaro & Scherre 2003, trend study of sixteen speakers of varying educational levels, recorded in early 1980s and again in 2000.
cAlmeida 2005, stratified sample of twenty-four speakers from São Miguel dos Pretos, RS, a community founded by ex-slaves in the nineteenth century.

percent) and verbal plurals were marked less than half the time (44 percent). Naro and Scherre's early 1980s data (2003) show higher rates of plural marking in both nouns and verbs, but this is probably more a consequence of the social makeup of the corpus rather than of the passage of five or six years of time: this sample included literate speakers of varying educational levels. Naro and Scherre's data collected in 2000 was a follow-up recontact of the same sixteen speakers interviewed in the 1980s, showing that their rates of plural marking jumped dramatically in less than twenty years to more than 80 percent marking in both nouns and verbs. Finally, Almeida's (2005) study of verbal agreement in an Afro-Brazilian community in southern Brazil in 2000 shows high rates of plural marking comparable to the Naro and Scherre 2000 data. Interestingly, Almeida's community is quite different in this respect from other Afro-Brazilian communities that have been studied (cf. Baxter 1992, 1995) in having a very high rate of plural marking. Almeida's discussion of the social characteristics of São Miguel makes it clear that this high rate of marking is associated with a high degree of integration with the wider society. São Miguel has a long history of people working outside the community and having frequent verbal interaction with outsiders. Other ex-slave communities studied in Brazil show both greater linguistic isolation and much lower rates of plural marking, as illustrated in figure 4.1 from Almeida's study.

This across-the-board increase in plural marking by itself represents a significant alteration in the behavior of the speakers in this community, taking them a long step in the direction of the standard. However, these figures are based on pooled data from a number of speakers. We might well ask "What are individual speakers doing, and what factors are causing them to change?" The Naro and Scherre panel study permits some answers to these questions. First, virtually all of the individuals in the study increased their rate of plural marking in the later sample, save only two speakers who declined by 1 percent in verbal marking. This clearly shows that standardization is affecting the behavior of the community as a whole. But the role of education as a driving force in standardization is also clear: the individuals in the study who spent at least some years in school in the interval between the two studies were the ones who increased plural marking the most, as can be seen in table 4.2, drawn from

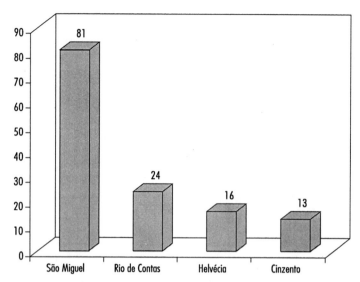

Figure 4.1 Verbal Plural Marking in Four Ex-slave Communities
Source: Almeida 2005.

Naro and Scherre (2003, 50–52). The average increase in plural marking for those who got more schooling was about double the increase for those who did not receive any more schooling.

Now let us consider the contextual constraints on plural marking. A striking result of recent research is that the increase in plural marking is concentrated in the most nonstandard contexts, having the effect of obscuring or minimizing the constraints on this process that have provided evidence for the debate on the origins of the dialect.

Consider in figure 4.2 the positional constraint on NP plural marking. Systematically, all studies of PBP have shown a powerful positional effect: plural markers are concentrated in prehead positions, especially the first word in an NP, while marking of head and posthead positions is much less frequent. The dashed line in figure 4.2 shows how strong this effect was in 1980, with rates of marking above 90 percent for prehead and headfirst positions, versus rates under 50 percent for other positions. But in 2000, while prehead plural marking is unchanged at a nearly categorical rate, there is an increase in all other positions, and the size of this increase keeps getting bigger, moving from left to right across the figure; in other words, the more nonstandard a category was in 1980, the more it has been corrected toward the norm in 2000. This has the effect of minimizing the positional constraint on plural marking, of flattening out the lines on the graph.

The same kind of leveling of constraint effects is evident in the Rio data on verbal plural marking. In figure 4.3 we see the effect of subject position on verbal marking. There is a substantial overall rise in plural marking for all subject positions, but the rise is most marked in those contexts that had the lowest levels of marking in the earlier period. Once again, the constraint effect is being minimized in the course of

Table 4.2
Table 4.2
Increase in Plural Marking in Rio by Individuals (percent)

	Nominal Plural Marking		Verbal Plural Marking	
	1980s	2000	1980s	2000
Subjects Who Increased Years of Schooling				
ADR57	43	75	38	58
ERI59	45	79	72	90
LEO38	62	93	71	92
ADR63	61	92	57	93
SAN39	84	95	76	93
FAT23	88	99	81	98
Average increase in marking		25		22
Subjects with no increase in years of schooling				
LEI04	45	64	56	59
JUP06	45	56	47	73
JOS35	57	67	52	70
NAD36	51	61	71	77
AGO33	53	66	57	83
DAV42	54	62	47	81
JAN03	62	71	46	54
VAS26	70	78	82	81
MGL48	89	98	93	95
EVE43	96	98	90	89
Average increase in marking		10		12

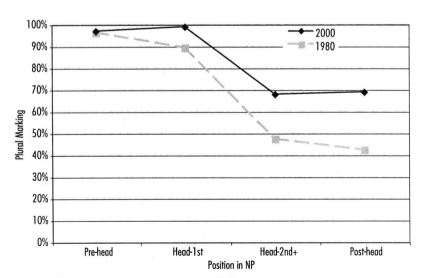

Figure 4.2 Advance of Standard Nominal Plural Marking in Rio, by Position in NP
Source: Naro and Scherre 2003.

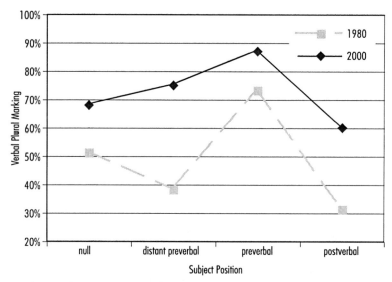

Figure 4.3 Advance of Standard Verbal Plural Marking in Rio, by Subject Position
Source: Naro and Scherre 2003.

the change. Plural marking in the disfavoring context of distant preverbal subjects (i.e., those that are separated from the verb by other words or phrases, such as adverbial phrases, relative clauses, etc.) has risen to more than 70 percent, a figure as high as what was found for the most favorable position in the earlier data—that of adjacent preverbal subjects. And postverbal subjects, which triggered agreement less than a third of the time in the 1980 corpus, are now getting 60 percent agreement. The line for 2000 is flattening out compared to the earlier data, again obscuring the effect of the context.

Finally, let us turn to the morphological saliency constraint. For this we will use apparent time data from São Miguel. This gives us a different perspective on the problem, but one that illustrates the same tendency toward assimilation and minimization of vernacular constraint effects. Figure 4.4 shows Almeida's data, for four saliency levels, broken down by age groups. The left edge of the graph shows the minimally salient morphological category, in which the opposition between singular and plural forms is unstressed and consists of simply an oral versus nasal vowel: for example, *come* (he eats) versus *comem* (they eat; a vowel followed by the letter *m* represents a nasal vowel in Portuguese orthography). The second level (Almeida's morphological categories 2 and 3) also involves unstressed desinences but with greater phonological contrast (e.g., *faz* "he does" vs. *fazem* "they do"). The third and fourth levels involve stressed desinences with progressively greater inflectional contrasts: the third level (Almeida's categories 4 and 5) have partial similarity between singular and plural desinences (e.g., *dá/dão* "gives/give"), while the fourth level (categories 6 and 7) have completely dissimilar inflections in singular and plural (e.g., *é/são* "is/are"). As we proceed from left to right, the more salient oppositions are always associated with higher levels of marking. However, note the differences among the

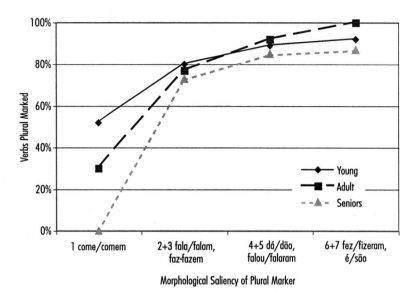

Figure 4.4 Verbal Plural Marking in São Miguel, by Age and Verbal Saliency
Source: Almeida 2005.

age groups. Overall the younger a speaker is, the more plural marking they do, but once again the greatest shift is in the most nonstandard environment. The oldest speakers showed zero plural marking in the first category, while the youngest speakers are already above the 50 percent rate here. Again the lines are flattening out, and younger speakers are moving in the direction of marking plurality without respect to morphological saliency. If the trend shown here continues into the next generation, we can expect an essentially straight line across the saliency categories, implying a plural marking rule that is no longer constrained by saliency.

In all of these cases, the diachronic tendency is toward the elimination of the constraint. As these constraints fade in local vernacular speech, the likelihood is that eventually they will not be acquired by a new generation of speakers. This will constitute a substantive change in the grammar of the community, a restructuring of the grammatical processes of agreement. Crucially, the constraints being eroded are precisely the ones of greatest proven interest to linguists, which have provided important evidence about the social history of the language.

The data that we have presented here thus show a general tendency toward increased use of agreement by speakers of very different social groups, stimulated by normative pressures. However, it should be noted that there is another change going on in the verbal system that indirectly affects the distribution of inflectional markers of agreement. This is the generalized use of a new first-person plural pronoun, resulting from the grammaticalization of what was historically a full NP *a gente* ("the people") replacing the historical pronoun *nós* (Zilles 2005a). This change matters here for two reasons. First it reduces the use of the traditional first-person plural desinence *–mos,* because verbs that take *a gente* as their subject appear in the unmarked form. This is the verb form that occurs with third-person subject pronouns *ele/ela* as well as with second-person *você,* and even with the traditional second-person subject pronoun *tu* for several Brazilian dialects. Second, many Brazilians spontaneously say they prefer using *a gente* because it avoids the worries about agreement that arise with using *nós.* This clearly demonstrates the linguistic insecurity that speakers feel about agreement. By adopting the innovative *a gente* they are effectively reducing their use of agreement marking by means of a parallel pathway that avoids the inconvenience of making "mistakes in agreement"—a highly undesirable error in view of the pronounced social stigma associated with lack of agreement that we document in the next section.

The Social Evaluation of Grammatical Agreement

We have implicitly asserted in this chapter that vernacular PBP speakers are responding to the higher social status and power of the dominant standard language when they increase their rates of agreement. We now present explicit evidence of the social evaluation of this variable. Grammatical agreement is the subject of overt social attention in Brazil, and Brazilian speakers often refer to the absence of agreement as a stereotypical marker of "bad" speech. Here are some examples from the data reported by Zilles in a recent paper on real-time change in PBP (Zilles 2005b).

The first example is from a woman recorded in 1990 in Porto Alegre, a city of about 1.4 million inhabitants in the southernmost Brazilian state of Rio Grande do Sul. She was interviewed for the Varsul ("Variation in the South") corpus, a database containing more than three hundred hours of interviews from twelve different cities and towns in the three southern states of Brazil. She is a widow, age sixty-eight, with an elementary education. The interviewer asks what she thinks it means to speak correctly. Without hesitation, she replies "Agreement." But strikingly, when pressed to elaborate, she tries to give an explanation of why agreement is so important but fails. This is very suggestive of a myth that she believes in but cannot explain—in other words, she recognizes the social norm for which superiority is asserted by the linguistically powerful but which in fact is simply arbitrary.

ENTREVISTADOR: O que que pra senhora assim é falar português corretamente?

FALANTE: A concordância.

E: A concordância?

F: A concordância, né? É muito importante, né? Porque- E escrever corretamente também, ler, saber ler . . .

(VARSUL corpus, RSPOA16, l. 1127–33)

INTERVIEWER: What is it for you to speak Portuguese correctly?

SPEAKER: Agreement.

I: Agreement?

S: Agreement, right? It's very important, isn't it? Because—And write correctly too, read, to know how to read . . .

Our second example comes from an interview conducted in 1970 in Porto Alegre, with a thirty-year-old professor of dentistry, himself no doubt an elite speaker. (This interview is drawn from the NURC project (Norma Lingüística Urbana Culta, "urban cultivated linguistic norms," project, which recorded the speech of samples of educated speakers from a number of major cities in Brazil.) The interviewer asks about "defects" in the way people speak, probably aiming at mannerisms such as stuttering and speech defects. The subject immediately and spontaneously talks about lack of agreement.

> *Entrevistador:* *Quais os defeitos mais comuns que você conhece no modo de*
> *falar?*
> *Falante:* *Quais os defeitos mais comuns no modo de falar? . . . éh . . .*
> *não há concordância . . . do verbo com a pessoa . . . às vezes a*
> *pes/ são várias pessoas e usa-se o verbo numa pessoa só . . .*
> *ou para uma pessoa . . . eu posso estar aqui . . . perfeitamente*
> *devido ao nervosismo estar falando erradamente . . .*
> (NUR—Porto Alegre inquérito 09 linhas 413–21)

After repeating the question presented to him, as if looking for a proper answer, the speaker says, "There is no agreement . . . of the verb with the person . . . sometimes the per—there are several people and one uses the verb for only one person . . . I may be here—just because of nervousness—speaking incorrectly."

Strikingly, this is a highly educated person displaying linguistic insecurity, fearing that he may be speaking "incorrectly" because he is nervous (although he is, in fact, using standard person/number agreement throughout). This bespeaks a powerful social stigma attached to lack of agreement. It is this stigma that is no doubt driving the assimilation evident in the data presented earlier.

Conclusions

Popular Brazilian Portuguese is among the most well-studied vernacular varieties in the world. Thirty years of sociolinguistic research have demonstrated a rich profusion of popular features, many of them strikingly at odds with the standard variety, and some of them typologically quite revealing or unusual. Numerous research projects—many of them completed, even more still under way, have investigated the sociolinguistic and dialectological landscape of Brazil. The data have revealed massive evidence bearing on the history and development of the Portuguese language in Brazil, and some of this evidence speaks directly to the social and cultural heritage of the great majority of Brazilians. Brazil manifestly possesses a culture and a population with a rich diversity of inputs from African, European, indigenous American, and even Asian roots, and the linguistic tapestry of Brazil has offered a colorful portrait of this diversity. But this tapestry is now being bleached of its color. Features of the standard language are spreading rapidly, and the grammars of Brazil are being homogenized. One consequence of this homogenization is that the linguistic contributions of some of the founding peoples of Brazil are being suppressed. The tapestry is turning monochromatic, and the color that is emerging is a lot paler than the population. The loss to linguistics and other social sciences from these processes of standardization will be substantial, but the loss to Brazilian society may be even greater.

REFERENCES

Almeida, Alessandra Preussler de. 2005. *A Concordância Verbal na Comunidade de São Miguel dos Pretos, Restinga Seca, RS* [Verbal agreement in the community of São Miguel dos Pretos]. MA thesis, Universidade Federal do Rio Grande do Sul.

Baxter, A. 1995. Transmissão geracional irregular na história do Português Brasileiro–divergências nas vertentes afro-brasileiras [Irregular generational transmission in the history of Brazilian Portuguese: Divergences in Afro-Brazilian outcomes]. *Revista Internacional de Língua Portuguesa* [International Journal of the Portuguese Language] 14:72–90.

Baxter, Alan N. 1992. A contribuição das comunidades afro-brasileiras isoladas para o debate sobre a crioulização prévia: um exemplo do estado da Bahia [The contribution of isolated Afro-Brazilian communities to the debate on prior creolization: An example from the State of Bahia]. In *Actas do colóquio sobre Crioulos de base lexical Português* [Proceedings of the Colloquium on Creoles with a Portuguese Lexical Base], org. E. d'Andrade and A. Kihm, 7–35. Lisboa: Edições Colibri.

Castilho, Ataliba. 1992. *O Português do Brasil* [Brazilian Portuguese]. In *Lingüística românica* [Romance Linguistics], ed. R. Ilari, 237–85. São Paulo: Ática.

Duarte, Maria Eugênia L. 1995. *A perda do princípio "Evite Pronome" no português brasileiro* [The loss of the "avoid pronoun" principle in Brazilian Portuguese]. Campinas, SP: Unicamp. Tese de doutorado.

———. 2000. The loss of the "avoid pronoun" principle in Brazilian Portuguese. In *Brazilian Portuguese and the null subject parameter,* ed. M. A. Kato and E. V. Negrão, 17–36. Madrid: Iberoamericana.

Gärtner, Eberhard. 2002. Tentativa de explicação diacrônica de alguns fenômenos morfossintáticos do Português Brasileiro [A possible diachronic explanation for certain morphosyntactic phenomena of Brazilian Portuguese]. In *Para a história do Português Brasileiro* [Toward a History of Brazilian Portuguese], org. Tânia M. Alkmin, 293–328. Vol. 3, Novos Estudos. São Paulo: Humanitas/FFLCH/USP.

Guy, Gregory R. 1981. *Linguistic variation in Brazilian Portuguese: Aspects of the phonology, syntax and language history.* PhD diss., University of Pennsylvania.

Holm, John. 1992. Popular Brazilian Portuguese: A semi-creole. In *Actas do Colóquio sobre crioulos de base lexical Portuguesa* [Proceedings of the Colloquium on Creoles with a Portuguese Lexical Base], ed. E. d'Andrade and A. Kihm, 37–66. Lisboa: Edições Colibri.

Kato, Mary. 2000. The partial pro-drop nature and the restricted VS order in Brazilian Portuguese. In *Brazilian Portuguese and the null subject parameter,* ed. M. A. Kato and E. V. Negrão, 223–58. Madrid: Iberoamericana.

Lemle, Miriam, and Anthony J. Naro. 1977. *Competências básicas do português* [Basic competencies in Portuguese]. Rio de Janeiro: MOBRAL.

Lucchesi, Dante. 2001. As duas vertentes da história sociolingüística do Brasil, 1500–2000 [The two currents of the sociolinguistic history of Brazil]. *Delta* 17:97–130.

Mattoso Camara, Joaquim. 1972. *The Portuguese language.* Trans. by A. J. Naro. Chicago: University of Chicago Press.

Mendonça, Renato. 1935. *A influência africana no português do Brasil* [The African influence on Brazilian Portuguese]. São Paulo: Editora Nacional.

Naro, Anthony J. 1981. The social and structural dimensions of a syntactic change. *Language* 57:63–98.

Naro, Anthony J., and Miriam Lemle. 1976. Syntactic diffusion. In *Papers from the Parasession on Diachronic Syntax,* ed. S. B. Steever, C. A. Walker, and S. S. Mufwene, 221–40. Chicago: Chicago Linguistic Society.

Naro, Anthony J., & Maria Marta P. Scherre. 2000. Variable concord in Portuguese: The situation in Brazil and Portugal. In *Language change and language contact in pidgins and creoles,* ed. John McWhorter, 235–55. Amsterdam: John Benjamins.

———. 2003. Estabilidade e mudança lingüística em tempo real: a concordância de número [Linguistic stability and change in real time: number agreement]. In *Mudança lingüística em tempo real* [Linguistic change in real time], org. M. C. Paiva and M. E. L Duarte, 47–62. Rio de Janeiro: Contra Capa Livraria.

Rodrigues, Aryon D. 1996. As línguas gerais sul-americanas [South American *lingue franche*]. *Papia* 4(2): 6–18.

———. 1993. Línguas indígenas: 500 anos de descobertas e perdas [Indigenous languages: 500 years of discovery and loss]. *D.E.L.T.A.* 9:83–103.

Schmidt-Riese, Roland. 2000. Perspectivas diacrônicas brasileiras: o rastro das línguas gerais [Brazilian diachronic perspectives: Traces of the *lingue franche*]. Unpublished manuscript.

Tarallo, Fernando 1995. Turning different at the turn of the century: 19th century Brazilian Portuguese. In *Towards a social science of language,* vol. 1, ed. G. R. Guy, C. Feagin, D. Schiffrin, and J. Baugh, 199–220. Amsterdam: John Benjamins.

Zilles, Ana Maria S. 2005a. The development of a new pronoun: The linguistic and social embedding of 'a gente' in Brazilian Portuguese. *Language Variation and Change* 17:19–53.

———. 2005b. Verbal agreement in spoken Brazilian Portuguese: Social practice and discourse representations. Paper presented at NWAV, New York University.

5

The Linguistic Negotiation of Complex Racialized Identities by Black Appalachian Speakers

CHRISTINE MALLINSON
University of Maryland, Baltimore County

THE DEBATE OVER "where sociolinguistics 'fits in' with the main currents of social theory and how it might become more substantively engaged in social theory" has pervaded the consciousness of sociolinguistics since the inception of the discipline (Coupland 2001, 2), and calls for sociolinguistics to advance its relationship with social theory seem recently to have become more urgent. Coupland, for example, specifically argues that current sociolinguistic research needs to incorporate "integrationist" social theories, which are balanced in their attention to structure and agency (i.e., they are neither overly structural nor overly constructivist). Similarly, Eckert (2003) has argued for sociolinguistics to adopt an integrated theoretical perspective that would take into account how social meaning is both locally situated and oriented toward a broader structure. To do so, Eckert suggests, would enrich sociolinguists' understandings of the power dynamics behind the social distinctions that emerge in field studies of minority or majority language varieties within any community.

Indeed, some recent research has begun to apply integrated theories of social action to refine how sociolinguists conceptualize the interrelationship between individual style, group linguistic norms, and social institutions and ideologies. Dodsworth (2005), for example, explores the concept of sociological consciousness—the recognition of links among different levels of social structure—as a factor conditioning variation in speakers' phonetic productions. Similarly, Dodsworth and Mallinson (2006) utilize intersectionality theory from sociology to frame apparently conflicting phonetic data from an individual speaker. They find that the phonetic data reflect this speaker's personal tensions as a marginalized member of his local community, which sheds light on the ways social structures interact with the privileges and inequalities of individual experience to produce unique practices, standpoints, and identities.

In addition, Mallinson (2006) incorporates two current social theories to analyze language variation in two women's communities of practice in the black Appalachian community of Texana, North Carolina. In the context of the communities of practice, the women construct social (including linguistic) distinctions based on lifestyle and presentation that serve as in-group and out-group markers and reinforce dominant ideologies about femininity, racial identity, and social status. Conclusions drawn from this study—which exemplify how social actors draw on a myriad of daily, locally meaningful, and ideologically laden practices and symbolic markers to create and maintain social boundaries—dovetail with the premises of intersectionality and structuration theories (Collins 2000; Giddens 1984).[1] Both theories hold that social structures such as race, class, and gender are multilevel. They interact to produce contextualized experiences of oppression and privilege for individuals and groups, who develop identities and standpoints and reproduce them in interaction, in ways that maintain or challenge status distinctions and hierarchies that are rooted in and support broader power relations.

In this study, the same theoretical lens—incorporating the perspectives of intersectionality and structuration theories—is applied to understand how the structure of race is constructed and articulated in the Texana community. Drawing on the idea that individuals and groups with unique social locations develop unique identities, I focus on four residents who articulated complex racialized standpoints during a three-year period of field research in Texana. The investigation is based on qualitative examination of interview and observational data, followed by a quantitative analysis (of the interview data) of four variables characteristic of African American English (AAE): third-person singular –s absence, copula and auxiliary absence with is and are, postvocalic r-lessness, and prevocalic syllable-coda consonant cluster reduction. Combining these multiple data sources—qualitative interview data, observational data, and quantitative (variationist) sociolinguistic data—allows an investigation of how the speakers use language as a symbolic vehicle to create racial distinctions that stem from and are relevant to their experiences as members of their community.

In this regard, like the studies outlined earlier, this study centralizes the fact that identities are not the "fallout" of external categorization.[2] Linguistic usages do not simply reflect social categories, as Eckert (2003, 115) explains; rather, they are part of what constructs them. Analyzing the processes is important for understanding how local meaning making interconnects with the meanings created in broader social systems—and, in turn, for investigating how the identity issues faced by many minority communities are expressed (and harnessed) in local language production.

Research Setting

This study focuses on the unique racial situation of African Americans in Appalachia. As Dunaway (2003) and others have noted, black Appalachians are a neglected U.S. racial minority within a neglected U.S. cultural minority—despite the fact that black outposts have existed in Appalachia since the early settlement period. One independent black community, Texana, is the largest black community in western North Carolina and is the focus of this study.[3]

Located in the Great Smoky Mountain region of North Carolina, which itself is located in the southeastern United States, Texana sits on the side of a mountain about a mile from the town of Murphy, the seat of Cherokee County.[4] Cherokee County is the state's westernmost county; it borders Georgia and Tennessee, and major urban areas such as Atlanta, Georgia, and Knoxville, Tennessee, are at least two hours away by car. Both Cherokee County and the town of Murphy are predominantly (over 90 percent) white. Texana proper has about 150 residents, all of whom are black except for about 10 whites. All of these whites are either partnered with black residents or are children of whites who moved into the Texana community to live with a black partner.[5]

Field Methods

To investigate the sociolinguistic situation in Texana, my research colleague Becky Childs and I made nineteen visits there between May 2002 and June 2005. The major components of our research strategy included conducting nonstructured interviews, interacting with and observing residents outside of interview settings, and participating in an oral history project designed and implemented with community residents. These elements are characteristic of the qualitative technique of naturalistic inquiry, which is less in depth than long-term participant observation but still entails attending to individuals' spontaneous behavior in their natural setting (Erlandson et al. 1993). In this process, we became familiar with residents while also accruing community-specific cultural information on social networks, contemporary situations, shared memories, and ways of life. These qualitative data provided substantive content for interpreting the aggregate patterns of linguistic variation that emerged in the subsequent quantitative analysis.

Racial and Ethnic Heritage

Details about the history of Texana are few and far between, documented in only some locally published books and in residents' memories.[6] Many Texana residents trace their heritage to a diverse group of African, Cherokee, Ulster Scots-Irish, and Irish-European ancestors—which is the case for many black Appalachians (Dunaway 2003). Texana's diverse history is not formally recognized, however. Although any individual might unofficially "claim" Cherokee heritage, applying for membership to the Cherokee nation entails a strict process. According to Gibson-Roles (2004), an applicant wishing to enroll with the Eastern Band of the Cherokee Indians must meet three criteria: be a direct lineal descendant of someone on the 1924 Baker Roll, possess at least 1/16 degree Eastern Cherokee blood, and apply for enrollment either within three years of his or her date of birth or within one year following his or her eighteenth birthday.[7]

According to Texana residents, individuals with black and Native American ancestry suffered prejudice and discrimination at the hands of both the Cherokee and the U.S. government. First, those with one-fourth black ancestry or more were deemed ineligible for the original Baker Roll—regardless of whether they had one-sixteenth (or more) Eastern Cherokee "blood." Second, families with black ancestors who lived on the reservation at the time the roll was created were forced off the local Cherokee reservation. Third, some individuals with black ancestry whose names made the original roll later learned that the records had mysteriously burned in a fire. Thus Texana residents are ineligible for federal funds, subsidies, and social services otherwise available to Native Americans today—services that, ironically, were first implemented to address the lingering effects of past discrimination.

As a result of their mixed ancestry and the history that has embittered many families, many Texanans now grapple with issues of ethnic identity and feel that their heritage is more diverse than the term "African American" denotes. As a result, most Texanans self-identify as "black," a term they prefer because it is a designation based on the color of their skin rather than on any single racial or ethnic identity. As Zora, a resident in her fifties, explained, "I call myself black because that's the color of my skin. Most everyone here is so mixed with black, white, and Indian blood. We aren't really one thing. So that's why I call myself black, it's the color of my skin and it describes me."[8] Similarly, the choice to call themselves black is, for some residents, a choice not to call themselves by another term. As Joan, a woman in her seventies, explained, "Our race is a welcoming race . . . So, I don't say that I'm Cherokee because the Cherokee people don't want me." Thus residents see "black" as more inclusive and representative of their mixed heritage and as a way to reject further involving themselves in the politics of naming.[9]

Yet despite how residents choose to self-identify, they still face the historic reality of race relations within the American South that is fundamentally based on a black–white dichotomy (Davis 1991). In some cases, Texanans' own conceptions of their race or ethnicity are usurped by outsider or institutional definitions—particularly for the youngest children, who are considered by the community to be multiracial. As Maggie Lou, a middle-aged resident, explained about children of "mixed" (typically black/white) race enrolled in the local school system, "They don't have them as mixed [on school records]. If their mother's white, they'll sign them in as white, as white kids. They don't ask. If the mother's black, then they'll register them as black." Thus, as Nagel (1994, 156) remarks, "While blacks may make intra-racial distinctions based on ancestry or skin tone, the power of race as a socially defining status in U.S. society makes these internal differences rather unimportant in interracial settings in comparison to the fundamental black/white color boundary."[10]

Speaker Profiles

Having framed my inquiry in an integrative theoretical perspective and situated Texana as a research setting, I move on to consider four speakers from the community. They were chosen for this analysis based on the complex racialized identities they each articulated during the three-year period of field research in Texana. All four of the individuals were born and raised in Texana, and I examine how they have experienced race and region in their local context and setting in order to shed light on their personal ideologies and standpoints about race and racial identity. For each speaker, I first present qualitative data from interviews and observations that include self-reference terms they use, stories they tell to express their affiliation to or distance from the Texana community, and the views they overtly espouse about race, racism, prejudice, and racial identity. These qualitative data contextualize the subsequent quantitative sociolinguistic data and thus allow for an examination of the connections between what speakers say substantively and the manner in which they say it.

Monica

The first speaker, Monica, is a self-identified black woman in her forties who was born and raised in Texana. After leaving the community during high school, she briefly moved to Atlanta, Georgia, but returned to Texana to marry a local man and raise a family. In the 1990s, however, she separated from her husband and moved to Dayton, Ohio, for about ten years. During her travels, she came to strongly identify with urban black culture. We interviewed Monica twice during a visit back to Texana (she now lives in Atlanta, Georgia). At first, Monica said, she found Dayton's fast pace to be hard to adjust to and frightening: "After the first two or three months up there, I was thinking, man I better get from here! [laughter] These folks are treacherous . . . too much game, it's a trick in just about everything they doing. . . . I'm just like, damn, this is much [even] for strong-willed me!" She also recounted how, when she first moved to Dayton, locals identified her as a Southerner and took advantage of her presumed naïveté: "They, where you from, Mississippi? Alabama? You know, stuff like that. And I says, why, you know, stop making fun of way I talk, you know, stuff like that. So it was obvious. And I think that's another reason why they zeroed in on me to take advantage, too, because I'm not from here, I'm easy prey, easy target. But I ain't easy prey, I ain't easy target, so you better think about that one, you know."

Monica quickly assimilated to city life by learning street smarts. After a year, she said, she had "finally established" herself as a woman who, on occasion and depending on the situation, was able to identify and behave as a *gangstress* and a *thug*. As she put it, "Now, it's a year later, and so, sometimes my cousin and I go to the hood, that's what we call, we go to the hood. I live downtown where it's real, real nice, saditty people.[11] And that's how they see me. But when I want to be gangstress, I go to the west side. You know what I'm saying? When I got to be the thug over there . . . And so after a year, I finally established myself that way."

Despite her assimilation to city life and her self-professed hardened attitudes and behaviors, Monica valued returning to her home community. She explained, "For the past 10 years, I've always had a prayer ritual. . . . Every time they say welcome to North Carolina, I send up my prayer. And then once I get here, I'm thankful and I mean that. But once I get here, where the liquor at, where the party at! [laughter]" Monica finds Atlanta, where she now lives, to be a balance between what she finds to be the fast-paced Ohio city and the slow-paced life she once knew in Texana.

Roger

The second speaker, Roger, is a self-identified black man in his early thirties who was born and raised in Texana and has never lived outside the community. Roger identifies strongly with local life and with mountain culture. When we first met him, for example, we had already interviewed his mother, father, and sister. He asked us when we were finally going to talk to him, jokingly explaining that he could give us the best information because he was the "mayor" of Texana.

Roger also self-identifies as a "hillbilly" and a "redneck," though for him, these terms do not seem to carry the racist connotations they do for many Americans.[12] During one interview he talked about how he works in construction and likes to hunt in his spare time, often killing wild boar, deer, and other animals that he then cooks for himself and his friends. Following this description, his girlfriend—a young white woman—explained to us that Roger is "the biggest redneck in Texana." Roger similarly called himself a redneck on another occasion when we asked him whether he used any of the current black slang terms we were discussing (cf. Childs and Mallinson 2006). He replied by shaking his head and saying "I'm redneck."

In further contrast, we also asked Roger how he felt about Atlanta—the city that the younger black teenagers cite often as being a place they want to visit. When we asked Roger whether he had ever been to Atlanta, he said he had "hung out" in cities before, but when asked if he would ever want to move there, he replied, "Hmm. Probably not. . . . I guess the, the [life's] too fast, the city's too fast. For me." Thus in his discourse Roger distances himself from wanting to live in a major black urban center and distances himself from using current black slang. At the same time, he self-identifies as black and also as "redneck"—a term that, for him, appears to indicate being "country," which indexes an insider status as being a member of Texana as well as of broader Appalachian culture.

Still, the fact that Roger identifies closely with the Texana community and disassociates himself from contemporary urban black life does not mean that he accepts uncritically the prejudice and discrimination he experiences in rural Cherokee County. In his interview, Roger recounted several stories of strong prejudice by whites toward interracial relationships he had had. On another occasion, Roger claimed that often "it's your last name that determines what job you get" in the Murphy area, indicating a type of social closure that converges with prejudice to structure job opportunities, particularly for young Texanans (Mallinson 2006). Roger's awareness of and insight into prejudice and discrimination suggests how the nuanced interplay of race, region, and rurality structure his life experiences and life chances as a young black Appalachian man.

Chris

The third speaker, Chris, is a self-identified black teenager who has also lived in Texana all his life. His mother is Monica, and when she moved to Ohio, Chris stayed to live with his father. Chris typically visits Monica once a year, and he sees her when she returns to Texana once or twice a year to visit. Despite the fact that Chris has not traveled much outside the Texana community yet, he says he is ready to leave, for reasons related to race and region. For one, he says, the local area is "broke down" as well as racist. As he puts it, "I don't like some of the people here. I really don't, I'm ready to leave. I don't like Murphy, period. It's boring, it's nothing to do. At all. Just wake up and sit. There's like no jobs that hire people or it's just. It's a sorry town. It's real racist and stuff. I don't like it." Chris told several stories about the prejudice and racism he has faced at school and in the local community, including once when he had to scare away "rednecks" who were driving through Texana waving rebel flags and once when he got into a fight at school after a white student used the "*n*-word." In this regard, we see that lexical items may be quite dynamic in their referential status and social meaning. In this case, Roger's use of *redneck* is distinctly different from the use of the term by Chris (and Heather; see following description). These differences may point to community-internal social divisions—that is, teenage residents may be adopting a more pejorative use of the word *redneck* as opposed to more inclusive meanings attributed to the term by older speakers and/or speakers with stronger local affiliation. Like other linguistic variables, lexical items may show the complex interaction of different social factors in accounting for their distribution (Johnson 1996).

Like Roger, Chris is acutely aware of local black-white dynamics that affect his experiences as a young black man in this predominantly white area. But unlike Roger, Chris strongly identifies with urban black culture. By virtue of living in the Texana community, Chris is at least two hours by car from any major metropolitan area that would readily provide him with firsthand knowledge of an urban lifestyle. However, Chris's mother and sister have lived in large cities, such as Atlanta. In addition to his ties to kin who have migrated to urban areas, Chris also says he learns about urban black culture by staying familiar with current hip-hop music and culture. The connection to popular black music and culture is a key transmitter of AAE lexical items to young Texanans, just as it is a venue for originating and spreading change in the larger black and/or young population in the United States more broadly (Childs and Mallinson 2006; Cutler 1999; Green 2002). Chris is one teenager who uses items from the AAE lexicon frequently (Childs and Mallinson 2006); for one, he refers to himself on occasion as *nigga*, particularly in instant messenger (IM) conversations, and says that he and his black male friends often say, "What's up my niggas," to greet each other and thereby mark their ethnic identities.

Heather

Heather, the fourth speaker, provides an interesting contrast to the other speakers because she is white and identifies as such. Like Chris, Heather is in her teens. She moved to Texana at the age of two with her sister when her mother married Chris's father, following his divorce from Monica. Heather's mother and Chris's father have since had children of their own; thus Heather has a blended family with black, white, and biracial siblings, step-siblings, and parents. Currently Heather and her older sister are the only white teenagers living in Texana. Based on the fact that she was raised there, Heather says she strongly identifies with Texana, but her alignment often causes some tension with her white peers in the surrounding area, who find it puzzling if not offensive that she takes "sides" with a black community. As she recalled, "Like down at the park . . . there was a bunch of black people, and all the rednecks were making fun of them and stuff and I was on the black people's side. And they was like, why you over there? Because." When probed, Heather continued, "[This is] where I live. I've known them almost all my life." Similarly, in one away message on IM, Heather posted "Texana is the city where we come from!" expressing her affiliation and dedication to Texana as her home community.[13]

Heather thus recognizes her marked status as a white member of a black community. Part of her awareness about white–black dynamics and white prejudice in this predominantly white region comes from stories she has heard about how whites used to go "coon hunting" for black people. Further awareness comes from prejudice she and her black friends have personally faced from white classmates. As Heather told us, "There's still racists in schools." She talked about classmates who used racial slurs and were "prejudiced," saying they get these ideas from their parents (i.e., that white racist sentiment is transferred intergenerationally). At the same time, her white classmates are not the only ones that have ethnic slurs at their disposal. In a joint interview with a black friend, Heather called local racist whites "rednecks" and "crackers," distancing herself from these whites. Similarly, just as Chris says he uses *nigga* with fellow black teenagers, Heather herself used the term in an IM away message, writing "1 my nigga" when leave-taking—presumably addressing black friends who she anticipated would read her away message (Childs and Mallinson 2006).[14] In sum, in response to her marginalization as a white individual member of a majority black community, Heather responds by distancing herself from local whites and claiming affiliation with Texana. These stances in particular can be seen both in the positive value she gives to terms such as "nigga" and in her pejorative use of "redneck."

Quantitative Analysis

This section turns from the qualitative analysis, which examined each speaker's background, standpoints, experiences, and ideologies about race and region, to the quantitative sociolinguistic analysis. The same corpus of interviews with each speaker profiled earlier also provided data from which tokens of four variables characteristic of AAE were extracted and tabulated. Quantitative data from each speaker are compared in this section to assess which speakers use different rates of the variables and to determine how these patterns relate to findings from the qualitative analysis. The four variables examined here are third-person singular *–s* absence (as in, *She work too much*), copula and auxiliary absence with *is* and *are* (as in, *He the man, She nice, They running*), postvocalic *r*-lessness in three contexts (stressed, unstressed, and nuclear, as in *car, mother,* and *hurt,* respectively), and prevocalic syllable-coda consonant cluster reduction (CCR) in monomorphemic and bimorphemic environments (e.g., *mist is, missed it*).

Previous research has found that each of these variables is characteristic of AAE (Bailey and Thomas 1998; Fasold 1972; Labov et al. 1968; Rickford 1999; Wolfram 1969) and occurs only rarely, if at all, in contemporary Southern white vernacular varieties (Wolfram and Fasold 1974; Wolfram and Schilling-Estes 2006), including Appalachian English (AppE) varieties, whether white or nonwhite. For one, third-person singular *–s* absence rarely surfaces in AppE, and when it does occur, it is generally restricted lexically to items such as the verbs *seem* and *don't* (Wolfram and Christian 1976; Wolfram and Fasold 1974). With regard to copula absence, absence with *are* has been found to some extent in white Appalachian speech in both West Virginia (Wolfram and Christian 1976) and North Carolina (Mallinson and Wolfram 2002) as well as in white Southern rural vernacular English in Alabama and Mississippi (Feagin 1979; Wolfram 1974). Yet copula absence with *is* continues to be considered a distinctive feature of AAE and an indexical ethnolinguistic marker (Fasold 1972; Labov et al. 1968; Rickford 1999; Wolfram 1969). Similarly, prevocalic CCR is considered to be a marker of AAE, as varieties of white speech, including AppE, are noted for their intact clusters in this environment (Wolfram and Christian 1976). Finally, regarding postvocalic *r*-lessness, this feature is also predominantly found within AAE and rarely, if at all, inAppE (Wolfram and Christian 1976), though it may be encountered in the coastal southeastern United States.

Some previous studies have investigated what the intersection of regional and ethnic dialect norms might look like in an Appalachian context. Mallinson and Wolfram (2002) found that multiracial Appalachian speakers show high levels of features associated with regional (white) varieties and extremely low levels of characteristic AAE features. Similarly, Childs and Mallinson (2004, 2006) found high levels of features characteristic of AppE and low levels of AAE features among Texana residents—and among the youngest generation in particular. These studies indicate that black Appalachians in general are not following a widespread movement toward a more urban version of AAE that has been noted for other African Americans, both urban and rural, in a variety of geographic locations (see Wolfram and Thomas 2002 for discussion). In both studies, these findings were attributed to sociopsychological factors such as local versus extralocal orientation and cultural values about identity, including but not limited to regional identity.

The analysis of the four previously listed AAE variables for the four Texana speakers considered in this study will thus suggest the extent to which each speaker's individual language patterns show alignment with a local AppE norm (as does most of the Texana community) or whether they show accommodation toward an AAE external norm. Table 5.1 presents data from each of the four variables for the four Texana speakers, and figure 5.1 displays the data graphically, showing percentages of total token count.

As the data in table 5.1 reveal, there is a distinct separation in that Monica and Chris exhibit the highest rates of nearly all of the AAE features, whereas Roger and Heather use these features rarely if at all. In other words, Heather and Roger closely align with each other in their low use of these variables, as do Monica and Chris in their higher use. Monica, who is the most mobile speaker, shows very high rates of all four of the AAE features. However, so does her son Chris, who has never lived outside Texana but does identify with urban black culture; knows urban residents,

Table 5.1
Rates of Characteristic AAE Variables, by Speaker

	Diagnostic AAE Variable					
Speaker	3sg -s absence	is absence	are absence	Postvocalic r-lessness	Prevocalic CCR, monomorph.	Prevocalic CCR, bimorph.
Monica	61.64% (45/73)	31.82% (14/44)	69.64% (39/56)	18.79% (31/165)	50.00% (4/8)	0.00% (0/5)
Roger	0.00% (0/15)	9.09% (1/11)	0.00% (0/3)	0.00% (0/22)	33.33% (1/3)	0.00% (0/1)
Chris	30.77% (8/26)	5.56% (2/36)	83.33% (10/12)	9.09% (6/66)	69.23% (18/26)	38.46% (5/13)
Heather	3.23% (1/31)	0.00% (0/19)	25.00% (1/4)	0.00% (0/53)	30.43% (7/23)	0.00% (0/11)

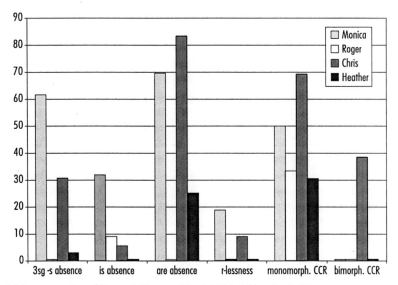

Figure 5.1 Representation of Rates of Characteristic AAE Variables, by Speaker

including former Texana residents; and has secondary and tertiary contact with AAE via hip-hop music and culture. Chris's case thus suggests that indirect language contact can affect an individual's dialect alignment.

Whereas token counts are low for several of these variables (see table 5.1), precluding definitive claims about similarities and differences in the use of these features by individual speakers, the quantitative data do suggest some parallels with the qualitative data. Examining both data sources together, we find that a range of symbolic vehicles and practices are employed as these four speakers create and negotiate complex social and linguistic identities. Monica and Chris show higher rates of third singular –s absence, *are* copula absence, postvocalic *r*-lessness, and prevocalic syllable-coda CCR in monomorphemic contexts.[15] Monica and Chris, who pride themselves on their connections to urban black culture, also employ racialized terms such as "gangstress" and "thug" (Monica) and "nigga" (Chris) to describe themselves. Finally, Chris also uses terms such as "redneck" to describe local racist whites and "broke down" to distance himself from the local area. Taken together the self-reference terms and higher rates of AAE features employed by Chris and Monica appear to be positive identity practices—those that individuals employ to orient themselves toward a favored (in this case, urban black) identity. In contrast, Chris's use of terms such as "broke down" to describe his local area is a negative identity practice—one that individuals employ to distance themselves from rejected identities (in this case, the white Murphy community, which Chris sees as "boring" and "racist").

Whereas Monica and Chris's ethnolinguistic identities are thus oriented more toward urban black culture and language patterns, Roger only rarely uses most of the analyzed morphosyntactic and phonological variables if at all, and he rejects current urban black slang terms. Roger also uses the terms "redneck" and "hillbilly"—not pejoratively but as a term highlighting his self-professed "country" identity that also presumably distances himself from the more urban identifications that he sees younger Texanans adopting. Finally, in yet another permutation, we consider Heather, the only white speaker in this analysis. Although she rarely uses the AAE variables analyzed here, she talks about learning new black slang terms from urban contacts, and she uses racialized or black slang terms such as "nigga" and "one" (see also Childs and Mallinson 2006). Like Chris, Heather also uses terms such as "redneck" and "cracker" to derogate local racist whites, and she ideologically locates herself "on the black people's side." Thus even though the quantitative data from Roger and Heather's interviews reveal that they both use low levels of characteristic AAE features, the qualitative data reveal that they use self-reference terms and other lexical items to lay claim to different racialized identities.[16] Whereas Heather works to establish herself as a legitimate member of a black community, orients herself toward a black identity, uses black slang and self-reference terms, and distances herself from local racist whites, Roger presents himself as an authentic local resident of a rural community and distances himself from an urban/younger black culture both in his ideological stance and in his linguistic practice.

As the quantitative and qualitative data reveal, social and linguistic differences abound within this group of four speakers. As they draw on a variety of linguistic symbols, the speakers construct and negotiate differing and complex social orientations toward race based on their own standpoints, life experiences, and racial identities.

Discussion and Conclusions

Studies of unique communities such as Texana have implications for future research on the intersection of language, race, and region. As the current analysis has revealed, the four Texanans discussed in this chapter hold different social attitudes and cultural orientations toward their local black Appalachian community, the broader African American community, and white Appalachia, as well as toward rurality and urbanity in general. In addition, the speakers have different life opportunities; different experiences with racism, prejudice, and discrimination; and different potential for and interest in developing contacts with outsiders to their community. All of these factors affect the racial identities, standpoints, and ideologies they develop—as well as, as this study suggests, the linguistic practices they adopt.

Thus individuals experience race (and its intersection with other social constructs) in ways that are deeply situational (Hartigan 1999)—but also structural/ideological (Collins 2000; Giddens 1979, 1984). On the one hand, the racialized standpoints and identities of the four individuals in this study are locally bound, having developed within the settings of Texana, western North Carolina, and Appalachia, in the U.S. context. At the same time, as these speakers use language variably to position themselves as members of a black community in a predominantly white area, their identities are created and negotiated within a racialized social system that, accordingly, infuses powerful racialized meanings into linguistic variables, features, and practices. As we have seen in the case of these Texanans, speakers recognize and participate in the ascription of racialized meaning to linguistic features, set linguistic and social boundaries based on perceptions of language use as a reflection of ethnic identity, use these parameters to construct their own linguistic and social identities, and subsequently reinforce these perceptions through differences in their own language practice. In short, speakers construct complex racialized identities by employing myriad variables as "heterogeneous resources for the construction of styles" (Eckert 2003, 115) in ways that are reflective of their different individual experiences while also shaped by power relations and power dynamics related to race and region (and other structures as well).

Although this study is limited in the extent to which its linguistic findings might be generalized to other language situations, it does suggest some avenues for future research on the situation of minority languages and communities in general. Comparative data provided by sociolinguists working in other communities whose speakers represent neglected racial minorities within neglected cultural minorities, or in other communities with biracial/biethnic or multiracial/multiethnic speakers, could enhance our understanding of the identity practices described here. Further detailed studies of local and broader processes of social identity construction, negotiation, and reproduction in minority communities around the world will help refine not only our sociolinguistic but our social theoretic conceptualizations of language use as simultaneously a negotiated product and tool of individual expression, group interaction, and intersecting determinants of social life.   ▨

ACKNOWLEDGMENTS
I gratefully acknowledge NSF Grant BCS-0236838 and the William C. Friday Endowment at North Carolina State University for funding this research. I would also like to thank Becky Childs for collaborating during the field research and data analysis process.

NOTES

1. See Mallinson 2006 for a discussion of intersectionality and structuration theories, including their similarities and differences, critiques of the theories, and their relationship to variationist sociolinguistics.
2. Other researchers, such as the social psychologist Erik Erikson (1959), conceptualize identity as a multilevel construct.
3. Texana is North Carolina's largest black community west of the town of Asheville.
4. The historic background of Texana dates to around 1870, when a black family, the McClellands, moved from elsewhere in western North Carolina and named the emergent community after their daughter, Texana.
5. Official census statistics for Texana apart from Murphy do not exist, as Texana is not an incorporated town. Based on the 2000 U.S. Census, 231 blacks/African Americans lived in Cherokee County, comprising just 1.6 percent of its total population. This number counts residents of Texana proper as well as a few other blacks who live in the same census tract.
6. See Mallinson 2006 for more information.
7. The 1924 Baker Roll is an official list of 3,146 names compiled and approved by U.S. Agent Fred A. Baker, pursuant to an act of Congress on June 4, 1924; it is considered the official base roll of the Eastern Band of Cherokee Indians of North Carolina (Blankenship 1998).
8. All names of speakers are pseudonyms.
9. Texanans who call themselves black may also be following a pattern of ethnic identification that differs in part by region and racial integration. Sigelman, Tuch, and Martin (2005) found that residents of nonlarge cities, Southerners, individuals who scored lower on a racial identification scale, and those whose grammar school had low degrees of racial integration were more likely to prefer "black"; these factors obviously relate to a setting like Texana, which is a small, Southern community with high numerical dominance by whites in local schools.
10. One trend in Texana, as the previous quotes attest, is an increase in black-white relationships and families. This demographic shift will undoubtedly have an effect on trajectories of language change

in Texana, and future research is needed to follow the coming generations and assess how ethnolinguistic identities are constructed among its "mixed" population.

11. Smitherman (1977: 68) defines *saditty* as "uppity-acting blacks who put on airs," although Monica's definition, from context, seems to mean "classy."

12. The *Dictionary of American Regional English* (*DARE*) defines *redneck* as a "poor, White, rural Southerner—used with a very wide range of connotations, but now [especially] applied as a [derogatory] term for a White person perceived as ignorant, narrow-minded, boorish, or racist." See Hartigan (2003) for a discussion of "redneck," "hillbilly," and "white trash" as racial terms.

13. Heather's line "Texana is the city where we come from" seems to reference a song called "East 1999," by the black rap group Bone Thugs-N-Harmony, which contains the line "Cleveland is the city where we come from." In this regard, Heather's away message would both claim Texana as her home community and make reference to broader urban black culture.

14. Texana teenagers often close their IMs with the leave-taking term *one*, which is derived from "One Love," a term popularized in reggae music. In this excerpt, we also see Heather use *nigga* to address a presumably black audience, in a way that also indexes her authenticity as a member of the black community with which she strongly identifies.

15. Monica and Chris also had several examples of habitual *be* during their interviews, which are not included here. Habitual (or invariant) *be* is a canonical feature of AAE; see Alim 2003.

16. Heather's sociolinguistic behavior shows some similarities and some differences to that of Mike, the white informant in Cutler's (1999) study of "crossing" (which refers to a speaker's use of a code associated with a group—often ethnic/racial—to which he or she does not belong). Mike's crossing into AAE was generally limited to vocabulary, *r*-lessness, and interdental fricative stopping. While Heather does use contemporary black slang, she makes far less use of the AAE phonological variables studied here, such as postvocalic *r*-lessness. At the same time, however, the black Texana speakers with whom she identifies and comes into contact also exhibit extremely low rates of these (and other) AAE variables.

REFERENCES

Alim, H. Samy. 2003. You know my steez: An ethnographic and sociolinguistic study of styleshifting in a Black American speech community. PhD diss., Stanford University.

Bailey, Guy, and Erik R. Thomas. 1998. Some aspects of AAVE phonology. In *African American English: Structure, history, and use*, ed. Salikoko Mufwene, John R. Rickford, Guy Bailey, and John Baugh, 85–109. London: Routledge.

Blankenship, Bob. 1998. *1924 Baker Roll: The final roll of the Eastern Band of Cherokee Indians of North Carolina*. Cherokee, NC: Cherokee Roots.

Childs, Becky, and Christine Mallinson. 2004. African American English in Appalachia: Dialect accommodation and substrate influence. *English World-Wide* 25:25–50.

———. 2006. The significance of lexical items in the construction of ethnolinguistic identity: A case study of adolescent spoken and online language. *American Speech* 81:3–30.

Collins, Patricia Hill. 2000. *Black feminist thought*. Routledge: New York.

Coupland, Nikolas. 2001. Introduction: Sociolinguistic theory and social theory. In *Sociolinguistics and social theory*, ed. Nikolas Coupland, Srikant Sarangi, and Christopher Candlin, 1–26. New York: Longman.

Cutler, Cecilia A. 1999. Yorkville crossing: A case study of hip hop and the language of a white middle class teenager in New York City. *Journal of Sociolinguistics* 3:428–42.

Davis, F. James. 1991. *Who is black? One nation's definition*. University Park: Pennsylvania State University Press.

Dodsworth, Robin. 2005. Attribute networking: A technique for modeling social perceptions. *Journal of Sociolinguistics* 9:225–53.

Dodsworth, Robin, and Christine Mallinson. 2006. The utility of intersectionality theory in variationist sociolinguistics. Paper presented at the Linguistic Society of America Annual Meeting, Albuquerque, January 8.

Dunaway, Wilma A. 2003. *Slavery in the American mountain South*. Cambridge: Cambridge University Press.

Eckert, Penelope. 2003. Social variation in America. In *Needed research in American dialects. Publication of the American Dialect Society* 88, ed. Dennis R. Preston, 99–122. Durham, NC: Duke University Press.

Erikson, Erik. 1959. *Identity and the life cycle*. New York: International Universities Press.

Erlandson, David A., Edward L. Harris, Barbara L. Skipper, and Steve D. Allen. 1993. *Doing naturalistic inquiry: A guide to methods*. Newbury Park, CA: Sage Publications.

Fasold, Ralph W. 1972. Tense marking in Black English: A linguistic and social analysis. Washington, DC: Center for Applied Linguistics.

Feagin, Crawford. 1979. *Variation and change in Alabama English: A sociolinguistic study of the white community*. Washington, DC: Georgetown University Press.

Gibson-Roles, Deanne. 2004. NC Cherokee reservation genealogy. Part of the North Carolina GenWeb project and the US GenWeb project. www.rootsweb.com/~ncqualla (accessed March 21, 2006).

Giddens, Anthony. 1979. *Central problems in social theory*. Berkeley: University of California Press.

———. 1984. *Constitution of society*. Berkeley: University of California Press.

Green, Lisa J. 2002. *African American English: A linguistic introduction*. New York: Cambridge University Press.

Hartigan, John, Jr. 1999. *Racialized situations*. Princeton, NJ: Princeton University Press.

———. 2003. Who are these white people? "Rednecks," "hillbillies," and "white trash" as marked racial subjects. In *White out: The continuing significance of racism*, ed. A. W. Doane and Eduardo Bonilla-Silva, 95–111. New York: Routledge.

Johnson, Ellen. 1996. *Lexical change and variation in the Southeastern United States, 1930–1990*. Tuscaloosa: University of Alabama Press.

Labov, William, Paul Cohen, Clarence Robins, and John Lewis. 1968. A study of the non-standard English of Negro and Puerto Rican speakers in New York City. United States Office of Education final report, research project 3288.

Mallinson, Christine. 2006. The dynamic construction of race, class, and gender through linguistic practice among women in a black Appalachian community. Ph.D. diss., North Carolina State University.

Mallinson, Christine, and Walt Wolfram. 2002. Dialect accommodation in a bi-ethnic mountain enclave community: More evidence on the development of African American Vernacular English. *Language in Society* 31:743–75.

Nagel, Joane. 1994. Constructing ethnicity: Creating and recreating ethnic identity and culture. *Social Problems* 41:152–76.

Rickford, John R. 1999. *African American vernacular English: Features, evolution, educational implications*. Malden, MA: Blackwell.

Sigelman, Lee, Steven A. Tuch, and Jack K. Martin. 2005. What's in a name? Preference for "black" versus "African American" among Americans of African descent. *Public Opinion Quarterly* 69:429–38.

Smitherman, Geneva. 1977. *Talkin and testifyin: The language of black America*. Detroit: Wayne State University Press.

Wolfram, Walt. 1969. *A sociolinguistic description of Detroit Negro speech*. Washington, DC: Center for Applied Linguistics.

———. 1974. The relationship of white Southern speech to vernacular black English. *Language* 50:498–527.

Wolfram, Walt, and Donna Christian. 1976. *Appalachian English*. Washington, DC: Center for Applied Linguistics.

Wolfram, Walt, and Ralph W. Fasold. 1974. *The study of social dialects in American English*. Englewood Cliffs, NJ: Prentice Hall.

Wolfram, Walt, and Natalie Schilling-Estes. 2006. *American English,* 2nd ed. Malden, MA: Blackwell.

Wolfram, Walt, and Erik R. Thomas. 2002. *The development of African American English*. Oxford: Blackwell.

6

Working at "9 to 5" Gaelic

Speakers, Context, and Ideologies of an Emerging Minority Language Register

EMILY McEWAN-FUJITA
University of Pittsburgh

SCOTTISH GAELIC is a minority language that has been undergoing language shift since approximately the twelfth century A.D. in Scotland (Withers 1984).[1] Gaelic is currently the focus of language planning and revitalization efforts in Scotland. One interesting aspect of these efforts is the emergence of an ethnolinguistically identified Gaelic-speaking middle class, a number of whom have become "professional Gaels," or "language workers" as I term them (after the "culture workers" of Whisnant 1983). This chapter explores the way these language workers negotiate the emergence of "professional Gaelic" as a register in the white-collar office workplace.

A register may be defined as "a variety of language associated with situation and purpose" (following Biber 1993; Lamb 1999, 141). Language shift entails an ongoing loss of registers as well as domains and speakers. In Scottish Gaelic, for example, Meek (1990, 11) has noted the progressive loss of command of an upper register of Gaelic based on the language of the Gaelic Bible among Protestant Gaelic speakers born after 1950. Language revitalization often leads to the deliberate or ad hoc creation of new registers that extend an endangered language into new areas of use. For example, Lamb (1999) has described and documented the emergence of "Gaelic news-speak" as a media register.

Register formation is a sociolinguistic process (Biber and Finegan 1993), as are the planning and development of minority and endangered languages. Thus an ethnographic perspective on register formation in a minority language situation can complement a purely linguistic description. In fact, an ethnographic perspective on language revitalization more generally is essential to a full understanding of the phenomenon. Only an ethnographic perspective can show us the processes of language revitalization: the motivations and the daily negotiations of speakers in their social and cultural contexts. My ethnographic analysis is based on four months of participant observation research and interviews conducted in 1999 and 2000 with workers at Comunn na Gàidhlig (CNAG), a Gaelic language planning organization in Scotland.

Description of Speakers

Prior to the eighteenth century, traditional Gaelic society was highly stratified (MacInnes 2006). During the social, economic, and military upheaval of the eighteenth century, Gaelic-speaking society lost its upper class (the clan chiefs, who became culturally and linguistically anglicized), its learned classes (including hereditary physicians, lawyers, poets, and pipers, whom the clan chiefs could no longer support), and its middle class (the tacksmen, or estate managers, who elected to emigrate). The remaining population of Gaelic speakers was disproportionately impoverished and oppressed, and Gaelic speakers became stereotyped as poor, illiterate peasants, the lowest of the low; Gaelic likewise was assigned the same social significance.

The relatively recent social restratification of Gaelic speakers as a group, with the emergence of an ethnolinguistically self-identified Gaelic middle class (MacKinnon 1996) may be organizing linguistic variation in Gaelic into a new register of professional Gaelic.[2] However, the stereotype of Gaelic as a peasant language remains strong in the Scottish public consciousness (McEwan-Fujita 2003).[3] Thus ambiguity and conflict among Gaelic speakers (to say nothing of non-Gaelic-speaking Scots) over the very meaning of the social restratification in relationship to ethnicity and language is part of the process of register formation. Therefore, my analysis of professional Gaelic focuses on the diverse speakers, sociocultural contexts, and conflicting ideologies of the emerging register.

Professional Gael is an ambiguous term; in theory it could refer to professionals of any kind who are Gaelic-English bilinguals. In practice it usually refers only to the relatively small group of Gaelic-English bilinguals professionally employed in the promotion of the Gaelic language. However, educated Gaelic-English bilinguals who work in white-collar professions of all kinds form the demographic basis for this smaller group, and they appear to be increasing in numbers in Scotland (MacKinnon 1996).

Professional Gael was not originally coined as a positive term. An anthropologist who studied the Gaelic college Sabhal Mòr Ostaig (SMO) on the Isle of Skye described the term as "a derogatory concept in the Gaelic community used to refer to people who have capitalized on their identity, especially their linguistic and cultural capital, to get involved in Gaelic development, Gaelic broadcasting, or comparable areas" (Gossen 2001, 314). Local Gaelic speakers on the Isle of Skye used the term "half mockingly, half enviously" to describe the ambitious administrators of the Gaelic college (314), and indeed many Gaelic speakers in the Hebrides have viewed economic and social success ambivalently (see, e.g., Jedrej and Nuttall 1996; Macdonald 1997). An ideology of egalitarianism has been enforced in Gaelic-speaking communities such that any individual who appeared to be more successful than others would be open to criticism in the community. Outsiders ("incomers") have often been encouraged to take positions of local leadership (Parman 1990), and locally born Gaelic speakers have achieved academic or professional success on the mainland, away from the Gaelic-speaking areas. In such circumstances it is not surprising that Gaelic speakers who have sought success openly, particularly through the promotion of Gaelic language and culture, have been criticized by other Gaelic speakers.

A major challenge for professional Gaels who are language workers is to create and negotiate in practice a "9 to 5" or professional Gaelic office environment. I use the American phrase "9 to 5" to evoke the type of compensated full-time white-collar work that is done in bureaucratically rationalized offices from 9:00 A.M. to 5:00 P.M., Monday through Friday, as opposed to shift work, agricultural work, domestic work, or any other type of work. A "Gaelic office" is a hybrid space: on the one hand, it is an office of the bureaucratically rationalized Western (and more specifically, British) type, a form of social, economic, and spatial organization where full-time, middle-class work is performed. As such it is embedded in a social and cultural infrastructure dominated by English: all of the workers are bilingual in English, and most of the goods and services received by such an office are provided by non-Gaelic speakers, including postal delivery, repair of office machines, and so forth.

On the other hand, a Gaelic office is also a site where the business of the office is deliberately conducted as much as possible through the medium of spoken and written Gaelic, and Gaelic linguistic activities are prioritized over English ones. But because the process of language shift has progressively restricted Gaelic language use, lexicon, and registers to noncommercial and informal contexts, most Gaelic speakers (and indeed most other Scots) have come to believe that Gaelic is not suitable for business. They associate Gaelic most strongly with domesticity and rural labor. The dual nature of a Gaelic office as both Gaelic-oriented and white-collar professional thus necessitates ongoing lexical and pragmatic innovations to extend Gaelic into the business domain. This means that on a daily basis the CNAG workers must negotiate between the practice of professional Gaelic and their own understandings of Gaelic developed mostly in the island-based domains of family and village-level community.

The Gaelic Office: Context and Description

Gaelic offices, defined as Gaelic-oriented bureaucratic professional work environments, are still rare in Scotland. The vast majority of offices, shops, and other businesses in Scotland use Scottish varieties of English; from the eighteenth century until recently, this even included organizations that concerned themselves explicitly with the support of Gaelic language and culture and the well-being of poverty-stricken Gaelic speakers in the Highlands. One of these organizations, An Comunn Gàidhealach (ACG), began to use Gaelic internally in its operations in the late 1980s, though not without objections from some staff and members who feared that this change would alienate the many ACG members who were "supporters" of Gaelic but unable to speak it themselves.

The English milieu in Gaelic-focused organizations changed relatively recently with the founding of the Gaelic-language planning organization CNAG in 1984. The first head of CNAG was the instigator of an informal Gaelic office policy within CNAG itself. By 1999–2000, most if not all of the organizations with deliberately Gaelic-oriented offices were the ones such as CNAG that were directly involved in Gaelic language revitalization efforts. They included ACG, Comataidh Craoladh Gàidhlig (the Gaelic Broadcasting Committee, formerly Comataidh Telebhisean Gàidhlig, the Gaelic Television Committee), Proiseact nan Ealan (the National Gaelic Arts Project, originally part of CNAG), Comhairle nan Sgoiltean

Àraich (the Gaelic Playgroup Association), and the BBC offices of Radio nan Gàidheal in Stornoway and Inverness, as well as BBC Alba (Scotland) in Glasgow.[4]

As part of a twelve-month period of anthropological research in Scotland for a larger project, I spent three months in 1999 and one month in 2000 based in the CNAG head office in Inverness. During this time I also made two one-week side trips to the Stornoway branch office on the Isle of Lewis.

When I arrived at CNAG in 1999, my communicative skills were typical of the classroom-educated language student; I spoke Gaelic hesitantly, although I could understand, read, and write it reasonably well. By the time I returned to CNAG in 2000 for the final portion of my field research there, I could speak Gaelic more fluently after having had more practice and experience over the year. I conducted my field research in both Gaelic and English, with the goal of being sensitive to the linguistic preferences of my interlocutors and the ways in which these preferences were shaped by context. However, the issue of language choice in field research on a minority language is a difficult one, and I further explore its implications elsewhere (McEwan-Fujita 2003).

While conducting research at CNAG, I went to the office nearly every weekday for participant observation and interviewing. While taking notes, doing research in CNAG's collection of press clippings, and making arrangements to interview people, I occasionally assisted with minor administrative tasks such as clipping newspaper articles, photocopying, and collating. During and in between these activities I had short conversations with participants on various topics relevant to my research.

In addition to participant observation, I formally interviewed every staff member based in the Inverness and Stornoway offices at least once, using a schedule including questions about linguistic upbringing, education, current linguistic usage, work history, and current activities at CNAG. I conducted four interviews entirely in English, six interviews almost entirely in Gaelic, and two in a combination of Gaelic and English.

The daily business of the CNAG office revolved around several areas. These included the promotion of Gaelic-medium education among Scottish parents and future primary-school teachers, lobbying with the Scottish Executive (formerly the Scottish Office) and the new Scottish Parliament for official status for Gaelic, and general activities to publicize Gaelic in Scotland. Personnel also administered a number of shorter term projects part-funded by the European Union.

The twelve people working at the headquarters of CNAG during my research were a diverse group of Gaelic speakers in terms of their geographical origins: they represented one mainland Gaelic-speaking area on the northwest coast and five Hebridean islands (Skye, South Uist, North Uist, Scalpay, and Lewis).[5] Ten of the twelve were fluent native speakers of Gaelic who had grown up in homes where both parents spoke Gaelic. Of the remaining two workers, one had grown up in a home with one Gaelic-speaking parent. By her own account she had not fully acquired Gaelic in the home but had learned Gaelic to fluency at SMO, the Gaelic college on the Isle of Skye. The other worker had grown up as a nonspeaker of Gaelic in a home without Gaelic and learned Gaelic to fluency as an adult. All of these people were also fully fluent and literate in English. Thus the CNAG office was a place where

Gaelic-English bilinguals speaking different Gaelic dialects mingled and spoke to one another face-to-face in Gaelic; this interdialectal interaction is another important aspect of Gaelic offices that I discuss elsewhere (McEwan-Fujita 2003).

The CNAG workers were also a diverse group in terms of their individual Gaelic linguistic abilities and habits. All of the CNAG workers were fully bilingual in Gaelic and Hebridean or Highland English (Clement 1997; Sabban 1984), as are the vast majority of present-day Gaelic speakers.[6] All of the island-born speakers spoke the particular Gaelic dialectal varieties associated with their district and island of origin. The mainland-born worker who was a nonnative fluent speaker made a choice to utilize the dialectal form of her district of residence. The other mainland-born worker spoke a form of Gaelic lacking distinctive dialect features.

Because of changes over the years in the geographical organization of the education system and in the role of Gaelic in the schools, workers of different ages had quite different experiences with Gaelic in their schooling. In addition, some workers born before about 1965 had been Gaelic monolingual when they entered primary school, although some with older siblings had learned English from them prior to entering school. They also had different experiences with Gaelic in their working lives; some had never worked in a Gaelic-related position prior to working for CNAG, while two had come to CNAG after working at a Gaelic publishing company. Two others had used spoken Gaelic occasionally in previous positions working with the public in the Highlands, specifically in interactions with elderly people who preferred speaking Gaelic.

Despite a wide range of schooling and employment experiences, all the CNAG workers appeared to be highly competent in Gaelic literacy skills.[7] For virtually all CNAG workers, as for most native Gaelic-English bilinguals, the use of written Gaelic was almost entirely confined to the work domain. They did not write extensive personal correspondence in Gaelic, although they might include a short phrase in a greeting card. Some individuals with prior Gaelic publishing experience or greater confidence in their Gaelic literacy skills were more involved in proofreading and correcting Gaelic grammar and spelling in written documents. Most of the workers had well-thumbed Gaelic-English dictionaries on their desks that I saw them consulting regularly.

In the office environment of CNAG, staff members would engage freely in English code-switching and borrowing in informal situations, as did Gaelic speakers in Uist, according to individual inclination and ability. The informal situations in which people spoke this "everyday" Gaelic peppered with English words and phrases included conversations and informal meetings between staff members and staff telephone conversations. As Dorian also noted for East Sutherland Gaelic (1981, 101), the number of English loanwords seemed to be a marker of the degree of formality of Gaelic in the CNAG office. During formal events and in written communications, CNAG workers minimized their use of English loans and avoided code-switching. The formal events included semiannual board meetings, the Annual General Meeting (AGM), public speaking engagements, and interviews on BBC Radio nan Gàidheal. The formal written communications, which included press releases, letters, minutes of meetings, and reports, were usually produced in a bilingual English-Gaelic format.

The daily activities of the office included the use of both spoken and written Gaelic. Spoken Gaelic was used in telephone conversations, in casual interactions and meetings between coworkers, and in interactions with other Gaelic speakers, whether they were employees of other Gaelic revitalization organizations or Gaelic speakers doing business with CNAG (e.g., by installing computer systems). Written Gaelic was used in the creation and distribution of letters, e-mail, faxes, and memos; telephone messages; and company publications including brochures, reports, and meeting minutes and agendas.

However, the CNAG office was completely encompassed by an English-speaking world, and English intruded frequently on the Gaelic office. All the computer software was English-based and included the widely used Microsoft word processing, spreadsheet, Internet browser, and e-mail programs.[8] The majority of the reference books in the office, apart from Gaelic dictionaries, were printed in English. The workers also had to accommodate to the world of English to communicate with service providers who could not speak Gaelic, including milk, parcel, and post delivery people.

Telephone callers who could not speak Gaelic were sometimes surprised by CNAG staff answering the phone in Gaelic. On one occasion, the receptionist, "Catriona," answered the phone as usual by saying *"Feasgar math, Comunn na Gàidhlig"* (Good afternoon, Comunn na Gàidhlig), and the person on the other end of the line said, "I'm sorry, I don't speak Gaelic. Do you speak English?"[9] Catriona, who had apparently grown frustrated with such reactions, told me what the caller said and complained, "I just speak Gaelic, I haven't got two heads, and I'm not thick!" My field research and regular review of the Scottish press in 1999 and 2000 indicated that average non-Gaelic speakers in Scotland, even the ones who telephoned CNAG, still perceived bilingualism or multilingualism as something rare and not always entirely welcome, particularly when it did not involve a European prestige language such as French or German.

Other callers as well as the postal service also regularly mistook Comunn na Gàidhlig for An Comunn Gàidhealach, whose headquarters were also located in Inverness. For example, in early October 1999 the CNAG receptionist was constantly interrupted by telephone callers requesting information about the Royal National Mòd—the annual Gaelic singing competition organized not by CNAG but by An Comunn Gàidhealach. The Royal Mail also regularly misdelivered correspondence to CNAG that was addressed to An Comunn Gàidhealach. This particularly seemed to happen when the envelope was addressed entirely in Gaelic, despite the fact that since the late 1980s the Royal Mail had officially allowed mail to be addressed in Gaelic as well as English, with the promise of accurate delivery contingent on the use of the postcode.

In the remainder of this chapter, I discuss two pragmatic aspects of the language workers' professional Gaelic in the workplace: workers' evaluations of their own and others' lexical choices and the problem of developing business etiquette in Gaelic, with a focus on greetings.

Evaluations of Lexicon in the Gaelic Office

On a daily basis the CNAG workers were negotiating between the practice of professional Gaelic on the one hand, and their own understandings of Gaelic developed for the most part in the island-based domains of family and village-level community on the other hand. The constitution of this new register involved an acceptance of the very possibility of Gaelic being used in an office domain, as well as the development of strategies to make it possible.

One aspect of this ongoing negotiation was the ambivalence that the fluent bilingual workers expressed about "new Gaelic" words and expressions. Some of my interviewees saw them variously as inauthentic, ridiculous, unaesthetic, viscerally unpleasant, or rigidly purist. In some cases they simply said they didn't like the words. For example, in a Gaelic conversation with "Dòmhnall," a part-time contract employee, about my research activities, I said *"Rinn mi mòran agallamhan"* (I did a lot of interviews). He repeated the word *"agallamhan"* (interviews) a few times, then commented in English, "I never heard the word until about two years ago. I don't like it very much." (#144).[10]

"Sìne," a full-time employee, expressed a desire for adult Gaelic learners to simply use an English word rather than a newly coined Gaelic word (#517). This was a sentiment I heard often in various contexts, for the workers themselves frequently used English words in their spoken Gaelic and considered this to be appropriate in everyday informal conversation—even in the Gaelic office. For example, in a casual Gaelic conversation that took place between Sìne, me, and a visiting local businessman, the visitor noted with amusement that a nonnative Gaelic speaker who was prominent in Gaelic language planning insisted on always calling the Apple Macintosh computer *Ubhal Mac an Tòisich,* a combination of the Gaelic word for "apple" and the original Gaelic form of the surname Macintosh (#72).[11] As the visitor related how he himself had insisted that an Apple Macintosh is an Apple Macintosh, Sìne and I laughed heartily, finding the earnest desire to translate absolutely everything into Gaelic amusing because it was out of keeping with the sociolinguistic norms of code-switching in the Gaelic-speaking areas from which most of the CNAG workers originated.

Sometimes the conflict between cultural authenticity and linguistic propriety was acute. One evening, just before leaving the office for the day, "Anna" asked her supervisor "Ailig," who was staying late, if she should put on the answering machine. Anna asked the question in Gaelic but used the English word *answering machine.* Ailig answered her in Gaelic, saying not to turn it on because he was expecting some phone calls. I then left the office with Anna, and as we were walking away and talking about something else, she suddenly said to me, *"Inneal-freagairt,* I should have said! But it sounds so silly to say it." She had just remembered that there was a new Gaelic word for answering machine, but she seemed to be caught between two genuine, strong, and conflicting impulses: a feeling of responsibility to use Gaelic and a feeling of ridiculousness for using new Gaelic. After some more thought, she said, "I know I should be saying them but it just sounds so strange to say these words. . . . My parents have a completely different way of speaking than I do." I asked her how so, and she just said that anything she said, they would have a different way of saying it in Gaelic (#129).

However, most of these same workers, working as they did with written Gaelic, did use the new Gaelic words themselves. When constructing documents with English-Gaelic parallel translations, they might use *An Stòr-Data Briathrachais*

Gàidhlig, the book form of the computerized database word list produced by SMO. The database includes many new Gaelic translations for "modern-day" proper nouns and other words including the names of U.K. acts of parliament and various Scottish national and voluntary bodies in English (Vathjunker 1992/93). Anna, who felt conflicted about the Gaelic word for answering machine, would also devise new Gaelic words herself if she did not like the new Gaelic words she found in the *Stòr-Data*—I observed her doing this while composing written documents. "Mairead," who fielded many telephone calls and processed a great deal of paperwork, noted all the new Gaelic words that she encountered in her work, such as *iomairt* (initiative), and complained that sometimes she needed a dictionary to decode them. But she followed this comment with, "The thing is, the more you do it, the more you get used to it." (#189). Indeed, I noticed that at other times Mairead used such words without comment. And a senior employee, "Donalda," who had a positive attitude about Gaelic language change, observed at length: "Feumaidh sinn faclan ùra . . . 's tha faclan ùra a'tighinn a-steach dhan a'chànan, dhomhsa, mar chomharradh gu bheil an canan beò, 's gun an cànan ga chleachdadh. 'S gum feum an cànan atharrachadh, mar a tha an dòigh beatha againn ag atharrachadh." (We need new words . . . and new words are coming into the language, to me, as a sign that the language is alive, and that the language is being used. And that the language must change, as our way of life is changing") (#546).

New words were more than acceptable to Donalda; they were a sign of the adaptation of both Gaelic and Gaelic speakers to a changing world, a positive sign of the continued existence of Gaelic. This shows the diversity of attitudes toward new lexical items, as workers negotiate a way forward through the conflicting demands of cultural authenticity and register development.

Professional Gaelic: Professional Manners, Gaelic Greetings

Verbal expressions of etiquette in the context of the Gaelic office are another important aspect of language workers' professional Gaelic where we can see the emergence of new usages as well as negotiation over the forms it should take and the meanings it should carry. When the practice and ideology of professional business are transplanted to a Gaelic-speaking domain, the professional manners must accompany them; or rather, when Gaelic language use is imported into a professional business domain, professionalism must be translated into Gaelic. One area in which we can examine this practice is the area of greetings. The particular greetings used at CNAG, and the commentary surrounding them, provided a way for workers to deal with the contradictions that characterize the extension of Gaelic into the professional realm. CNAG workers were essentially negotiating a way between the ideal of an all-Gaelic office that encompasses linguistic practices of professionalism and business manners, and the ideal Gaelic core of authenticity that indexes a rural, agricultural, domestic island-based environment and their own origins in that environment.

Telephone greetings provide one example of this negotiation between professional Gaelic and rurally based Gaelic. Catriona, the receptionist at the main CNAG office in Inverness, always answered the telephone before noon with, "*Madainn mhath, Comunn na Gàidhlig*" (Good morning, Comunn na Gàidhlig). After noon, she would say, "*Feasgar math, Comunn na Gàidhlig*" (Good afternoon, Comunn na Gàidhlig). Mairead, mentioned earlier, did the same. This telephone greeting served the purpose of communicating to callers that the organization was a Gaelic one. It also signaled to Gaelic-speaking callers that they could conduct the telephone conversation in Gaelic. This was important, as Gaelic speakers generally tended to assume that people unknown to them could not speak Gaelic. A bilingual English-Gaelic greeting was not used; the rationale for this was never discussed, but I hypothesize that if English was used at all, it could very likely have prompted even many Gaelic-speaking callers to accommodate to the English usage and therefore in some sense could have compromised the mission of the office. No doubt it could also be cumbersome to say.

It must be noted that without the receptionist specifically answering the phone in Gaelic, the fact of CNAG being a "Gaelic organization" would not in itself have guaranteed to potential callers, or created the expectation in them, that the person who answered the phone could actually speak Gaelic. For example, as previously mentioned, the nearby headquarters of An Comunn Gàidhealach in Inverness had been an English-speaking office for many years.

"*Madainn mhath*" and "*Feasgar math*" were presented as standard Gaelic greetings in many Gaelic courses for adult language learners. They are the first phrases listed under the "Meeting Friends/Getting Acquainted" section in the phrase book *Everyday Gaelic* (MacNeill 1991). During my research in the CNAG office, several workers and the chief executive would often greet me with "*Madainn mhath* Emily" in the morning when I first came into the office.

However, Anna contested the practice of saying "*Madainn mhath*" on the telephone. She said that she wouldn't say "*Madainn mhath*" when she answered the phone because it sounded wrong, unnatural, and artificial. She interpreted it as a direct calque on English and a sign of English manners:

> *Madainn mhath* doesn't make sense. *Madainn mhath* is something that makes you stick out as a learner. If you're only wanting to be polite, to me "good morning" is an English thing to say. . . . For me, I find *madainn mhath* and *feasgar math,* I find that so daft saying it. And people kind of look at you. . . . If I want to say it, I'll just say "Good morning, Comunn na Gàidhlig" [on the telephone], but [*pause, change to a musing tone*] that gives the wrong impression. But then, Gaelic has changed so much that in the business world it's almost acceptable to say, *madainn mhath* and *feasgar math* (#36).

Anna was again caught between the conflicting requirements of cultural authenticity and Gaelic professionalism. Implicit in Anna's backtracking on the preference for "Good morning" in English was the idea that it would give the wrong impression to callers to greet them in English, because CNAG was supposed to be a Gaelic organization. I noticed that Anna had in fact developed her own strategy for answering the phone to avoid "*Madainn mhath*" while still greeting callers appropriately as the representative of a Gaelic organization. She said "*Hallo, Comunn na Gàidhlig,*" using the Gaelicized form of *hello,* which was a borrowing from English and a common greeting in Gaelic-speaking areas (MacAulay 1982, 29). "*Hallo*" could be perceived as more linguistically neutral: a more authentically Gaelic greeting than "*madainn mhath,*" less obviously English than "good morning," and indeed Gaelic enough not to trigger Gaelic speakers to accommodate to a perceived use of English.

Anna seemed to be thinking through the issue as she talked, and in her extended commentary there was an acknowledgment of the professionally motivated language change wrought by the Gaelic revitalization movement, together with a resistance to that change. Anna recognized the necessity of corpus planning and language change in order to utilize Gaelic in new domains; she noted, for example, that a college economics course would require the use of a standardized academic language and that a Gaelic-medium economics course at SMO, where she had studied, would therefore require the use of a standardized Gaelic academic language. However, she resisted the idea of change in the dialectal, spoken form of Gaelic: "But I don't accept that you have to have spoken Gaelic standardized. . . . I just see this kind of nightmare scenario where they only . . . understand what they hear on the radio." By "they" she meant young people learning Gaelic in the present.

The question of standardization, together with the different social values assigned to Gaelic and English codes (Blom and Gumperz 1972), were the issues at the heart of our discussion of greetings. When I asked Anna what the preferable alternative to *madainn mhath* would be in daily face-to-face Gaelic conversation, she said that people would simply comment on the weather as a greeting, rather than saying "good morning." She then related the use of comments on the weather as greetings to the social context of older Gaelic speakers living around the house where she grew up, in a rural district of a Hebridean island. She observed that in 1999 her parents' three closest sets of neighbors were in their fifties, seventies, and eighties, respectively, "so this whole concept [of saying *madainn mhath*] doesn't work" for Anna to greet her parents' neighbors in the Gaelic-speaking area in which they live when she visits. This rural island context, both familial and familiar, as well as the particular age range of the interlocutors, is the context that "authentic" Gaelic indexes for many fluent native speakers. Anna's dichotomy between the "crazy" standardized spoken Gaelic greeting "*madainn mhath*" and the authentic, nonstandardized comments on the weather is one example of how the native Gaelic speakers working at CNAG remain partial to the idea of Gaelic as a spoken variety of idiomatic Gaelic with dialectal features indexing their rural, island district of origin and an older age set.

However, while Anna valued this particular context for Gaelic language use, she also recognized reluctantly that it was changing: "Over the last ten years things have changed drastically. It's more anglified. There's not the same amount of mixing as there used to be, [with] people going around to each other's houses. So there's not as much mixing of generations" (#36). In fact, she said that when she was young the same neighbors of her parents would only speak English to her. She explained that "older people don't expect children to speak Gaelic, so they just speak to them in English."[12] But, she noted, once the neighbors knew she worked "in Gaelic," they spoke Gaelic to her with no problem.

If "*madainn mhath*" was considered inauthentic Gaelic by some Gaelic-English bilinguals, how did it come to be part of the canon of Gaelic greetings taught to adult Gaelic learners and an acceptable way to answer the telephone in a Gaelic office?

According to the ideology of standard language (Silverstein 1996, 292), there ought to be a Gaelic equivalent for every English word and expression (see, e.g., Paterson 1964). Every foreign-language dictionary and phrasebook constructs its equivalencies according to this ideology. Moreover, because traditional interlocutor-specific greetings are not so easily taught or learned, teachers of Gaelic may have wished to provide a simpler standardized Gaelic morning greeting equivalent to the standard English one.

The linguistic standardization of Gaelic greetings is also an aspect of professionalization, the issue most relevant to the institutional context of Gaelic language use at CNAG. One fluent Gaelic speaker who had learned Gaelic as an adult attributed the promotion of the use of "*madainn mhath*" as a substitute for the English "good morning" to SMO, the Gaelic college in Skye. This explanation relates to SMO's original mission from its founding in 1974, which was to provide business education through the medium of Gaelic and thus transform the Gaelic language into a viable tool for business in Scotland. This required transposing Gaelic from the family domain to a white-collar office domain, creating a new lexicon—and pragmatics—as part of a new register of Gaelic.[13] The chief executives of CNAG continued this mission by professionalizing their language revitalization efforts in the 1980s and 1990s.

Conclusion

This ongoing effort to professionalize Gaelic highlights the linguistic and social change that Gaelic-speaking areas in particular, and Gaelic speakers in general, have been undergoing in the latter half of the twentieth century. More and more Gaelic speakers are becoming professionals of various kinds, and most of them are still moving up and moving out of the traditionally Gaelic-speaking areas of the Hebrides and settling across the mainland of Scotland. Those among them who become professional Gaels, earning a livelihood by contributing to the project of Gaelic language revitalization, must negotiate in practice how best to extend the language into a new register. As they see it, they must find a way to "professionalize" Gaelic while remaining true to their own authentic—and nonprofessional—Gaelic ethnic origins.

ACKNOWLEDGMENTS

The author is grateful to the Society for the Anthropology of Europe and Council for European Studies for a Pre-Dissertation Research Grant, the Social Science Research Council and American Council of Learned Societies for an International Dissertation Research Fellowship, the National Science Foundation for a Dissertation Improvement Grant (No. 9974337), and the University of Chicago for a Markovitz Dissertation Writing Fellowship, all of which generously supported and made possible the research on which this chapter is based. I appreciate the comments made by the anonymous reviewers. Any errors or omissions are my own responsibility.

NOTES

    1. Gaelic dialects have become obsolescent in most of the formerly Gaelic-speaking areas of Scotland (e.g., Dorian 1981). Offered here only as a rough guide, the 2001 UK Census results list 58,652 Gaelic speakers in Scotland; this is just over 1 percent of Scotland's population of about 5.06 million. A further 33,744 census respondents indicated that they could understand, read, or write Gaelic, or some combination of these, but not speak it.

2. This contrasts with the situation of dialect death as described by Nancy Dorian in the localized and isolated Gaelic-speaking area of East Sutherland, where Gaelic speakers all belonged to the same lower socioeconomic class throughout most of the twentieth century (Dorian 1981, 152).
3. This sentiment was articulated, for example, in a 1995 editorial in *The Scotsman* newspaper, which stated that the Gaelic language is "a low level peasantish sort of debris." A columnist named Margaret Morrison, writing in the *Daily Mail* tabloid newspaper in 1996, declared that when her ancestors "made their escape from the backbreaking labour of croft life, they left behind the language and culture which went with it."
4. One former BBC Radio nan Gàidheal employee told me that he believed that the Gaelic radio division had struggled with maintaining a Gaelic-medium office, however, because they shared work space with English-language BBC radio divisions. My limited observation seemed to support this idea: in 1999 I attended a BBC staff party in Inverness, where colleagues from Radio Highland and Radio nan Gàidheal mingled. Nearly all conversation during the party was conducted in English.
5. All of these people did not have the same employment status with CNAG. Nonetheless they all maintained office space at CNAG or regularly used CNAG facilities and, in so doing, interacted on a regular basis with one another. To highlight this common experience they shared in the workplace, while recognizing the differences in their employment status, as a group I term them "workers" rather than "employees."
6. The only exceptions are some preschool-age children.
7. However, other Gaelic-speaking professionals who did not work in directly Gaelic-related jobs had widely varying levels of literacy.
8. The national Scottish curriculum development organization Learning and Teaching Scotland launched a Scottish Gaelic version of Open Office software in 2005. However, the field research on which this article was based was conducted in 1999 and 2000, before this software existed.
9. A gender-matched and culturally appropriate Gaelic pseudonym was used for each participant to preserve anonymity.
10. Numbers in parentheses are the author's field note record numbers. Long quotations are given exactly as transcribed from tape-recorded interviews, whereas short quotations are from written field notes.
11. This literal but grammatically incorrect translation thus brought full circle the international linguistic transformation of the Gaelic surname *Mac an Tòisich*, meaning "son of the chief": from its beginning as a Gaelic clan or family name, to anglicized Scottish surname (variously spelled MacIntosh, Macintosh, or McIntosh), to a U.S. American surname (again MacIntosh, Macintosh, or McIntosh), to the name of a variety of apple popular in the United States (Macintosh apple), to the appellation of a globally popular U.S. brand of personal computer (Apple Macintosh), which was then translated back to Gaelic (*Ubhal Mac an Tòisich*), albeit ungrammatically, as the construction should have used the genitive case: *Ubhal Mhic an Tòisich*. It should be noted that the person reporting this usage may have been the one responsible for omitting the genitive case, rather than the original user.
12. A CNAG employee from a different Hebridean island also noted the same phenomenon with her own children and her neighbors.
13. However, SMO was not the sole origin of this practice. Nancy Dorian (personal communication) notes that a native Gaelic-speaking teacher at a school in Sutherland enthusiastically used and promoted the expression "*madainn mhath*" as a greeting in his community, decades before the founding of SMO.

REFERENCES

Biber, Douglas. 1993. An analytical framework for register studies. In *Sociolinguistic perspectives on register,* ed. Douglas Biber and Edward Finegan, 31–56. New York: Oxford University Press.

Biber, Douglas, and Edward Finegan, eds. 1993. *Sociolinguistic perspectives on register.* Oxford: Oxford University Press.

Blom, Jan-Petter, and John J. Gumperz. 1972. Social meaning in linguistic structure: Code-switching in Norway. In *Directions in sociolinguistics: The ethnography of communication,* ed. John Gumperz and Dell Hymes, 407–34. New York: Holt, Rinehart and Winston.

Clement, David. 1997. Highland English. In *The Celtic Englishes,* ed. H. L. C. Tristram, 301–7. Heidelberg: Carl Winter Universitatsverlag.

Dorian, Nancy C. 1981. *Language death: The life cycle of a Scottish Gaelic dialect.* Philadelphia: University of Pennsylvania Press.

Gossen, Andrew. 2001. *Agents of a modern Gaelic Scotland: Curriculum, change, and challenge at Sabhal Mòr Ostaig, the Gaelic college of Scotland.* Ph.D. diss., Harvard University.

Jedrej, Charles, and Mark Nuttall. 1996. *White settlers: The impact of rural repopulation in Scotland.* Luxembourg: Harwood Academic.

Lamb, William. 1999. A diachronic account of Gaelic news-speak: The development and expansion of a register. *Scottish Gaelic Studies* 19:141–71.

MacAulay, Donald. 1982. Register range and choice in Scottish Gaelic. *International Journal of the Sociology of Language* 35:25–48.

Macdonald, Sharon. 1997. *Reimagining culture: Histories, identities and the Gaelic renaissance.* Oxford: Berg.

MacInnes, John. 2006. *Dùthchas nan Gàidheal: Selected essays of John MacInnes.* Ed. Michael Newton. Edinburgh: Birlinn.

MacKinnon, Kenneth. 1996. Social class and Gaelic language abilities in the 1981 census. *Scottish Gaelic Studies* 17:239–49.

MacNeill, Morag. 1991. *Everyday Gaelic.* Glasgow: Gairm.

McEwan-Fujita, Emily. 2003. *Gaelic in Scotland, Scotland in Europe: Minority language revitalization in the age of neoliberalism.* Ph.D. diss., University of Chicago.

Meek, Donald E. 1990. Language and style in the Scottish Gaelic Bible (1767–1807). *Scottish Language* 9:1–16.

Morrison, Margaret. 1996. My family left behind the old back-breaking work of croft life. If the language now dies too, then so be it. *Daily Mail,* August 15.

Parman, Susan. 1990. *Scottish crofters: A historical ethnography of a Celtic village.* Fort Worth: Holt, Rinehart and Winston.

Paterson, John M. 1964. *The Gaels have a word for it! A modern Gaelic vocabulary of 2000 words.* Glasgow: Dionnasg Gàidhlig na h-Alba (The Gaelic League of Scotland).

Sabban, Annette. 1984. Investigations into the syntax of Hebridean English. *Scottish Language* 3:5–32.

Silverstein, Michael. 1996. Monoglot "Standard" in America: Standardization and metaphors of linguistic hegemony. In *The matrix of language: Contemporary linguistic anthropology,* ed. Donald Brenneis and Ronald S. Macaulay, 284–306. Boulder, CO: Westview Press.

Vathjunker, Sonja. 1992/93. Review of *An Stòr-Dàta Briathrachais Gàidhlig—The Gaelic Terminology Database, Vol. I. Scottish Language* 11/12:181–82.

Whisnant, David E. 1983. *All that is native & fine: The politics of culture in an American region.* Chapel Hill: University of North Carolina Press.

Withers, Charles. 1984. *Gaelic in Scotland 1698–1981: The geographical history of a language.* Edinburgh: John Donald.

7

▉ Voice and Biliteracy in Indigenous Language Revitalization

Contentious Educational Practices in Quechua, Guarani, and Maori Contexts

NANCY H. HORNBERGER
University of Pennsylvania

▉ **TWENTY YEARS AGO**, I wrote the following, based on my two-year comparative ethnographic study in two highland Quechua communities of Puno, Peru, and their schools, one in the midst of implementing an experimental Quechua–Spanish bilingual program and the other following the traditional Spanish-only curriculum, a study in which I had found greater oral and written pupil participation—in absolute, linguistic, and sociolinguistic terms—when Quechua was the medium of instruction:

> It is often said that Quechua children, and indigenous children in many parts of the world, for that matter, are naturally shy and reticent, and that that is why they rarely speak in school; therefore we should not interfere with their cultural patterns by encouraging them to speak out more. In light of observations such as those outlined above, however, I think we should ask ourselves whether at least some of that reticence is due to the fact that the school language in many of these cases is a language entirely foreign to the child.
>
> Of course, more may be involved than language. In some parts of the world, children are shy in school even though the home language and the school language are the same. Philips (1983) has shown that, for the case of the Native American children at Warm Springs, at least, it is the cultural patterns themselves which are precisely the key to the children's participation. Given participation structures which are more congruent with their own cultural patterns, Warm Springs children do participate more in school. Participation structures may also be a factor in the case of Quechua children. Nevertheless, an even more fundamental issue seems to be language. Who, after all, can speak out in a language which they do not know?
>
> For example, I had opportunity to observe one little girl in both classroom and home settings. This little seven-year-old rarely, if ever, spoke in class; yet, at home, she was something of a livewire. She talked non-stop to me (in Quechua), telling me all about the names and ages of her whole family,

showing me the decorations on the wall of her home, the blankets woven by her grandmother, borrowing my hat—all this while she jumped on the bed, did somersaults, cared for her two baby brothers, and so on. (Hornberger 1988, 194, based on Hornberger 1985, 498–99)

Then, as now, it struck me that this little girl, whom I call Basilia, lost her voice at school and found it at home and that use of her own language in familiar surroundings was key in the activation of her voice. In the intervening twenty years, our notions of voice have developed and filled out, largely due to the influential work of Russian Mikhail Bakhtin. Here I consider this opening instance from twenty years ago, along with three other, more recent instances of educational practice in indigenous contexts, all in light of our developing understanding of voice.

The two grand questions driving me in that study twenty years ago, and in much of my work since then, have been "What educational approaches best serve (indigenous and immigrant) language minority children?" and "What policies, programs, and circumstances encourage or contribute to (indigenous and immigrant) minority language maintenance and revitalization?" I have argued through my empirical and theoretical work that multilingual language policies implemented through bilingual education can be a positive factor in answering both those needs, that is, in enhancing children's learning and in promoting language maintenance and revitalization (Hornberger 1988, 1998, 2002, 2003).

In the first instance, that is, the role of mother-tongue-based bilingual education (Alexander 2003) in enhancing language minority children's learning, my argument is supported by my own and others' work as analyzed through the continua of biliteracy framework (Hornberger 1989, 2003; Hornberger and Skilton-Sylvester 2000), which in a very fundamental sense is built on the commonsense premise that we learn best based on what we already know. In the second instance, that is, the role of mother-tongue-based bilingual education in promoting language maintenance and revitalization given a supportive policy and societal context, my argument is further backed by Fishman's Reversing Language Shift framework (Fishman 1991, 2000), which has as one of its key planks that children must learn to speak the heritage language if it is to survive into the next generation.

My continuing quest for a more complete understanding of the role of multilingual language education policies in indigenous language revitalization has coincided with a dramatic increase in instances of multilingual language policy around the world, even while (and perhaps because) the English language continues its seemingly inexorable trajectory toward becoming the most global language the world has ever known. Three indigenous contexts of multilingual language policy are the Andes, Paraguay, and Aotearoa/New Zealand. In the Andes, language education policy of the 1970s in Peru opened the way for implementation of internationally funded experimental bilingual education programs in Quechua and other indigenous communities in the 1980s; and in Bolivia, the National Education Reform of 1994 sought to implant bilingual education nationwide, incorporating all thirty Bolivian indigenous languages, beginning with the three largest—Quechua, Aymara, and Guarani (Hornberger and López 1998; López and Küper 2004). In Paraguay, the demise of a multidecade dictatorship in the early 1990s ushered in a new democratic language education policy that seeks to implant instruction through the medium of Guarani alongside Spanish in all grades and in all schools of the nation incrementally, one year at a time (Choi 2003, 2004; Corvalán 1998; Gynan 2001a, 2001b). In Aotearoa/New Zealand, a grassroots movement was born in the 1980s among the Maori to save their language from further decline; these were the preschool language nests, or *kohanga reo,* where English-speaking Maori children are immersed in Maori language and culture using a total immersion approach that goes way beyond language to other media, modes, and content. That early initiative has in turn spawned the development of Maori-medium primary, secondary, and most recently tertiary level education as well, now overseen by the national Ministry of Education and the Education Review Office (Durie 1999; May 1999, 2004; Spolsky 2003).

In these indigenous contexts of sociohistorical and sociolinguistic oppression, the implementation of multilingual language policies through bi/multilingual education brings with it choices, dilemmas, and even contradictions in educational practice. In Basilia's instance, her class and school had been in the midst of implementing an experimental Quechua–Spanish bilingual education program that was discontinued the following year in her community, under contentious circumstances (Hornberger 1987). In what follows, I consider examples of such contentious educational practices in this and three more recent instances observed in indigenous Quechua, Guarani, and Maori contexts. In doing so, I adopt an ecological perspective, using the continua of biliteracy and Bakhtinian notions of voice as analytical heuristics, in seeking to understand how it is that the use of indigenous languages as a medium of instruction in indigenous communities can contribute to both enhancing children's learning and revitalizing the indigenous language.

An Ecological Perspective on Indigenous Language Revitalization and Biliteracy

An ecology of language perspective can be succinctly characterized in terms of three themes salient in both early (Haugen 1972) and more recent (Hornberger 2002; Kaplan and Baldauf 1997; Mühlhaüsler 1996; Phillipson and Skutnabb-Kangas 1996; Ricento 2000) writings. The first theme is that languages, like living species, evolve, grow, change, live, and die in relation to other languages—the language evolution theme. Second, languages interact with their environment (sociopolitical, economic, cultural, educational, historical, demographic, etc.)—the language environment theme. A third theme is the notion that some languages, like some species and environments, may be endangered and that the ecology movement is about not only studying and describing those potential losses but also counteracting them; I call this the language endangerment theme.

Ecology of language, then, recognizes that planning for any one language in a particular context necessarily entails planning for all languages impinging on that one. The power relations and dynamics among languages and their speakers cannot be ignored. It is precisely because of those unequal relations of power and the increasing recognition that an alarming portion of the world's languages are endangered (Krauss 1992) that language revitalization, and in particular indigenous language revitalization, arose as a scholarly and activist focus of concern primarily in the 1990s. Defined as "the attempt to add new linguistic forms or social functions to an embattled minority language with the aim of increasing its uses or users" (King 2001, 23), language revitalization is closely related to earlier sociolinguistic concerns with vitality (Stewart 1968) and revival (Edwards 1993; Fellman 1974), and with more recent notions of renewal (Brandt and Ayoungman 1989, 43) and reversing language shift (Fishman 1991).

Language revitalization goes one step further than language maintenance in that it implies recuperating and reconstructing something that is at least partially lost, rather than maintaining and strengthening what already exists. Whereas work on language maintenance (and shift) has focused as much on immigrant as on indigenous languages (or perhaps more so), language revitalization work carries a particular emphasis on indigenous languages. Likewise, while research on language maintenance and shift has been biased toward documenting cases of shift rather than maintenance (Hyltenstam and Stroud 1996, 568), documentation on language revitalization emphasizes the positive side of the equation, despite seemingly insurmountable odds against survival of the languages in question. Another difference between maintenance and revitalization work is the relative emphasis placed on conscious and deliberate efforts by speakers of the language to affect language behavior, that is, on language planning. While language maintenance has long been recognized as a language planning goal (e.g., Nahir 1977, 1984), and language revitalization only more recently so, nevertheless it is also true that maintenance can describe a "natural" language phenomenon that does not require any deliberate planning on the part of its speakers, whereas revitalization cannot. Finally, where language maintenance efforts have often tended to emanate from the top-down (in which someone takes benevolent initiative in "maintaining" someone else's language), language revitalization efforts tend to originate within the speech community itself (e.g., Reversing Language Shift, see Fishman 1991, 2000) as counterhegemonic social movements (Alexander 2003).

Indeed, King and I have argued that it is crucially important that the speakers of the language be involved in revitalization, as it entails altering not only the traditional language corpus but also how it is traditionally used, both at the micro level in terms of interpersonal discourse patterns and at the macro level of societal distribution; in other words, it is not so much about bringing a language back as bringing it forward. Who is better or more qualified to guide that process than the present and future speakers of the language, who must and will be the ones taking it into the future (Hornberger and King 1996, 315)? This recognition sets the stage for understanding the role of biliteracy and voice in contributing to indigenous children's learning and, in turn, to indigenous language revitalization.

The continua of biliteracy model is an ecological framework for situating educational research, policy, and practice in linguistically and culturally diverse settings around the world. The framework incorporates the language evolution, language environment, and language endangerment themes of the ecology of language. The very notion of bi- or multiliteracy assumes that one language and literacy is developing in relation to one or more other languages and literacies (language evolution); the model situates biliteracy development (whether in the individual, classroom, community, or society) in relation to the contexts, media, and content in and through which it develops (i.e., language environment); and it provides a heuristic for addressing the unequal balance of power across languages and literacies (i.e., for both studying and counteracting language endangerment).

Biliteracy in this framework refers to "any and all instances in which communication occurs in two (or more) languages in or around writing" (Hornberger 1990, 213). Specifically, the continua of biliteracy depict the development of biliteracy along first language–second language, receptive–productive, and oral–written language skills continua; through the medium of two (or more) languages and literacies whose linguistic structures vary from similar to dissimilar, whose scripts range from convergent to divergent, and to which the developing biliterate individual's exposure varies from simultaneous to successive; in contexts that encompass micro to macro levels and are characterized by varying mixes along the monolingual–bilingual and oral–literate continua; and with content that ranges from majority to minority perspectives and experiences, literary to vernacular styles and genres, and decontextualized to contextualized language texts (Hornberger 1989; Hornberger and Skilton-Sylvester 2000; also see figure 7.1).

These twelve continua can be conceptualized as four nested sets of three intersecting continua each. The nested sets represent development, media, contexts, and content of biliteracy respectively, each set made up of a cluster of its three intersecting continua. Not only is the three-dimensionality of any one set of three intersecting continua representative of the interrelatedness of those three constituent continua, but also the interrelationships extend across the four sets of continua, hence the nesting of the three-dimensional spaces.

The notion of continuum conveys that all points on a particular continuum are interrelated, and the intersecting and nested relationships among the continua convey

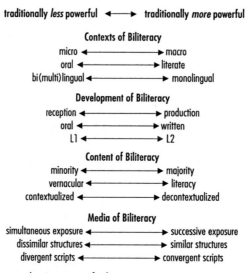

traditionally *less* powerful ◄──► traditionally *more* powerful

Contexts of Biliteracy

micro ◄──► macro
oral ◄──► literate
bi(multi)lingual ◄──► monolingual

Development of Biliteracy

reception ◄──► production
oral ◄──► written
L1 ◄──► L2

Content of Biliteracy

minority ◄──► majority
vernacular ◄──► literacy
contextualized ◄──► decontextualized

Media of Biliteracy

simultaneous exposure ◄──► successive exposure
dissimilar structures ◄──► similar structures
divergent scripts ◄──► convergent scripts

Figure 7.1 Power Relations in the Continua of Biliteracy

that all points across the continua are also interrelated. The model suggests that the more their learning contexts and contexts of use allow learners and users to draw from across the whole of each and every continuum, the greater are the chances for their full biliterate development and expression (Hornberger 1989, 289). Implicit in that suggestion is a recognition that there has usually not been attention to all points and that movement along the continua and across the intersections may well be contested. In educational policy and practice regarding biliteracy, there tends to be an implicit privileging of one end of the continua over the other such that one end of each continuum is associated with more power than the other (e.g., written development over oral development); there is a need to contest the power weighting in any given instance by paying attention to, granting agency to, and making space for actors and practices at the less powerful ends of the continua (Hornberger and Skilton-Sylvester 2000, 99).

In order to understand any particular instance of biliteracy, be it at the level of individual actor, interaction, event, practice, activity, program, site, situation, society, or world, we need to take account of all dimensions represented by the continua. At the same time, the advantage of the model is that it allows us to focus for analytical purposes on one or selected continua and their dimensions without ignoring the importance of the others; that is precisely what we will do in the following section in relation to Bakhtinian notions of voice.

Voice and Contentious Biliterate Educational Practices

Voice is what seven-year-old Basilia in my opening quote joyfully expresses through the medium of her own language in her own home, surrounded by familiar people and objects. She vividly exemplifies the individual in active dialogue with her environment, that is, the dialogism that is a prominent theme of Bakhtin's work and "begins from the premise that sentient beings—alone and in groups—are always in a state of active existence; they are always in a state of being 'addressed' and in the process of 'answering'" (Holland and Lave 2001, 9–10). Holquist put it this way:

> Existence is addressed to me as a riot of inchoate potential messages, which at this level of abstraction may be said to come to individual persons much as stimuli from the natural environment come to individual organisms. Some of the potential messages come to me in the form of primitive physiological stimuli, some in the form of natural language, and some in social codes or ideologies. So long as I am in existence, I am in a particular place, and must respond to all of these stimuli either by ignoring them or in a response that takes the form of making sense, of producing—for it is a form of work— *meaning* out of such utterances. (Holquist 1990, 47, cited in Holland and Lave 2001, 10)

It would appear that seven-year-old Basilia was perhaps ignoring the stimuli at school while responding actively to those at home; the voice that was lost at school was exuberantly found at home.

Voice, in Bakhtin's concept, is the speaking consciousness, articulated as social practice, in dialogue with others and in situated contexts. These notions have increasingly found their way into a reconceptualization of voice in language and education, in which learners can be seen as engaging in dialogical struggles for speaking consciousness (Norton 1997; Solá and Bennett 1985; Walsh 1991).

Beginning from dialogism as the first theme in Bakhtin's concept of voice, Holland and Lave (2001) highlight three additional dialogical themes in Bakhtin's writings. Self-authoring is the second theme; in the making of meaning, we author the world and ourselves in it and, in doing so, draw on languages, dialects, cultural genres, and the words of others to which we have been exposed as the media through which our senses of self and group are developed. A third theme is that "all dialogic engagements of self . . . are struggles across and about differences between self and others," animated by "discourses widely circulating locally and beyond" while a fourth highlights the active stances persons take toward others and the dialects, languages, genres, and other cultural forms they produce (Holland and Lave 2001, 10–14).

Holland and Lave elucidate these themes in their edited volume, *History in Person,* where they posit the "mutually constitutive nature of language and complex social, political, and economic struggles and the historically fashioned identities-in-practice and subjectivities that they produce" and suggest an analytic approach that starts with "local struggles"—that is, struggles in particular times and places (2001, 109). They tell us that enduring struggles are crucibles for the forging of human subjects' identities through contentious local practice. Borrowing from their approach, I am here interested in the forging of indigenous children's voices in the crucible of indigenous people's enduring struggles through contentious local practice in schools.

I examine instances of contentious biliterate educational practice in contexts of indigenous language revitalization, using the continua of biliteracy and the four Bakhtinian themes as analytical heuristics to understand the ways in which the use of indigenous languages as medium of instruction in indigenous language communities may contribute to both enhancing children's learning and revitalizing the indigenous language through the activation of voice. Specifically, I suggest that activation of indigenous children's voices enables them to negotiate along and across the various continua making up the development, contexts, content, and media of biliteracy.

Biliteracy Development and Dialogic Voices: Quechua in Peru in the 1980s

We saw earlier how little Basilia's active engagement in the dialogical process of being addressed or answering/responding contributes to her lively oral interaction in Quechua at home, while her more passive engagement at school, where Spanish is dominant, leaves her silent. In the Bakhtinian sense, her voice is activated at home but silenced at school. In terms of the consequences of this loss of voice for her biliteracy development, until she can use her first language (L1) in productive and receptive, written and oral modes at school, it will be difficult for her to develop her second language (L2) to its fullest.

Biliteracy Content, Cultural Genres, and Self-Authoring: Quechua in Bolivia in the 1990s

The second instance of contentious biliterate educational practice comes from a visit to a rural school in the department of Cochabamba in Bolivia.

After about an hour's drive from Cochabamba in the luxury of a project jeep, chauffeur Elio and I arrive at Kayarani school at about 10:30 A.M. and are greeted in the schoolyard by several dozen children rushing over to the car to shake our hands. We approach the low adobe building where the teachers live during the school week and are met at the door by head teacher Berta and Angélica who is currently substituting for the K–1st grade teacher on maternity leave. A third teacher is absent today. Berta, a native of Tarija, has been teaching here at Kayarani for three years, implementing bilingual education under the 1994 National Education Reform. She began with her class from the start of their schooling; they are now in 2nd–3rd grade.

A new school building was inaugurated last year and the rooms are nice, with tables and chairs that can be set up for group work. Berta's classroom, the only one I observed, is decorated with a lot of posters she's made in Quechua, including models of a story, a poem, a song, a recipe, a letter, as well as both the Quechua and Spanish alphabets (which she has the students recite for me later). Also on the wall is the class newspaper, *Llaqta Qapariy* (Voice of the People), featuring an article in Quechua written by student Calestino about farmers' wanting better prices for their potatoes.

A key provision of the Bolivian Education Reform is the establishment of a library in every primary classroom of the nation, each one stocked with a collection of 80 books provided by the Ministry of Education through the auspices of UNESCO. Included are 6 Big Books in Spanish, 3 of them based on oral traditions in Quechua, Aymara, and Guarani, respectively: *El Zorro, el Puma y los Otros* "The Fox, the Puma, and the Others"; *La Oveja y el Zorro* "The Sheep and the Fox"; *La Chiva Desobediente* "The Disobedient Goat." The Big Books are approximately $18'' \times 24''$, with large print text and colorful illustrations, such that the pictures can be seen by the whole class if the teacher holds the book up in front of the class in a reading circle. Berta's classroom, too, has a library corner housing a small collection including a couple of Big Books, and she calls on a child to come to the front of the class to read one of the Big Books aloud to his classmates. Later, after the class leaves for recess, a couple of the children notice my interest in the Big Books and come over to gleefully hold the books up for a photo. (August 14, 2000, Kayarani)

The instance of contentious biliterate educational practice I am drawing attention to here is the use of indigenous oral tradition within the Spanish language literacy materials of the National Education Reform—an instance of minority, vernacular, contextualized content in the second language. This practice might be doubly contentious with, on the one hand, a purist indigenous perspective rejecting the presentation of indigenous content in a nonindigenous language, and on the other hand, a hispanicist-assimilationist perspective rejecting the inclusion of indigenous content in Spanish language texts. Yet from the point of view of biliteracy development, this practice constitutes a strong support for the learner or user of the texts. Given that, in the Bakhtinian sense, an individual develops a sense of self through incorporating the languages, dialects, genres, and words of others to which she has been exposed, this biliterate practice offers a familiar voice for indigenous children to incorporate in their own voices.

Biliteracy Context, Dialogic Engagement, and Circulating Discourses: Guarani in Paraguay in the 1990s

The third instance of contentious biliterate educational practice emerged in a meeting of the curricular team of the Ministry of Education and Culture of Paraguay.

> I spent one morning with members of the Curriculum team at the Ministry of Education and their consultants Delicia Villagra and Nelson Aguilera, brainstorming the design for Guarani and Spanish language and literature curriculum for the secondary level. Paraguay's Bilingual Education Reform introduced Guarani as language of instruction alongside Spanish, beginning in 1st grade in 1993 and progressively adding one grade each year; 2001 would complete the primary cycle (grades 1–9), and Guarani instruction at the secondary level was to be introduced for the first time in February 2002.
>
> The complexity of issues needing to be addressed [is] staggering; not only is this the first time in South America (to our knowledge) that an indigenous language with relatively little tradition of technical, scientific, or literary use will be introduced into the secondary curriculum, but there are also unresolved issues lingering from the past nine years of primary bilingual education in Paraguay, including a lack of bilingual teacher preparation, inadequate language teaching methodology, lack of consensus on which Guarani to use in the schools, and negative attitudes towards the use of Guarani in the schools from some parents and communities. Not to mention the exponentially escalating demand for and market in English language education in the schools. None of these challenges is unique to Guarani; in fact these "problems in the socio-educational legitimization of languages / varieties" (Fishman 1982, 4–6) regularly attend the introduction of vernacular languages into education worldwide, historically and in the present. Nevertheless, they are very real challenges which the Curriculum Department must address in order to advance the use of Guarani in secondary education.
>
> For the time being, as a pragmatic measure, the team has opted to require the teaching of Guarani literature through the medium of Guarani, while leaving the medium of instruction for other curricular areas at the secondary level—such as math, science, and social studies—up to the decision of each school. As a strategy toward the promotion of Guarani, the team plans to orient the Guarani language and literature curriculum strongly toward production of texts in a variety of genres, the goal being to create a generation of confident and prolific Guarani writers who will in turn develop and intellectualize the language, so that it can subsequently be introduced into all areas of the secondary curriculum. (October 4, 2001, Asunción)

The instance of contentious biliterate educational practice I am drawing attention to here is the ecological approach to use of Spanish as medium of instruction alongside Guarani, even in the midst of a reform calling for the strengthening of Guarani. In terms of the continua of biliterate context, this is a case of ceding some ground to the more powerful monolingual, literate, macro contexts while simultaneously attempting to gain ground at the multilingual, oral, micro contexts. Given that, in Bakhtinian terms, dialogic selves are animated by discourses circulating locally and beyond, such a practice attempts to offer a chance for Paraguayan students to incorporate both local Guarani and wider Spanish discourses in their own, thereby contributing to their academic and biliteracy development.

Biliteracy Media and the Active Stance: Maori in Aotearoa/New Zealand Beginning in the 1980s

The fourth instance of contentious biliterate educational practice is seen in a Maori immersion primary school in Aotearoa/New Zealand.

> We three—my colleague Stephen May of the University of Waikato, his colleague Karaitiana Tamatea, parent and former *whanau* (extended family) leader at the school, and I—enter the *kura kaupapa Maori* (Maori immersion school) following the traditional protocol (*powhiri*), which means that the assistant principal (in the principal's absence) greets us with a chant while we are still outside the premises, and then we slowly enter, exchanging chants with her as we do. After a continuation of this protocol inside one of the classrooms where all 80 children (grades 1–6) are gathered for our visit, we are invited to a different room for refreshments. Because of the strict prohibition on the use of English anywhere on the school premises at all times, this is the only room where I, a non-Maori speaker, can have a conversation with teachers, staff, and leadership of the school.
>
> I am introduced to the current *whanau* leader. Here, as is the case for the 58 other *kura kaupapa* schools in Aotearoa/New Zealand, the *whanau* has been indispensable in the establishment and existence of the *kura kaupapa*. The school exists in the first place only by initiative of the *whanau;* and only after two years of running the school themselves may they appeal for government recognition and support. This school was founded in 1995 and gained recognition and its own school building and grounds several years ago.
>
> The *whanau* leader asks me, "What do you think of bilingual education?" As I formulate my answer and engage in further dialogue with him, it suddenly dawns on me that for him, bilingual education and Maori immersion are opposites, while for me they are located on a continuum. Maori-only ideology is of such integral and foundational importance to Maori immersion that the use of two languages (English and Maori) suggested by the term *bilingual* is antithetical to those dedicated to Maori revitalization. (June 28, 2002, Hamilton)

The instance of contentious biliterate educational practice I am drawing attention to here is the absolute prohibition of English language use on the *kura kaupapa* grounds, an instance, in terms of the continua of biliteracy, of successive exposure to the media of biliteracy, strictly enforced. The prohibition is controversial in a nation where English is socially and educationally dominant and highly desirable for academic and social advancement, and all the more controversial considering that the Maori children attending the school arrive as English speakers. Nevertheless, Maori immersion education, with its strict Maori-only enforcement, has been highly successful in bringing the Maori language back from the brink of disappearing. Given that, in Bakhtinian terms, speakers not only use the words of others but also take active stances with respect to those words, this contentious practice, I suggest, represents an active stance taken by the *kura kaupapa* to maximize activation of indigenous student voice and heritage indigenous language revitalization.

A famous teacher of Maori children, Sylvia Ashton-Warner, understood the importance of indigenous children's voice, even though, ironically, she taught through the medium of English. In the 1930s, she developed and used an approach she called organic reading and organic writing, described in her book *Teacher*. She writes: "First words must mean something to a child," and again, "first words must have intense meaning for a child. They must be part of his being" (1963, 33). She continues, commenting on the writings of her Maori students: "These books they write are the most dramatic and pathetic and colourful things I've ever seen on pages. But they are private and they are confidences and we don't criticize their content. Whether we read that he hates school or that my house is to be burned down or about the brawl in the *pa* (Maori village) last night the issue is the same: it is always not what is said but the freedom to say" (52–54).

By extraordinary measures she was able to activate her indigenous students' voice, even without primary use of their language. How much more often is it the case that denial of students' language also strips them of their voice?

Conclusion

Haugen argued that language itself is not a problem, but language used as a basis for discrimination is (1973). McCarty, considering the struggle for self-determination among Native people in the United States, concludes that while "language *can* be an instrument of cultural and linguistic oppression, [it] can also be a vehicle for advancing human rights and minority community empowerment" (2003, 160). It is, I suggest, the activation of indigenous voice that tilts use of the indigenous language away from discrimination and oppression and toward emancipation, self-determination, and empowerment.

Giroux tells us that "Language represents a central force in the struggle for voice . . . language is able to shape the way various individuals and groups encode and thereby engage the world" (Giroux 1986, 59, cited in Ruiz 1997, 320). This is as true for immigrant as for indigenous language minority students. Maxine Hong Kingston, who wrote the forward for the republication of *Teacher* in 1963, writes in her novel *Woman Warrior* about silencing and voice for Chinese children in school in America:

When I went to kindergarten and had to speak English for the first time, I became silent. . . . My silence was thickest—total—during the three years that I covered my school paintings with black paint. . . . During the first silent year I spoke to no one at school, did not ask before going to the lavatory, and flunked kindergarten. . . . I enjoyed the silence. At first it did not occur to me

I was supposed to talk or to pass kindergarten. I talked at home and to one or two of the Chinese kids in class. I made motions and even made some jokes. . . . I liked the Negro students (Black Ghosts) best because they laughed the loudest and talked to me as if I were a daring talker too. . . .

It was when I found out I had to talk that school became a misery, the silence became a misery. I did not speak and felt bad each time that I did not speak. . . . The other Chinese girls did not talk either, so I knew the silence had to do with being a Chinese girl.

After American school, we picked up our cigar boxes, in which we had arranged books, brushes, and an inkbox neatly, and went to Chinese school, from 5:00 to 7:30 P.M.. There we chanted together, voices rising and falling, loud and soft, some boys shouting, everybody reading together, reciting together and not alone with one voice. . . . Not all of the children who were silent at American school found voice at Chinese school. (Kingston 1975, 165–68)

True enough, not all indigenous or language minority children find voice through use of their own language in school. "It's much more than language," ethnographer Freeman is told as she sets out to document Washington, D.C., Oyster School's bilingual language plan and ends up writing about their identity plan (Freeman 1998). Ruiz, too, has warned us:

As much as language and voice are related, it is also important to distinguish between them. I have become convinced of the need for this distinction through a consideration of instances of language planning in which the "inclusion" of the language of a group has coincided with the exclusion of their voice. . . . Language is general, abstract, subject to a somewhat arbitrary normalization; voice is particular and concrete. Language has a life of its own—it exists even when it is suppressed; when voice is suppressed, it is not heard—it does not exist. To deny people their language, as in the colonial situations described by Fanon (1967) and Macedo (1983), is, to be sure, to deny them voice; but to allow them "their" language . . . is not necessarily to allow them voice. (Ruiz 1997, 320–21)

Perhaps it is not necessarily so, but what I suggest here is, though it may be that not all indigenous children find voice through use of their language, many of them do, and when they do it is perhaps because of the ways that the biliterate use of their own or heritage language as medium of instruction alongside the dominant language mediates the dialogism, meaning making, access to wider discourses, and taking of an active stance that are dimensions of voice. Indigenous voices thus activated can be a powerful force for both enhancing the children's own learning and promoting the maintenance and revitalization of their languages.

ACKNOWLEDGMENTS

Deepest thanks to Professors Kendall King and Natalie Schilling-Estes for inviting me to present this plenary at GURT 2006 and for including it in the present GURT volume. It is reprinted from the *Journal of Language, Identity, and Education* 5(4), with permission from Lawrence Erlbaum Associates.

The paper draws on my recent opportunities to revisit the Andean Quechua context and to make personal acquaintance with the Paraguayan Guarani context and the Aotearoa/New Zealand Maori context. My gratitude goes to the Fulbright Senior Specialists Program, which provided grants for my visits to Paraguay in October 2001 and Aotearoa/New Zealand in July 2002.

Earlier versions of the paper were presented at the Fourth International Symposium on Bilingualism in Arizona in May 2003, at the IX International Conference on Minority Languages in Kiruna, Sweden, in June 2003, and at the International Conference on Language, Education and Diversity at the University of Waikato, Hamilton, Aotearoa/New Zealand, in November 2003. My heartfelt thanks to my colleagues Professor Terrence Wiley of Arizona State University, Professor Birger Winsa of Stockholm University, and Professor Stephen May of Waikato University, respectively, for inviting me to reflect on and talk about these matters in such inspiring venues.

REFERENCES

Alexander, Neville. 2003. *Language education policy, national and sub-national identities in South Africa.* Strasbourg: Council of Europe: Language Policy Division, DG IV—Directorate of School, Out-of-School and Higher Education.

Ashton-Warner, Sylvia. 1963. *Teacher.* New York: Simon & Schuster.

Brandt, E. A., and V. Ayoungman. 1989. Language renewal and language maintenance: A practical guide. *Canadian Journal of Native Education* 16:42–77.

Choi, Jinny K. 2003. Language attitudes and the future of bilingualism: The case of Paraguay. *International Journal of Bilingual Education and Bilingualism* 6:81–94.

———. 2004. La planificación lingüística y la revivificación del Guaraní en el Paraguay: Comparación, evaluación e implicación [Language planning and revitalization of Guaraní in Paraguay: Comparison, evaluation and implications]. *Language Problems and Language Planning* 28:241–59.

Corvalán, Graziella. 1998. La educación escolar bilingüe del Paraguay: Avances y desafíos [Bilingual school education of Paraguay: Advances and challenges]. *Revista Paraguaya de Sociología* 35:101–18.

Durie, Arohia. 1999. Emancipatory Maori education: Speaking from the heart. In *Indigenous community-based education,* ed. Stephen May, 67–78. Clevedon, UK: Multilingual Matters.

Edwards, John. 1993. Language revival: Specifics and generalities. *Studies in Second Language Acquisition* 15:107–13.

Fanon, Frantz. (1967). *Black skin, white masks.* Trans. C. L. Markmann. New York: Grove Press.

Fellman, Jack. 1974. The role of Eliezer Ben Yehuda in the revival of the Hebrew language: An assessment. In *Advances in language planning,* ed. Joshua Fishman, 427–55. The Hague: Mouton.

Fishman, Joshua A. 1982. Sociolinguistic foundations of bilingual education. *The Bilingual review/ La revista bilingüe* 9:1–35.

———. 1991. *Reversing language shift: Theoretical and empirical foundations of assistance to threatened languages.* Clevedon, UK: Multilingual Matters.

———, ed. 2000. *Can threatened languages be saved? "Reversing language shift" revisited.* Clevedon, UK: Multilingual Matters.

Freeman, Rebecca D. 1998. *Bilingual education and social change.* Clevedon, UK: Multilingual Matters.

Gynan, Shaw N. 2001a. Language planning and policy in Paraguay. *Current Issues in Language Planning* 2:53–118.

———. 2001b. Paraguayan language policy and the future of Guaraní. *Southwest Journal of Linguistics* 20:151–65.

Haugen, Einar. 1972. *The ecology of language.* Stanford, CA: Stanford University Press.

———. 1973. The curse of Babel. In *Language as a human problem,* ed. Morton Bloomfield and Einar Haugen, 33–43. New York: W. W. Norton and Co.

Holland, Dorothy, and Jean Lave, eds. 2001. *History in person: Enduring struggles, contentious practice, intimate identities.* Santa Fe, NM: School of American Research Press.

Holquist, Michael. 1990. *Dialogism: Bakhtin and his world.* London: Routledge.

Hornberger, Nancy H. 1985. Bilingual education and Quechua language maintenance in Highland Puno, Peru. PhD diss., University of Wisconsin–Madison.

———. 1987. Bilingual education success, but policy failure. *Language in Society* 16:205—26.

———. 1988. *Bilingual education and language maintenance: A southern Peruvian Quechua case.* Berlin: Mouton.

———. 1989. Continua of biliteracy. *Review of Educational Research* 59:271–96.

———. 1990. Creating successful learning contexts for bilingual literacy. *Teachers College Record* 92:212–29.

———. 1998. Language policy, language education, language rights: Indigenous, immigrant, and international perspectives. *Language in Society* 27:439–58.

———. 2002. Multilingual language policies and the continua of biliteracy: An ecological approach. *Language Policy* 1:27–51.

———, ed. 2003. *Continua of biliteracy: An ecological framework for educational policy, research and practice in multilingual settings.* Clevedon, UK: Multilingual Matters.

Hornberger, Nancy H., and Kendall A. King. 1996. Bringing the language forward: School-based initiatives for Quechua language revitalization in Ecuador and Bolivia. In *Indigenous literacies in the Americas: Language planning from the bottom up,* ed. Nancy H. Hornberger, 299–319. Berlin: Mouton.

Hornberger, Nancy H., and Luis Enrique López. 1998. Policy, possibility and paradox: Indigenous multilingualism and education in Peru and Bolivia. In *Beyond bilingualism: Multilingualism and multilingual education,* ed. Jasone Cenoz and Fred Genesee, 206–42. Clevedon, UK: Multilingual Matters.

Hornberger, Nancy H., and Ellen Skilton-Sylvester. 2000. Revisiting the continua of biliteracy: International and critical perspectives. *Language and Education: An International Journal* 14:96–122.

Hyltenstam, Kenneth, and Christopher Stroud. 1996. Language maintenance. In *Contact linguistics,* ed. Hans Goeble, Peter Nelde, A. Stary, and Wolfgang Wölck, 567–78. Berlin: Walter de Gruyter.

Kaplan, Robert B., and Richard B. Baldauf. 1997. *Language planning from practice to theory.* Clevedon, UK: Multilingual Matters.

King, Kendall A. 2001. *Language revitalization processes and prospects: Quichua in the Ecuadorian Andes.* Clevedon, UK: Multilingual Matters.

Kingston, Maxine Hong. 1975. *The woman warrior: Memoirs of a girlhood among ghosts.* New York: Vintage International.

Krauss, Michael. 1992. The world's languages in crisis. *Language* 68:4–10.

López, Luis Enrique, and Wolfgang Küper. 2004. *La educación intercultural bilingüe en América Latina: Balance y perspectivas* [Intercultural bilingual education in Latin America: Outcomes and outlooks]. La Paz-Cochabamba: Cooperación Técnica Alemana (GTZ)-PINSEIB-PROEIB Andes.

Macedo, Donaldo P. (1983). The politics of emancipatory literacy in Cape Verde. *Journal of Education* 165:99–112.

May, Stephen, ed. 1999. *Indigenous community-based education.* Clevedon, UK: Multilingual Matters.

———. 2004. Accommodating multiculturalism and biculturalism in Aotearoa/New Zealand: Implications for language policy. In *Tangata, tangata: The changing ethnic contours of Aotearoa/New Zealand,* ed. Paul Spoonley, Cluny McPherson, and David Pearson, 247–64. Southbank, Victoria: Thomson/Dunsmore Press.

McCarty, Teresa L. 2003. Revitalizing indigenous languages in homogenizing times. *Comparative Education* 39:147–63.

Mühlhaüsler, Peter. 1996. *Linguistic ecology: Language change and linguistic imperialism in the Pacific region.* London: Routledge.

Nahir, Moshe. 1977. The five aspects of language planning: A classification. *Language Problems and Language Planning* 1:107–22.

———. 1984. Language planning goals: A classification. *Language Problems and Language Planning* 8:294–327.

Norton, Bonny. 1997. Critical discourse research. In *Research methods in language and education,* ed. Nancy H. Hornberger and David Corson, 207–16. Dordrecht: Kluwer Academic.

Philips, S. 1983. *The invisible culture: Communication in classroom and community on the Warm Springs Indian Reservation.* New York: Longman.

Phillipson, Robert, and Tove Skutnabb-Kangas. 1996. English only worldwide or language ecology? *TESOL Quarterly* 30:429–52.

Ricento, Thomas. 2000. Historical and theoretical perspectives in language policy and planning. *Journal of Sociolinguistics* 4:196–213.

Ruiz, Richard. 1997. The empowerment of language-minority students. In *Latinos and education: A critical reader,* ed. Antonia Darder, Rodolfo Torres, and Henry Gutierrez, 319–28. New York: Routledge.

Solá, Michelle, and Adrian Bennett. 1985. The struggle for voice: Narrative, literacy and consciousness in an East Harlem school. *Journal of Education* 167:88–110.

Spolsky, Bernard. 2003. Reassessing Maori regeneration. *Language in Society* 32:553–78.

Stewart, William. 1968. A sociolinguistic typology for describing national multilingualism. In *Readings in the sociology of language,* ed. Joshua Fishman, 531–45. The Hague: Mouton.

Walsh, Catherine E. 1991. *Pedagogy and the struggle for voice: Issues of language, power, and schooling for Puerto Ricans.* New York: Bergin and Garvey.

Developing

8

Endangering Language Vitality through Institutional Development

Ideology, Authority, and Official Standard Irish in the Gaeltacht

TADHG Ó hIFEARNÁIN
University of Limerick

CURRENT PERSPECTIVES on language policy suggest that, in order to be effective, govern-mental planning efforts must be consistent with a given community's language prac-tices and beliefs along with other contextual forces that are in play (Spolsky 2004) and that official language policies make up only one aspect of what is often a deeply rooted system of overt and covert practices and beliefs of both government bodies and community members (Shohamy 2006). This chapter reports on a three-and-a-half-year-long survey of members of a specific community in the Irish Gaeltacht to determine how language revitalization efforts by the state have affected the language practices of community members. This study draws attention to a mismatch between Irish national language policy and the apparent language policy of a Gaeltacht com-munity with regard to Official Standard Irish and its role in language revitalization and analyzes the ways in which government policies—specifically the development of a national standard for the language—have paradoxically affected the language in the Múscraí Gaeltacht region.

Since its foundation in 1922, the Irish state has sought to influence the belief systems in Irish-speaking communities, which had experienced a massive language shift from Irish to English. The focus has been on both Irish language attitudes and usage patterns. The goals of state planning efforts have been concentrated on revers-ing the declining use of Irish as the primary community language and revitalizing it for use both by the traditional community of speakers and as a fit medium for all the needs of a modern state. The strengthening of the status of Irish in the speaker com-munity and the expansion of its domains of usage nationally has thus always been a fundamental pillar of the Irish national language ideology, although the practice of formulating specific language policies has varied in scope and application through time. The national ideological commitment to Irish revival is particularly clear in language in education policies from the 1920s and 1930s, including making Irish compulsory in primary schools as well as for the postprimary Leaving Certificate (Kelly 2002, 18). A move toward Irish medium education nationally in the first thirty years of statehood meant that just under one-third of schools were teaching through

Irish only by the late 1930s. When this number peaked in the 1950s, a further one-fourth of schools were teaching some subjects through the Irish medium (Ó Riagáin 1997, 16).

The cultivation of the Irish language in the Gaeltacht population served as a resource to fuel the national policy. One policy initiative that shows this clearly was the establishment from 1927 to 1960 of dedicated secondary schools, *Coláistí Ullmhúcháin* (preparative colleges) in the Gaeltacht. These schools fed the primary teacher training colleges so that up to 50 percent of trainees should be native Irish speakers (Kelly 2002, 69), which was hugely disproportionate to the number of native Irish speakers in the general population. National language policy, as experienced in the ideology behind legislation but also as a manifestation of majority public opinion, differs subtly from Gaeltacht community policy in the mechanisms of language management employed. When there are mismatches, often unseen but with potentially conflictual consequences, the national policy has always had the stronger position.

National Language Policy and the Gaeltacht

There have been a number of distinct periods of national language policy since the 1920s, which can be tracked by changes in the state's practice with regard to educational planning and provision, Gaeltacht administration structures, and Irish language broadcasting in particular, all of which reflect both government politics and majority public opinion on these questions (Ó hIfearnáin 2000). The state's early language ideology was rooted in national language revivalism, and so official responsibility for the Gaeltacht and language questions was dispersed throughout all departments of government and state agencies. While departments that physically had a presence in the Gaeltacht, such as the ministries responsible for agriculture, fisheries, and forestry, were particularly concerned with language issues, the brief included all areas of government activity, especially the national departments of education and of finance.

1926–1956

As a result of the Gaeltacht Commission's report of 1926, the government recognized areas where approximately 80 percent or more of the population spoke Irish as being *fíor-Ghaeltacht* (true Gaeltacht). It was intended that these areas should be administered through Irish alone and that all education would also be in Irish only. Surrounding areas where Irish was spoken by more than 25 percent of the population were called *breac-Ghaeltacht* (partial Gaeltacht), where administration and education was to be developed rapidly toward Irish-medium provision. The rest of the country was an area targeted for full language revival rather than language preservation and development. The underlying ideology was one of a belief in language revitalization at the national level, with more or less specific plans according to the presence of Irish as a community language at the local level. These geographic divisions were not meant to be set in stone but to change in favor of Irish, the *breac-Ghaeltacht* and the rest of the country to become *fíor-Ghaeltacht* in the course of time.

1956–Present

A full Department of the Gaeltacht, *Roinn na Gaeltachta,* was set up in 1956. Since then the administration and development of the Gaeltacht has been the direct responsibility of a named government ministry, currently a major division of the Department of Community, Rural and Gaeltacht Affairs. A dedicated state development authority, *Údarás na Gaeltachta* (The Gaeltacht Authority), was created in 1979. Until it became the remit of a particular ministry, the Gaeltacht was geographically defined in a loose yet potentially dynamic way.

Extracting the Gaeltacht from national language policy and defining it for the focused language management purposes of a named government ministry in 1956 was not a simple task. As the result of policy being dispersed to all areas of government, in the course of the thirty years between the report of the Gaeltacht Commission (1926) and the setting up of the ministry for the Gaeltacht, a multitude of definitions of the Gaeltacht had evolved. A memorandum prepared for the government dated January 19, 1956 (National Archives, Department of the Taoiseach, S15811A), suggests that as many as twelve different understandings of where the Gaeltacht was to be found were in circulation at the time, from the first official usage that is contained in the Local Offices and Appointments (Gaeltacht) Order, 1928, through various acts on housing, school meals, vocational education, to the different operating structures of the Garda Síochána and the Defence Forces. The Gaeltacht was only first officially defined in 1956 by the Gaeltacht Areas Order (Statutory Instrument no. 245/1956) for the purpose of giving *Roinn na Gaeltachta* a precise geographical definition of its operational area.

The Gaeltacht Areas Order is based on the townland as a unit, being the traditional rural land division that most of the population recognize, and lists these as whole or parts of the smallest administrative areas used by the state, the district electoral divisions, as "determined to be Gaeltacht areas for the purposes of the Ministers and Secretaries (Amendment) Act, 1956 (No. 21 of 1956)," being the act that set up the Gaeltacht ministry. Although public opinion in Ireland generally assumes that the Gaeltacht was defined as those areas where Irish was the primary community language, this definition is hard to sustain under close examination. Indeed, although the reason for existence of the Gaeltacht as a statutory area is linguistic, from 1956 it was far from being an exclusively Irish-speaking or even bilingual community. The area it encompassed contains many townlands where Irish was certainly spoken but as a minority language.

The Gaeltacht area, so defined, was a result of a special language census of households that were deemed to be in the Gaeltacht in 1956 by one or more of the dozen or so definitions that had been identified as being in use. This special census, basically a report by the house to house enumerators who collected the general census of population forms that year, was then further verified by selected reexamination visits by three specially selected school inspectors and further referral to government experts. The original draft of the Gaeltacht map (available in the National Archives) prepared on September 8, 1956, included core areas where Irish speakers were in a clear majority, typically surrounded by larger areas that were recommended to be kept under review for potential inclusion. As such, the proposed definition of the Gaeltacht prepared internally for the government already recognized that language ideology and management were the driving forces in describing the Gaeltacht rather than the more objective criteria of actual language ability and practice. When the government's order was enacted, on September 21, 1956, nearly all the "potential areas" were included, as were some contiguous townlands that had not previously even been considered for possible inclusion. The only exclusions from the original draft were isolated townlands where Irish was observed to have been spoken as a native language but that were not contiguous to core Gaeltacht areas, a fact that further confirms the Gaeltacht boundaries to be driven by policy for area language management, or the intention to develop such plans rather than being simply linguistic reservations for the management of a residual bilingual population.

Ideologies behind the Mapping of the Gaeltacht
The inclusion of the linguistically peripheral areas was not entirely cynical or illogical. Most of the secondary schools were located in these areas, as they tended to be in the villages and small towns that were population centers where the English language had made most advances since the mid-nineteenth century. Equally, inclusion of such areas meant that many parishioners were not separated from their churches, and sports fields and other amenities remained within the jurisdiction of the Gaeltacht and so could benefit from subsidy and improvement as amenities for the Irish-speaking population. All this sought to maintain the rural communities to which the Irish-speaking communities belonged and to bring them under one government ministry responsible for their economic and social development, which were seen as the primary contexts for linguistic preservation and expansion. The central, though slightly ambiguous status of Irish as a community language, particularly in the geographical margins of the core Gaeltacht areas, was confirmed by the wording used by the government when further extending the Gaeltacht boundary to some adjacent areas in 1967, 1974, and 1982 (Statutory Instruments 200/1967, 192/1974, and 350/1982): "Whereas the areas specified in the Schedule to this Order are substantially Irish speaking areas or areas contiguous thereto which, in the opinion of the Government, ought to be included in the Gaeltacht with a view to preserving and extending the use of Irish as a vernacular language."

The emphasis is plainly on the Gaeltacht as a planning area where Irish is to be preserved and extended, even to areas that are contiguous to areas where it is spoken by a substantial part of the population.

The official Gaeltacht thus has a complex relationship with Irish. It contains regions where Irish is still a major, if not entirely dominant, community language and others where Irish is only the first language of a very small percentage of the local population. Gaeltacht community language policy, being the people's beliefs about and practices with regard to Irish, to English, to bilingualism, and to language questions generally, and specifically the status and roles of the languages, is a multifaceted combination of the national process of language shift toward English that has taken place, the communities' own conscious or accidental bucking of the trend, and the region's position as the target of specific language policies since the foundation of the Irish state. Although both the local communities of the Gaeltacht and the majority of the Irish public have as a common goal the preservation and promotion of Irish, an analysis of several aspects of state policy reveals a divergence between the language policy of the local speech communities and that of the national collective (i.e., the state and majority public opinion), particularly with regard to the role and form of the standard national language and to the practice of bilingualism at home and school (Ó hIfearnáin 2007). As a result of underlying differences in language ideology, these subtle mismatches between the de facto language policy of many Irish speakers in the Gaeltacht and the rest of the population may have actually reinforced the pattern of linguistic decline in a covert way, in Shohamy's (2006) terms, counter to the apparent desires of community and state. The following discussion is based on the hypothesis that positive language development in the Gaeltacht and throughout the nation requires consensus between language planners and individual community members on the cultivation of the linguistic ambitions of speakers and potential speakers of Irish and on the target variety or varieties of the language that can be cultivated for this purpose. The discussion is based on fieldwork between the summer of 2000 and the spring of 2004 in the Múscraí Gaeltacht region in the southwestern province of Munster and an analysis of the ideology behind the official standard language, *an Caighdeán Oifigiúil.*

The Múscraí Gaeltacht Study

Múscraí provides an example of a small Gaeltacht region where the community use of Irish is under great pressure from growing English language dominance. Its western townlands around Cúil Aodha and north of Béal Átha an Ghaorthaidh were unquestionably in the Gaeltacht according to the early 1956 government report, while the rest were originally in the "potential inclusion" category, and some eastern townlands were simply added on the publication of the Gaeltacht Areas Order. The area was expanded in 1982 to include remaining parts of a parish on its eastern border. Múscraí is a landlocked mountainous area on the Cork side of the boundary between Counties Cork and Kerry. The area had a population of 3,401 according to the 2002 Census of Ireland (CSO 2004). Some 2,707 or 79.6 percent of the total population claimed to be able to speak Irish on census day, but only 1,207 (35.5 percent) said they did so on a daily basis (table 8.1). The area can be divided into four linguistic zones consistent with the percentage of daily users of Irish according to the census, and these areas correspond closely to local perceptions of language vitality in the area.

Fieldwork for this study was conducted over three and half years. The first thirty months, from the summer of 2000 to the spring of 2003, were spent gathering data by a quantitative questionnaire, which was followed by qualitative interviews with selected informants from the quantitative study. The project investigated the language abilities, practices, and ideologies of fluent Irish speakers in the region, not those of the population as a whole. It is thus not methodologically wholly comparable to the work of Ó Riagáin (1992), conducted in the Corca Dhuibhne Gaeltacht region in Kerry, further to the west, in the 1980s, which was based on a sample of the whole population, including Irish speakers and non-Irish speakers and concentrated on the dynamics of language transmission from parents and the broader community. The

Table 8.1
Population Claiming Ability to Speak Irish in Múscraí (percent)

	15–19 Years	20–29 Years	30–44 Years	45–59 Years	60+ Years
Cúil Aodha	100	91.4	84	70.3	91.3
	(64)	(48.3)	(49.4)	(46)	(40.2)
Béal Átha an Ghaorthaidh	98.6	90.6	79.9	75.9	78.7
	(65.8)	(22.9)	(51.1)	(28.3)	(27.4)
Baile Mhic Íre	95.5	83.7	79	76.8	84.4
	(59.8)	(13.2)	(26.7)	(25.8)	(28.7)
Cill na Martra	81.4	78.6	73	67.7	72.2
	(42.4)	(12.6)	(12.8)	(14.5)	(15.2)

Source: Special Calculation by Central Statistics Office from Census 2002.
Note: The percentage who say they use the language daily is given in parentheses.

quantitative questionnaire did, however, take many elements of Ó Riagáin's as its core subject matter.

The initial aim was to interview one-third of all the daily Irish speakers in the area over fifteen years old, in proportion to their distribution by age group and gender. Broadly speaking, this was achieved (table 8.2), although it was difficult to locate enough fluent Irish speakers to complete the quota in the eastern area where the language was least used, and some oversampling occurred in circumstances where the number of very fluent speakers was shown to be much higher than the number

Table 8.2
Daily Speakers of Irish in Each Area within the Múscraí Gaeltacht (Census of Population 2002) and the Numbers in the Valid Survey

	Age Group (years)				
Region	15–19	20–29	30–44	45–59	60+
Cúil Aodha					
Census	25	28	40	34	37
Survey: 56	8	17	10	7	14
Béal Átha an Ghaorthaidh					
Census	48	22	64	41	45
Survey: 89	15	17	25	13	19
Baile Mhic Íre					
Census	67	25	65	69	66
Survey: 75	16	9	21	17	12
Cill na Martra					
Census	25	13	25	18	23
Survey: 19	7	3	4	3	2

Source: Census Statistics from Special Tabulation by the Central Statistics Office.

who claimed to use the language daily in the census. A total of 239 valid questionnaires were completed. They were conducted face-to-face by the author and local fieldwork assistants in interviews in Irish that lasted between twenty minutes and several hours. The sample was built using the snowballing, or friend-of-a-friend, technique, whereby local knowledge enabled us to make initial contact in each age cohort in each subarea, and then informants suggested the names of others, who were interviewed until the quota was reached. This is a very effective way to engage with a very small population, and nobody who was approached to complete the quantitative questionnaire refused to cooperate. The resultant data reflect the attitudes and practices of a significant proportion of the most fluent regular speakers of Irish in this Gaeltacht area.

Irish Speakers in Múscraí
According to these findings, the strongest Irish-speaking areas within Múscraí are the communities to the northwest (Cúil Aodha) and southwest (Béal Átha an Ghaorthaidh) of the region. The Cúil Aodha area has a population of 438 and is the strongest Irish-speaking community, with some 83.3 percent who claim to speak Irish, 246 or 56.2 percent of whom say they do so on a daily basis. Béal Átha an Ghaorthaidh is a village and surrounding mountainous countryside with a population of 863, where some 40.6 percent claim to use Irish on a daily basis. The practice of intergenerational transmission is under great pressure in Béal Átha an Ghaorthaidh, all informants in the present study placing great importance on schooling and social clubs in maintaining Irish as a community language among the young. The schoolgoing populations of these two areas, although physically in proximity, rarely meet as they attend their local primary schools and then postprimary schools in Baile Bhuirne and Béal Átha an Ghaorthaidh, respectively. As a result, the small group of thirty-nine Irish speakers in the fifteen- to nineteen-year-old cohort from Cúil Aodha and the seventy-two in Béal Átha an Ghaorthaidh (table 8.1) remain linguistically isolated. To the east of these two core areas lies Baile Bhuirne/Baile Mhic Íre, an urbanized area on the main Cork to Killarney road, with a population of 1,297 and some 34.4 percent daily Irish speakers. Further east and to the south lies a fourth area in the electoral divisions of Cill na Martra, Doire Finín, and Ceann Droma, where only 25.7 percent of the 820 people claim to use Irish daily, a percentage that drops in some parts among certain age groups.

The Múscraí region is clearly a bilingual community where Irish is under great pressure as a community language, but it is also one that played an important role in the revival movement of the nineteenth and early twentieth centuries. Many revivalists attended summer colleges in the area. Father Peadar Ua Laoghaire, born locally, was one of many writers from the area and one of the leaders of the *caint na ndaoine* (speech of the people) movement that established the basis of the Irish language and literature revival on the contemporary language of the native speakers rather than on the earlier literary variety. The Irish Folklore Commission, founded in 1935, also collected a large amount of material from storytellers and tradition bearers in all parts of Múscraí, proving the vigor and scope of the Irish language oral tradition in this area in comparatively recent times. The regional variety of Irish is, however, perceived locally as significantly distant from the standard language, particularly with regard to verbal forms, vocabulary, and syntax.

Irish as a Home Language

Unlike some other recent studies (Ó Giollagáin 2002, 2005), this research did not seek to categorize Gaeltacht Irish speakers as native or neonative speakers along anthropological grounds according to the language of their parents or the length of time that their families had been in the area. Instead, the aim was to collect data on the practices of fluent speakers in this Gaeltacht region, and informants were included based on residency in the area and their competence to use Irish fluently and well enough to discuss some quite sophisticated sociolinguistic issues. The questionnaire and interview thus performed a gate function in selecting highly competent language users. Only a handful of informants were not originally from the area, and all had ties to the region through family or marriage. Informants were asked to say which language or combination of languages they learnt first at home. There was a marked difference between those in the fifteen- to nineteen-year-old category and those over twenty years old. Only 28 percent of the younger informants, most of whom were in their final year at school or had left school the previous year, thought that they had learnt Irish first, while 52 percent thought that English was the first language or dominant language in their youth. Although still a significant proportion, only 26 percent of those over twenty years old thought that English was their only or dominant first language, 37 percent saying that Irish was their first language, and a further 37 percent saying that they spoke both at home. Only a few individuals in the sixty plus age group of Irish speakers claimed to have spoken English or a mixture of the two languages as their first language.

It is not appropriate to describe the younger speakers as semispeakers. In her studies of Scottish Gaelic communities in northeastern Scotland, Nancy Dorian (1981, 107) describes semispeakers as not being fully proficient in Gaelic, their speech being marked by what the fully fluent speakers described as "mistakes." While one could argue that the younger speakers in this study were semispeakers of Múscraí dialect Irish, they were for the most part very articulate in Irish, and while their speech style might not be as rich in idiom as that of the older speakers, it is nevertheless functional and expressive. If a comparison can be made to Dorian's models of speaker types, they most closely resemble the "young fluent speakers" of the Embo area (Dorian 1981, 116), their linguistic "faults" passing unremarked in everyday conversation with older speakers until a question of authenticity or idiom might actually be discussed. One older informant suggested that theirs was a form of youth speak, common in local English too. An analysis of younger Gaeltacht speakers, especially in the more strongly Irish-speaking areas, would be a fruitful area for further research.

Children's Language Competence

Parents of pupils of school age during the survey believed that their children had a reasonably good command of both Irish and English, although more felt that their English was "very good" compared with their Irish (table 8.3, cf. Ó Curnáin 2007).

Table 8.3
Parents' Perceptions of School-Going Children's Language Proficiency

	Irish	English
Very good	66.7	86.4
Quite good	31.8	7.6
Not too good	1.5	4.5
Bad or None	—	1.5

Note: Parents' perceptions are presented in percentages. $N = 71$.

The qualitative interviews showed that participants' criteria for describing a child as competent in the two languages, Irish and English, were different. Irish ability in the younger children in particular tended to be assessed by parents according to the child's ability to conduct everyday conversations in the language, whereas skills in English were often connected to more formal reading and writing. English ability was also often expressed in comparative terms, a child's progress being compared to that of the peer group and relations living elsewhere in Ireland or abroad. This is natural in that English-speaking society is much broader but also displays a more targeted approach to English acquisition, with greater value being placed on English literacy and education for wider communication.

Irish Literacy

Actual ability in reading and writing Irish is a good indicator not just of a person's literacy skills but also of their experience with the standard language, as this is the variety that they are most likely to encounter in written form.

Table 8.4 reveals some stark facts. Only just over half of the fifteen- to nineteen-year-olds claim to have no problems in reading Irish, despite the fact that the survey sample is of fluent Irish speakers who live in an environment where Irish is spoken as a community language and who have done all their schooling through the medium of Irish. Those who are least confident about their reading skills are actually those who have the most contact with the written word—the school-age category (fifteen- to nineteen-year-olds) and that of the majority of the parents of younger

Table 8.4
Self-Assessment of Reading Ability in Irish (percent)

	15–19 Years ($n = 46$)	20–29 Years ($n = 46$)	30–44 Years ($n = 60$)	45–59 Years ($n = 40$)	60+ Years ($n = 47$)
I can only read it when it is a local variety of Irish	17.4	6.5	15.0	7.5	17.0
I can read Irish well, but sometimes have problems	23.9	28.3	20.0	15.0	12.8
I have no problems in reading Irish	52.2	60.9	50.0	70.0	59.6

children in the survey (thirty- to forty-four-year-olds). It is in these two groups that there is also a small peak in the percentage claiming that they can only read a local variety of Irish. The peak in the sixty plus group can be attributed to the most elderly in this open-ended group, some of whom did not attend school in their youth or for whom their only reading materials in Irish are collections of local history and folk-tales published in the dialect. Difficulty in reading Irish is not just associated with the problems of the standard but also is associated with aliteracy in Irish, literacy in Irish being tied to schoolwork and to only very limited usage beyond. Indeed, those who claim to have no difficulty in reading Irish may not actually read very much in the language in their everyday lives. Nevertheless, the official standard is the only writ-ten form of the language experienced by the vast majority of informants. The qualita-tive data clearly show that there is alienation with the written word because it is in what is perceived to be an inauthentic variety. Exclusive use of the official standard in schooling since the 1950s is clearly an element in the complex matrix of language endangerment, particularly for the younger age groups and their parents who are most in contact with it.

Language Standardization and Irish Dialects

It is not unusual for a recently coined standard variety to create ambiguity about au-thenticity in communities undergoing language loss and revitalization. Fañch Broudic (1995a) observes that revived standardized Breton, which accounts for most of what is written and published in the language, is not accepted as authentic by the majority of native speakers but that with few exceptions these speakers have not transmitted any variety of their language to their children (Broudic 1995b). In Ecuador, field research (King 2001, 93–99) has shown that the main point of contention between older native Quichua speakers and their younger relatives who have learnt the Unified variety is perceived authenticity, notably in respect of neologisms and pronunciation. The Irish of the Munster Gaeltacht regions, including Múscraí, differs in this dynamic from other minorized languages in that there was a relatively strong written tradition in the dialect that is perceived to have been replaced by the official standard while the contin-uing processes of language shift have taken place. The official standard is not deemed to be dialect neutral; one informant from Cúil Aodha explains his reasons for speaking (local) Irish only to his children thus: "Déinim é chun an teanga a choimeád beo agus gan an droch-Ghaoluinn chaighdeánach nó Chonamarach a bheith i Múscraí" [I do it to keep the language alive and to avoid bad Standard or Conamara type Irish coming into Múscraí].

Language revitalization is the overt aim of the state and is widely supported in national surveys (Ó Riagáin and Ó Gliasáin 1994). While there is no evidence that the vast majority of Irish speakers in the Gaeltacht are not in favor of the preservation and development of Irish, there is strong evidence that the speech community and the national collective diverge significantly on the role and form of the target variety to be revitalized. Whereas the language policy of the state is explicit in this respect, the standard language being the only variety used in administrative publications and the school curricula, the unwritten but nevertheless forceful language policy of the com-munity does not totally accept the dominance of the standard. There is also an important mismatch between the community's own ideology and practice: the continuing decline in the vitality of localized Gaeltacht varieties of Irish is evidence of the language community's estrangement from the home variety in favor of English. This drift away from robust dialectal use is reinforced by schooling, where only the standard language is used in reading and writing. The authority of the standard language is, however, ambiguous. It requires practitioners to accept it as a subtle, dialect-neutral, and effective tool for national communication, yet this goal is quite abstract as, even among highly competent Gaeltacht Irish speakers, productive reading and writing in Irish is linked to schooling and not widely practiced by the majority after school years (Ní Mhianáin 2003; Ó hIfearnáin 2005). It requires effort to acquire a command of the standard, a variety that is seen as somewhat synthetic and of limited practical use in their daily lives. Estranged from their home variety through the dynamics of language shift and because it is not reinforced at school, the standard is equally rejected by some as a legitimate and useful target variety because of its distance from local authentic speech, adding to the spiral of linguistic marginalization.

The Authorship and Authority of Official Standard Irish

The development of *an Caighdeán Oifigiúil,* Official Standard Irish, was driven by the needs of statehood and the role ascribed to Irish as the national and first official language by the constitution. Its development conforms closely to the stages of language planning in Haugen's model (1959), based on Norwegian, with which it was contemporary. The modern standard's origins are in the cultural nationalist movement of the nineteenth century, and it represents a fundamental paradox. The revival movement was built on an ideological commitment to the revitalization and development of *caint na ndaoine* (the speech of the people), a dialectally diverse language with an impoverished spread of domains of usage, as a unified national language. The full version of the standard was first published in 1958 (Rannóg an Aistriúcháin 1958). It has been reprinted many times and is still the authoritative handbook, although there are frequent debates about its reform (e.g., Ó Ruairc 1999; Ó Baoill 2000; Williams 2006). The 1958 volume covers mainly grammar and orthography, complementing a document published some eleven years earlier that dealt only with spelling reform (Rialtas na hÉireann 1947). By the 1970s the standard spelling and grammar were firmly established as the only authoritative variety in the state administration and education, the key domains of Irish language policy.

The authorship of standard Irish is officially anonymous. It is the work of *Rannóg an Aistriúcháin* (the "Translation Section"), which is a service of the Houses of the Oireachtas, being the *Dáil* (National Representative Assembly), *Seanad* (Senate), and *Oifig an Uachtaráin* (the President's Office). The handbook's origins, and so those of the standard itself, are thus in Rannóg an Aistriúcháin's desire for internal consistency in the provision of Irish versions of government and legislative documentation. The first version of the full standard was published in 1953 with the more tentative title of *Gramadach na Gaeilge—Caighdeán Rannóg an Aistriúcháin* [Irish Grammar—The Translation Section's Standard]. This was seen by Rannóg an Aistriúcháin as the first step in a national consultation about the standard. They write (Rannóg an Aistriúcháin 1958, viii) that the opinions and suggestions they received as a result of that publication formed the basis for the next draft, which was itself then given to un-named people who they knew to be interested in grammar and who had expertise in the field. The major work in establishing the standard then took place in 1957 as all the previous work and input were reassessed. They declare further that "helpful advice was given by native speakers from all the Gaeltacht areas, from teachers, and from other people who had particular knowledge of the language, and it was agreed with the Department of Education that this booklet should be published as a standard for official usage and as a guide for teachers and the general public" (translation from Rannóg an Aistriúcháin 1958, viii). The standard was thus developed by a small group of language professionals who sought advice from unnamed experts and ac-quaintances for the specific purposes of government administration. Having devel-oped this useful tool for internal use, it was crucially then adopted by the Department of Education, and so guaranteed its central position through schooling.

The standard is constructed on four basic principles, translated here from Ran-nóg an Aistriúcháin (1958, viii):

1. As far as possible not to accept any form that does not have good authority in the living language of the Gaeltacht;
2. Choose the forms which are most widely used in the Gaeltacht;
3. Give appropriate importance to the history and literature of the Irish language;
4. Seek regularity and simplicity.

Although these guidelines show that Gaeltacht Irish varieties played a key role in the founding ideology of the standard, and the authors themselves do say that all its forms and rules comply with the usage of good Irish speakers in "some part" of the Gaeltacht, each of the decisions on the standard form can be contested. For exam-ple, no definitions are given of "good authority" as opposed to any other kind of authority. Although using the most widely used form of a word or grammatical struc-ture may seem democratic, it is not stated whether this means that which is under-stood most widely throughout the country or that which is used by the largest number of Gaeltacht Irish speakers. The latter might leave the authority consistently with the dialect(s) of Conamara, which although only one part of the Gaeltacht contains about half of all of the Gaeltacht's Irish speakers.

While setting out its preferred forms, the standard professes not to impose itself as the only acceptable form of the language: "Tugann an caighdeán seo aitheantas ar leith d'fhoirmeacha agus do rialacha áirithe ach ní chuireann sé ceartfhoirmeacha eile ó bhail ná teir ná toirmeasc ar a n-úsáid" (Rannóg an Aistriúcháin 1958, viii). [This standard gives recognition to particular forms and rules but it does not remove the validity of other correct forms, nor does it forbid their usage.]

However much the authors may have wished to reconcile the existence of the standard with the continued vitality of the regional dialects, the two have not existed in total harmony. The dialects, being the native forms of Irish, have continued to lose their vitality as part of a well-documented language shift that continues in the Gaeltacht while they benefit from negligible recognition from the education system and state agencies. The decline of the dialects is not simply a coincidence, but in part a consequence of the promotion of the standard as a prestige form. It has its roots in the national language ideology.

Niall Ó Dónaill, a native of the Donegal Gaeltacht in the northwest of the province of Ulster, was an intellectual and creative writer but also a state-employed translator and lexicographer. He was the chief editor of the Irish-English Dictionary *Foclóir Gaeilge-Béarla,* which was first published in 1977 and is still the standard reference. He was an active member of the milieu that was working to produce the standard in the 1950s and was one of its champions. In his provocative and highly influential essay on the development of Irish, *Forbairt na Gaeilge* (Ó Dónaill 1951), he clearly articulates his belief that although those who are developing the Irish language must be careful to cultivate its native roots, they should cut and prune it to make it develop in more useful ways: "Is cosúil teanga le habhaill. Is é an bás di scaradh lena fréamhacha, ach is troimide a toradh na géaga a bhearradh aici" (Ó Dónaill 1951, 12). [A language is like an apple tree. Break its roots and it dies, but its fruits are heavier for cutting its branches.]

Ó Dónaill makes the point forcefully in this work that the future of Irish is in the cities and on the national stage and that the promotion of the dialects through an overindulgence of *caint na ndaoine* is a danger to its progress: "Is é bun agus barr mo scéil go gcaithfear foréigean a dhéanamh ar chanúnachas leis an teanga Ghaeilge a shlánú" (Ó Dónaill 1951, 56). [The basis of my message is that we must assault dialectal traits/fondness for dialects if the Irish language is to be saved.]

Nevertheless, Ó Dónaill observed the power that the standard quickly acquired some thirty years later when he was editing a modern edition of a book by an author from his own area that was written in the early twentieth century. Writing in the literary and current affairs magazine *Comhar,* he commented on some local dialect forms that clearly were correct and held authority locally, but which were now frowned upon by editors as being illegitimate or displaced by the standard: "Ní 'ceartfhoirmeacha eile' a bhí iontu, ag cuid mhaith de lucht eagair na Gaeilge, ach foirmeacha réamhchaighdeánacha ar fáisceadh an muinéal go reachtúil acu sna caogaidí i dTeach Laighean" (Ó Dónaill 1981, 21–22). [Many Irish language editors decided they were not "other correct forms," but prestandard forms whose necks had been legislatively wrung in the 1950s in Leinster House (i.e., seat of the Dáil and Seanad).]

It is clear that although the authors of the standard explicitly stated that they did not intend to undermine any dialectal form that had a historical basis and was part of the living language of the Gaeltacht, after having been adopted by the education system and by all the state agencies, the standard took on its own dynamic to become the only acceptable form in most domains of written Irish usage. The fact that the standard is primarily a written variety has also led to a diglossic situation for the varieties of Irish in the Gaeltacht, where spoken Irish takes as its basis the regional dialect, while all forms of written language tend toward the standard, as this is what is to be found in textbooks and in most published material. Although the standard is flexible to the extent that local dialect words and idiom can be used in a standardized text, there is an observable dualism is its application, the point that Ó Dónaill (1981) highlights. Although many forms are "acceptable," clearly standard usage has determined the "preferred" forms for schools and official documentation. The association

of the standard with written Irish and the popular perception of its prescriptive nature
are especially cause for concern in populations where the local variety has been
weakened through language shift and dialect attrition. As the standard variety of Irish
has not developed as a spoken variety outside school-learner circles, it challenges regional dialects but does not offer a complete alternative model—in effect imposing a
form of silence on native dialect speakers.

The perception that the local variety is distant from the new prestige forms of the
standard may also actually contribute to decline in the vitality of the spoken language.
Nancy Dorian (1987, 59) has observed that teaching a grammatically standardized
prestige version of a language to a community who speak a tangibly different variety
only emphasizes the marginal nature of their own dialect in their eyes and further un-
dermines their belief in the language's role and legitimacy. This is certainly a factor
that can be observed in the Múscraí study but not one that applies to the whole of the
Irish-speaking population. In broad terms, it seems that those whose language skills
are strongest, typically the older generations, have little difficulty in understanding
the standard language or indeed other regional varieties of Irish. In the course of fieldwork it became increasingly apparent that the older speakers had a much deeper well
of passive knowledge of the language, based on oral tradition, the heavy literature
content of Irish schooling before the 1960s, and exposure in their youth to relatives
and neighbors who had little command of English. The dynamics of language marginalization and the strengthening of the role of English in this bilingual society, coupled with widespread aliteracy in Irish (i.e., most speakers have the ability to read and
write Irish but few develop the habit of using these skills), mean that the opportunity
to exercise these language skills is limited. While few outside the language-centered
professions are productive users of the standard in their everyday lives, the elders tend
to see it as a form they can understand that is a useful unifying tool for the national
language. In contrast, many younger speakers fall between two camps.

With some rare exceptions, younger Irish speakers do not have such a deep
knowledge of their regional variety because the bilingual society in which they live is
now dominated by English and the opportunities to obtain the profound passive
knowledge that older members of the community had are no longer available due to
social changes such as the fragmentation of extended families, the concentration of
shops and social venues outside the local communities, and the diversification of
professions from farming and trades that kept people close to their homes. The older
speakers are mostly confident enough in their own variety, have enough residual linguistic resources to understand interlocutors who speak other varieties, and have less
of a problem reading written Irish in the standard, a situation that is akin to what
Haugen (1966), when discussing semicommunication between speakers of related
language varieties, described as the trickle of sufficient messages through a rather
high level of code noise. The difference between these older speakers and the younger speakers is that the latter have to make a conscious effort to acquire either the local variety or the standard, or both, and are thus limited in the important passive ability to accommodate other language varieties, whether written or spoken. In the
formulation of language management policies, the target variety for revitalization is
thus ambiguous.

Conclusion

Grenoble and Whaley (2006, 154–56) have argued that although standardization has undeniable benefits for minorized languages, the very process can facilitate continued language loss for a wide variety of reasons. Written standards in particular unavoidably reduce variation and create new hierarchies of linguistic prestige. The standard is an essential tool for the continued development of Irish as a national language. It has served the national language community well, and modern Irish is now a highly developed and subtle medium that can and is regularly employed to discuss all contemporary issues from politics and intellectual and academic questions, through legislature and governance, to all facets of daily life. However, in those regions where Irish is endangered as a community language, the power of the standard as a prestige written variety does itself contribute to the multifaceted process of linguistic endangerment because of the ambiguity of a target language for Gaeltacht speakers faced with a shift or revitalization scenario. Language management has been shown to consist of sustaining or changing language practices and ideologies of the speaker community to achieve certain linguistic goals (Spolsky 2004). In the case of Irish, the evidence would suggest that creators of a national language policy should seek a compromise that would reinforce intergenerational transmission of the local variety through schooling so as to avoid conflict in the target variety and to encourage community language development. This would, however, require a change in the driving language ideology of the national collective to accommodate the uncodified, yet deeply rooted language ideology of the Gaeltacht in a productive way that would not undermine the national development of Irish that the national standard has manifestly facilitated.

REFERENCES

Broudic, Fañch. 1995a. Langues parlées, langues écrites en Basse-Bretagne 1946–1990 [Spoken languages and written languages in Lower Brittany 1946–1990]. *La Bretagne Linguistique* 10:69–79.
———. 1995b. *La pratique du breton de l'Ancien Régime à nos jours* [Breton usage from the Ancien Régime until the present]. Rennes: Presses Universitaires de Rennes.
CSO (Central Statistics Office). 2004. *Census of Ireland 2002, Vol. 11. Irish language.* Dublin: Government of Ireland.
Dorian, Nancy. 1981. *Language death: The life cycle of a Scottish Gaelic dialect.* Philadelphia: University of Pennsylvania Press.
———. 1987. The value of language-maintenance efforts which are unlikely to succeed. *International Journal of the Sociology of Language* 68:57–67.
Grenoble, Lenore, and Lindsay Whaley. 2006. *Saving languages: An introduction to language revitalization.* Cambridge: Cambridge University Press.
Haugen, Einar. 1959. Planning for a standard language in modern Norway. *Anthropological Linguistics* 1:8–21.
———. 1966. Semicommunication: The language gap in Scandinavia. *Sociological Inquiry* 36:280–97.
Kelly, Adrian. 2002. *Compulsory Irish: Language and education in Ireland, 1870s–1970s.* Dublin: Irish Academic Press.
King, Kendall. 2001. *Language revitalization processes and prospects: Quichua in the Ecuadorian Andes.* Clevedon, UK: Multilingual Matters.
Ní Mhianáin, Róisín, ed. 2003. *Idir Lúibíní. Aistí ar an Léitheoireacht agus ar an Litearthacht* [Between brackets: Essays on reading and literacy]. Baile Átha Cliath: Cois Life.

Ó Baoill, Dónall. 2000. Athchaighdeánú na Nua-Ghaeilge [The restandardizing of Irish]. In *Aimsir Óg 2000 Cuid a dó*, 128–40. Baile Átha Cliath: Coiscéim.

Ó Curnáin, Brian. 2007. *The Irish of Iorras Aithneach*. Dublin: Dublin Institute for Advanced Studies.

Ó Dónaill, Niall. 1951 *Forbairt na Gaeilge*. Baile Átha Cliath: Sáirséal agus Dill.

———. 1981. *Comhar* vii:21–22.

Ó Giollagáin, Conchúr. 2002. Scagadh ar rannú cainteoirí comhaimseartha Gaeltachta: Gnéithe d'antraipeolaíocht teangeolaíochta phobal Ráth Chairn [A critical examination of the classification of contemporary Gaeltacht speakers: Aspects of the linguistic anthropology of Ráth Cairn]. *Irish Journal of Anthropology* 6:25–56.

———. 2005. Gnéithe d'antraipeolaíocht theangeolaíoch Phobal Ros Muc, Co. na Gaillimhe [Aspects of the linguistic anthropology of the parish of Ros Muc, Co. Galway]. In *Legislation, literature and sociolinguistics: Northern Ireland, Republic of Ireland and Scotland*, ed. John Kirk and Dónall Ó Baoill, 138–62. Belfast Studies in Language, Culture and Politics 13. Belfast: Cló Ollscoil na Banríona.

Ó hÍfearnáin, Tadhg. 2000. Irish language broadcast media: The interaction of state language policy, broadcasters and their audiences. *Current Issues in Language and Society* 7:2.92–116.

———. 2005. Adult literacy in Irish in the bilingual Gaeltacht region. In *Bilingualism and education: From the family to the school*, ed. Xoán Paulo Rodríguez-Yáñez, Anxo M. Lorenzo Suárez, and Fernando Ramallo, 325–32. Munich, Germany: Lincom.

———. 2007. Raising children to be bilingual in the Gaeltacht: Language preference and practice. *International Journal of Bilingual Education and Bilingualism* 10:4.510–28.

Ó Riagáin, Pádraig. 1992. *Language maintenance and language shift as strategies of social reproduction: Irish in the Corca Dhuibhne Gaeltacht, 1926–86*. Baile Átha Cliath: Institiúid Teangeolaíochta Éireann.

———. 1997. *Language policy and social reproduction: Ireland, 1893–1993*. Oxford: Clarendon Press.

Ó Riagáin, Pádraig, and Micheál Ó Gliasáin. 1994. *National survey on languages, 1993: Preliminary report*. Baile Átha Cliath: Institiúid Teangeolaíochta Éireann.

Ó Ruairc, Maolmhaodhóg. 1999. *I dTreo Teanga Nua* [Toward a new language]. Baile Átha Cliath: Cois Life.

Rannóg an Aistriúcháin [The Translation Division]. 1958. *Gramadach na Gaeilge agus Litriú na Gaeilge. An Caighdeán Oifigiúil [Irish grammar and orthography: The official standard]*. Baile Átha Cliath: Oifig an tSoláthair.

Rialtas na hÉireann [Government of Ireland]. 1947. *Litriú na Gaeilge: Lámhleabhar an Chaighdeáin Oifigiúil*. Baile Átha Cliath: Oifig an tSoláthair.

Shohamy, Elana. 2006. *Language policy: Hidden agendas and new approaches*. Oxford: Routledge.

Spolsky, Bernard. 2004. *Language policy*. Cambridge: Cambridge University Press.

Williams, Nicholas. 2006. *Caighdeán Nua don Ghaeilge?* [A new standard for Irish?] An Aimsir Óg, Páipéar Ócaideach 1 [An Aimsir Óg, Occasional Paper 1]. Baile Átha Cliath: Coiscéim.

9

Scandinavian Minority Language Policies in Transition

The Impact of the European Charter for Regional or Minority Languages in Norway and Sweden

LEENA HUSS
Uppsala University

THIS CHAPTER is devoted to recent developments regarding the situation of linguistic minorities in two neighboring countries in northern Europe: Norway and Sweden. In these countries formerly existing minority language policies, both overt and covert, have been challenged by the Charter for Regional or Minority Languages (or the Charter), which was created by the Council of Europe (CoE) in 1992 and entered into force in 1998 after ratification by five countries. Norway was among the early ratifiers (1993), while Sweden joined in somewhat later (2000). In addition to the Charter, the two countries also signed and ratified another CoE minority rights instrument, the European Framework Convention for the Protection of National Minorities, which has a wider scope than the Charter but also includes some paragraphs pertaining to linguistic rights.[1]

In the following I give a short description of the charter, which is the main theme of this chapter. Then I move on to a general presentation of the situation of the minority languages before and after the ratifications, with a special focus on three minority languages in the far North: Kven, Meänkieli, and Saami.

The Charter

The purpose of the Charter is to protect and promote regional or minority languages as a threatened aspect of Europe's cultural heritage. As defined in its text, regional or minority languages are languages that are "traditionally used within a given territory of a state by nationals of that state who form a group numerically smaller than the rest of the state's population," that are "different from the official language(s) of that state, and they include neither dialects of the official language(s) of the state nor the languages of migrants."[2] This definition, however, does not culminate in a preconceived list of such languages and concomitant protective measures. Rather, the ratifying states are free to decide which languages are to be protected and on what level. Thus, following a preamble and some introductory provisions, the Charter is segmented into two main sections: part II, which states the principles that are applicable to all ratifying states and all regional or minority languages, and part III, which lists detailed practical commitments that may vary according to the state and the language. Part II includes eight main "objectives and principles" that the ratifying states must follow and that are considered necessary for the maintenance of regional or minority languages everywhere. These eight objectives and principles are the recognition of regional or minority languages as an expression of cultural wealth; the respect for the geographical area of each regional or minority language; the need for resolute action to promote such languages; the facilitation and/or encouragement of the use of such languages, in speech and writing, in public and private life; the provision of appropriate forms and means for the teaching and study of such languages at all appropriate stages; the promotion of relevant transnational exchanges; the prohibition of all forms of unjustified distinction, exclusion, restriction, or preference relating to the use of a regional or minority language and intended to discourage or endanger its maintenance or development; and the promotion by states of mutual understanding between all the country's linguistic groups.[3]

Part III of the Charter consists of sixty-eight detailed practical measures that states can take to further implement the principles in part II. States decide individually which provisions from part III they wish to apply. After specifying which languages are to be covered not only by part II but also by part III, the states have to choose at least thirty-five provisions with respect to each language. Most provisions include several options, one of which has to be chosen "according to the situation of each language."[4] The areas of public life covered by part III are education, judicial authorities, administrative authorities and public services, media, cultural activities and facilities, economic and social life, and transfrontier exchanges. The ratifying states are obliged to choose specific undertakings in all of these areas.

There is a built-in monitoring system attached to the Charter that includes a first monitoring round one year after the ratification and subsequent rounds every three years. The monitoring process demands that every government that has acceded to the Charter has to submit a report on the situation of minority languages to the CoE. The report is then studied by the Committee of Experts, which usually pays a visit to the country concerned, discusses minority language issues with the minorities as well as with the relevant authorities, and then, accordingly, evaluates the situation for minority languages and/or how the states have succeeded in implementing the provisions they have subscribed to. During the country visits, the committee in particular tries to determine whether prior critique and recommendations from the CoE have actually led to improvements in the situation of the minorities. Minority nongovernmental organizations (NGOs) are invited to submit additional information during the process if they wish to do so. After this information collection, the committee prepares its own report, with suggestions and recommendations to the government. This report has to be adopted by the Committee of Ministers at the CoE, who finally decide whether or not to make the report public and pass along the recommendations to the government concerned.[5]

Three Minority Languages in Northern Scandinavia

In this discussion of the impact of the Charter on linguistic minorities in Norway and Sweden, I focus on the specific cases of Kven, Meänkieli, and Saami. All three are Finno-Ugric languages with deep roots in Scandinavia.

Meänkieli and Kven have developed from Finnish varieties and have been spoken for centuries within what today are the countries of Sweden and Norway. Meänkieli is spoken by Tornedalians—people traditionally living in the Tornedalen area by the Finnish border in northeastern Sweden. The Kven live scattered across the coastal regions of northernmost Norway.

The original Saami population was divided into four parts when state borders were drawn between Norway, Sweden, Finland, and Russia, the four countries with indigenous Saami populations. In Norway and Sweden, there are at least four Saami languages: North, Lule, and South Saami are spoken in both Norway and Sweden, and Eastern Saami is spoken in Norway.

The estimated numbers of the Kven, Saami, and Tornedalians (see table 9.1) may seem low at first glance but should be considered against the background that the areas concerned are on the whole very sparsely populated; thus a small minority may actually form a majority locally. This is the case, for instance, in the municipalities of Kautokeino and Karasjok in northern Norway, where the North Saami are in majority. In Kautokeino, 85 to 90 percent of the inhabitants (of 2,998 total inhabitants in 2006) are reported to be Saami speaking (and, in practice, Saami), while the estimation given for the number of Saami in Karasjok is 80 percent (of 2,916 inhabitants in 2000).[6] However, in many other municipalities, ethnicity and competence in the original language of the ethnic group do not always correspond. The number of people who categorize themselves or are categorized by others as being Kven, Saami, or Tornedalians is often much bigger than the number of those who actually *speak* Kven, Saami, and Meänkieli (see table 9.2).

Table 9.1
Numbers of Saami, Kven, and Tornedalians in Northern Scandinavia

Group	State	Estimated Numbers
Saami	Norway	40,000
Saami	Sweden	15,000–20,000
Kven	Norway	2,000–8,000
Tornedalians	Sweden	70,000

Sources: Data from MINLANG/PR 1999, report 5; ECRML 2001, report 6; and ECRML 2003, report 1.
Note: As there is no ethnic census in either Norway or Sweden, the estimates given in the table were taken from the previous sources.

▥ Table 9.2
Numbers of Speakers

Language	Estimated Numbers of Speakers
North Saami, Norway	20,000*
Saami, Sweden[a]	9,000–10,000
Lule Saami, Norway	600*
Lule Saami, Sweden	600–800
South Saami, Norway	400*
South Saami, Sweden	400–500
Kven, Norway	2,000–8,000
Meänkieli, Sweden	40,000

Note: There is no language census in either Norway or Sweden. The estimates marked with * in the table are provided by Torkel Rasmussen, personal communication December 11, 2006, for North, Lule, and South Saami in Norway; the estimates for Kven are provided by MINLANG/PR 2005, report 3; and all figures for Sweden are from ECRML 2003, report 1.

[a]Note that according to the information given in report 1 in ECRML 2003:1, there are 9,000–10,000 speakers of Saami in Sweden. Of them, 600–800 speak Lule Saami and 400–500 South Saami. No separate figure is, however, given for North Saami speakers.

Situation before the Ratifications

In contrast to Sweden, Norway has a long tradition of official language policies. The parliamentary decision on the equality of the two written standards of Norwegian (Bokmål and Nynorsk) dates back to 1885. However, it was not until 1992 that specific regulations pertaining to the Saami language were implemented as part of the Saami Law (1989).[7] Language policies and language issues are frequently discussed in the Norwegian media. Attitudes toward regional varieties of Norwegian appear more favorable than in many other European countries, where dialects have long been negatively labeled. According to a parliamentary decision in 1878, teachers are to adapt their own language to that of the (spoken) language of the children in the classroom, thereby acknowledging and respecting the local variety. However, traditionally, minority-language speakers have not benefited from this regulation because it has only been applied to varieties of Norwegian.

Official language policy in Sweden is more recent and mainly dates back to the mid-1970s, when the new Immigrant Policy was introduced. Among the three basic principles of this policy—equality, freedom of choice, and collaboration—the notion of freedom of choice was interpreted as giving immigrants the right to choose to what extent they wanted to maintain their original identity (including language) and to what extent they wanted to become Swedish. "Home language support," mostly given in the form of weekly lessons at school in the home languages of immigrant children, was seen as the main means to achieve freedom of choice. The goal of the educational policy toward immigrant children has been, and still is, to develop "active bilingualism" in Swedish and the home language and has long been considered generous in international comparison.

When home language instruction at school was introduced in Sweden, it was also extended to the children of historical minorities, who thus came to benefit from the new immigrant policy and its linguistic implications. Nevertheless, there was neither a special language policy for minority languages nor an official minority policy in Sweden before the country ratified the European minority rights instruments mentioned earlier and recognized five national minorities and minority languages: Jews/Yiddish, Roma/Romani, Saami/Saami, Finns/Finnish, and Tornedalians/Meänkieli.[8]

Special Issues Connected to the Ratifications

In Norway, Saami had a relatively high status even before the ratification of the European Charter while no other minority languages were officially recognized. Thus discussion in Norway regarding the ratification came to focus mainly on Kven, and especially the question of whether Kven should be considered a dialect of Finnish or a language in its own right.

The Swedish ratification was preceded by a corresponding discussion on Meänkieli, or "Tornedalian Finnish." The Kven had formerly been regarded as fairly recent immigrants speaking a dialect of Finnish; in contrast, the Swedish authorities did not question the long history of Tornedalians in Sweden. Yet just like Kven, the Tornedalian language Meänkieli was traditionally considered a Finnish dialect, a vernacular used in the northern villages and sprinkled with loanwords taken from the majority language. Tornedalian and Kven language activists argued that their language varieties had in the course of time gradually grown apart from Finnish and thus could—and should—achieve formal language status under the Charter.

Questions concerning language versus dialect and historical language versus immigrant language are, as we know, very difficult to settle, and as noted earlier, the creators of the Charter had decided not to touch them but to leave the interpretation of the criteria to the discretion of the individual governments concerned. Thus the ratifying states have the right to pick and choose between languages and to find their own interpretations of Charter definitions (see Article 1) of such concepts as "traditionally used" and even "language." As a prevention against abuse, however, there is the instrument of the relatively rigorous monitoring mechanism built into the Charter, which allows the Committee of Experts from the CoE to report on apparent incongruities and malpractices (see earlier discussion).

When the governmental committees in Norway and Sweden began discussing the status of Kven and Meänkieli under the Charter, Kenneth Hyltenstam, a Swedish professor in bilingualism, was consulted to make an inquiry in this matter, first in Sweden and then in Norway (Hyltenstam 1996; Hyltenstam and Milani 2003). This represented an effort on the part of the governments to use linguistic scientific evidence when deciding whether the varieties were to be given the status of languages. As a result of the inquiries and suggestions made by Hyltenstam, both Meänkieli and Kven were finally recognized as languages in their own right, to be maintained and developed as part of the national cultural heritage in their respective countries.

The two minority languages in Sweden I focus on in this chapter, Saami and Meänkieli, were given protection according to part III of the Charter, that is, the higher level of protection. To implement the new policy, the first language laws (numbers 1175 and 1176) in Swedish history came into force in April 2000: "Law on the right to use Saami with administrative authorities and courts" (SFS 1999:1175), in force in four northern municipalities, and "Law on the right to use Finnish and Meänkieli with administrative authorities and courts" (SFS 1999:1176) in force in five northern municipalities. These laws also give speakers the right to receive all, or a substantial part, of day care and elder care through the medium of these languages. School education is not covered. In Norway, Kven was given protection only according to part II of the Charter and therefore became the only one among the languages in question to be given protection according to the lower level.[9]

Although Saami was included as a part III language in both countries, some representatives of the minor Saami languages protested against the fact that their varieties were not listed as separate languages under the Charter. (Thus "Saami" was used instead of "North Saami," "South Saami," or "Lule Saami.") Even in the smallest language communities, feelings for the local Saami variety are very strong, and the speakers claimed that their languages, although they were in fact treated separately in connection with many specific obligations under the Charter, were rendered more vulnerable than if they had been listed separately overall. Many feared that the biggest Saami language, North Saami, would overshadow the smaller Saami languages under the present provisions.

Indeed, these fears were not totally without grounding, as the traditional South Saami areas were excluded from the area where the Saami Language Law was put into force in Sweden. (In Norway, the Lule and South Saami areas were excluded even earlier, in connection with the language regulations pertaining to the Saami Law; see earlier discussion). This issue was one of the first to be brought up during the initial monitoring process. The Norwegian and Swedish governments were advised to intensify their efforts to protect and promote the minor Saami languages, and in the case of Sweden, it was explicitly suggested that that country widen the Saami administrative area to cover traditional South Saami municipalities. As of November 2006, part of the Lule Saami area in Norway has been included in the area where the language regulations of the Saami Law are in force, and a further widening is under discussion. In Sweden, a governmental investigation on the possibilities of widening the Saami administrative area was published in the nineteenth report in April 2006 (SOU 2006, report 19). Should the recommendations become reality, the four municipalities where the Saami language law is currently in force would be increased by a further twenty municipalities, in line with the fact that the South Saami in Sweden live scattered across a very large area.

Minority Languages, National Languages, and the "Threat of English"

The question of national minority languages is not the only language issue under discussion in Scandinavia over the last few years: one could indeed claim that it has been at least partly intertwined with and implicated in a simultaneous and much broader discussion on the status of *national* languages. In Norway and Sweden, as well as in many other European countries, a debate focusing on the perceived threat English poses for national languages has been going on since the late 1980s. English is seen to be gaining in popularity and spreading almost "uncontrollably" to new societal domains, such as to higher education (especially natural sciences), secondary schools where English-medium instruction in various subjects is becoming increasingly popular, big multinational organizations, and popular culture (e.g., Hyltenstam 1999). Meanwhile, the national languages are perceived as correspondingly losing ground. In July 1999, a headline in one of the biggest Swedish newspapers, *Svenska Dagbladet,* read, "The Position of Swedish Must Be Legalized." Two former members of the Swedish Language Council emphasized the importance of giving Swedish a stronger position vis-à-vis English, inter alia, by giving it official position in society confirmed by a language law. They suggested that the measures "should be seen in the light of the Government Bill on Minority Languages. If Saami, Finnish, Meänkieli (Tornedalian Finnish), Romani Chib, and Yiddish will get a legally based position as minority languages in Sweden—which is a good thing—it will surely be a bit strange that we do not have a majority language with a legalized position. Will Swedish only be an official language within the European Union and in Finland?"[10]

Both in Norway and in Sweden, these discussions have led to major investigations on the situation of the national languages, including proposals for measures to curb the growing dominance of English. In Sweden, a governmental committee published a report (number 27) in 2002, *Mål i mun* (SOU 2002, report 27) that proposed numerous measures to secure the position of Swedish vis-à-vis English but also emphasized everybody's individual language rights: a right to Swedish, a right to one's mother tongue, and a right to foreign languages.[11] A similar comprehensive view on language policy and linguistic rights was reflected in *Norsk i hundre!* (2005), the Norwegian equivalent of *Mål i mun,* with the main focus on the national language, Norwegian.[12]

In Sweden, some critics feared that a promotional program for Swedish could, in some cases, render the weak situation of immigrant and minority languages even weaker (e.g., Boyd and Huss 2001). In response, one of the persons responsible for *Mål i mun* emphasized that the program was for, not against, minority languages; indeed, linguistic diversity was seen as a factor working against a growing dominance of English.[13] (The final version of *Mål i mun* did contain a number of proposals to promote and develop minority languages in the media, at school, and in other venues as well as to strengthen school education in immigrant languages—a fact that strongly supports this statement.)

As a result of *Mål i mun* and the Government Bill (2005) following it, language planning in Sweden has been totally reorganized.[14] In July 2006, a new language council, Språkrådet, was established as the primary institution for language planning and "language cultivation" in Sweden.[15] The council is a department within an official language authority, Institutet för språk och folkminnen (The Institute of Language and Folklore), and replaces the former Swedish Language Council and the Sweden Finnish Language Council. According to the information on its website, its mission is "to monitor the development of spoken and written Swedish and also to monitor the use and status of all other languages spoken in Sweden. Primarily, that means promoting the use of sign language and our five official minority languages, Finnish, Meänkieli, Sami, Romani and Yiddish."[16] In actuality, the cultivation of Saami is not included in the regular work of the new Council but remains, according to the wishes of the Swedish Saami Parliament, the responsibility of the Saami Parliament only.[17] However, both parties have recently expressed a strong will to cooperate with each other on language cultivation issues.

The Impact of the European Charter on Minority Language Protection

The ratification of the Charter (and the Framework Convention) in Norway and Sweden has proved significant in many respects. Instead of a situation where minorities are negotiating with the government in a very asymmetric position, we now witness a somewhat more sophisticated negotiation process with three parties involved: the government, the minorities, and the CoE. The governments are expected to maintain a continuous dialogue with the minority groups to find out what their wishes are, while the representatives of the minorities are getting more and more familiar with the negotiation process and the opportunities offered by it. This is especially true of the groups that were formerly invisible or largely neglected as to language issues, including the Kven in Norway and the Tornedalians in Sweden. Ethnopolitical discussions have been intense within both groups, and there has been a virtual explosion of cultural activities and manifestations. The first novel ever written in Kven, *Elämän jatko: Kuosuvaaran takana* (The Continuation of Life: Behind Kuosuvaara), was published in 2004; the film *Det tause folkets stille død* (The Silent Death of a Mute People), a documentary on the Kven produced by Kven, was shown in the Tromsø Film Festival in 2004. Niemi (2006) mentions that new economic subsidies available for cultural activities among the national minorities have resulted, inter alia, in increased activity at the Ruija Kven Museum in Vadsø, the establishment of the Kainun Institutti (Kven Institute), a language and culture center in the municipality of Porsanger, and specific Kven initiatives at the Nord-Troms Museum. The Tornedalians now have a research and culture institute of their own, Nordkalottens Kultur-och Forskningscentrum; several Tornedalian culture festivals have been held in Stockholm; and the award-winning novel *Populärmusik från Vittula* (Popular Music from Vittula), depicting life in Tornedalen and originally written in Swedish in 2000, was published in Meänkieli in 2002 by the major Swedish publishing house Nordsteds as a gesture of thanks to the successful novelist and his region. "The Wind Is Blowing Our Way Now!" read a headline in the Tornedalian journal *Met-Aviisi* in 2001.[18]

As far as those languages are concerned that already had a relatively strong position before the ratification of the Charter, somewhat different developments can be seen. For the Saami, a tradition of protection was already in place in the two countries when it was ratified, but the level of that protection was not equal in both countries. Norwegian Saami had a stronger position both legally and numerically, and there was a much higher number of schoolchildren taking part in Saami-medium education in Norway. In addition, in Norway, Saami media were better developed, more cultural events were taking place in Saami, and there was a more extensive Saami youth culture than in Sweden. However, the CoE evaluation reports about the Nordic countries now gave the members of the Saami communities in both countries a better opportunity to compare in detail the situation of their languages across state borders and to cooperate with and inspire one another. The speakers of the minor varieties of Saami had a new possibility to make their voices heard, and in fact, in connection with the Charter, the focus has partly been shifted from the dominant North Saami to the minor, very endangered Saami varieties, including, for example, a focus on widening the official Saami areas in Norway and Sweden to include all Saami languages, as noted earlier.[19]

As already mentioned earlier, there are signs of growing awareness and activity within the minority populations as direct or indirect consequences of the ratifications. It is easy to spot strengthened revitalization efforts in education and among adults who have lost or never learned their ancestral language. A case in point is the new Kven language and culture course at the University of Tromsø, northern Norway, which attracted fifty students in 2006–7, making the Kven course one of the most popular language courses within the Faculty of Humanities that year. University courses in Meänkieli in three universities in Sweden and a number of evening classes for adults in speaking or reading/writing Meänkieli or Saami have also been developed since the Swedish ratification of the Charter in 2000. In both countries, cooperation between minority groups has been strengthened, in some cases between groups that had never met to discuss their common problems before the governments began gathering them together for joint negotiations.

Another sign of growing activity among the minorities are special action plans for language maintenance and revitalization among minorities. Such action plans have been created by the Norwegian and Swedish Saami, with the purpose of boosting Saami language use among various target groups. The Norwegian plan *Samisk er tøft!* (Saami Is Cool!) from 2004 is mainly directed at creating new positive attitudes toward the Saami language among the young. The Swedish plan, *Start för en offensiv samisk språkpolitik* (Launching a Strong Saami Language Policy Effort; Teilus 2004) has applied some of the main points from the *Mål i mun* report (see earlier discussion) to the situation of Saami. It is written for all Saami and offers a detailed program of activities designed to revitalize Saami in Sweden within the next ten years. The program was commissioned by the Swedish Saami Parliament. The task of language planning for Meänkieli, with the aim of standardizing the language, has been given to the recently established Language Council of Sweden (see earlier discussion). Language planning for minority languages, including standardization and terminology issues, is indeed central to the current situation. For several minority groups, the ratification of the Charter has meant that their languages are for the first time used in official contexts, such as in legal texts and municipal websites. Language courses, interpreter and translator education, and teaching materials in these languages necessitate further corpus development of the languages concerned. For this reason, the establishment of the Language Council of Sweden, where language planners for Finnish, Meänkieli, Romani, and Yiddish can work together and establish links to the language cultivators within the Saami Parliament, is generally welcomed by minority organizations in Sweden.

In Norway as in Sweden, language planning for Saami was in place before the ratification of the Charter entered into force. Likewise as in Sweden, the Norwegian

Saami Parliament has today the sole responsibility for Saami language planning, including all varieties. The Kven situation is much more complicated.[20] A plan for the development of the Kven language has been presented by the Kven Alliance, but so far there is no official language planning body for this language.

Some aspects of the new minority language policies have been heavily criticized. In Sweden, members of the minority language groups and reports by the government and the Committee of Ministers have repeatedly pointed out that the minority language laws adopted in connection with the Charter are not implemented in practice as they were expected to be. A major investigation consisting of several independent studies was recently published by the Constitutional Council of the Swedish Parliament (KU 2004–5). One of these studies (Elenius 2005) demonstrates that various shortcomings are due in large part to a general lack of information on the rights of the speakers of the minority languages, as well as a lack of language competence among civil servants or minorities themselves. Generally public services in Meänkieli are reported to be more accessible and more utilized than those in Saami (Elenius 2005, 183), partly because even though the Saami have greater political power, they are linguistically weaker. In addition, Meänkieli and Finnish are mutually comprehensible, and therefore Meänkieli-speakers can use their language with Finnish-speaking personnel.

Another study by Hyltenstam and Milani (2005) pinpoints a number of structural hindrances leading to considerable difficulties in fulfilling the obligations of the new minority policy, a major one being the decentralized decision-making process in Swedish society. While the state adopts obligations on the national level, the practical implementation takes place on municipal or local levels. Hyltenstam and Milani (2005, 69–70) mention examples concerning minority language education in schools and universities where local decisions fail to support or, in some cases, actually weaken the situation of minority languages. They conclude that outcomes are highly dependent on the attitudes and values of individual decision makers and their understanding of the goals of the new policies.

Municipalities, local schools, and other parties may cite economic problems as obstacles to policy implementation, or the persons in charge are not familiar with the national minority language policy and do not know what their obligations are in this context. Still others point out that the state cannot adopt obligations without ensuring that regions and municipalities are provided with adequate funding for the new tasks. (The economic consequences of the new policy, not yet fully appreciated by the Swedish state, are also discussed in Hyltenstam and Milani 2005).

Further, there are civil servants who have been reported not to distinguish between immigrant policies on the one hand and minority policies on the other. Consequently, they claim that they do follow the new policy, but because there are not adequate resources to meet the linguistic needs of all groups, they often choose to support those who have the greatest needs, that is, refugees and newly arrived immigrants. Complaints about this kind of reasoning have been brought to the Committee of Experts by Finnish and Saami parents whose children have been refused the right to mother tongue instruction in school for financial reasons and also from a former minority-language-medium preschool class in Stockholm that was integrated into the larger Swedish-medium class against the wishes of the parents, with the motivation that the preschool "did not wish to segregate minority children from the others."[21]

In Norway, similar criticisms have been voiced, mostly concerning the Kven situation, but also concerning the minor Saami languages. As for North Saami, the Committee of Experts note in their first report on Norway (ECRML 2001, report 6) that support is satisfactory in many respects but that there are "some difficulties in the implementation of undertakings related to the judicial and administrative authorities as well as some aspects of economic and social life. The main problem seems to be a lack of employees' having a command of Saami and a sufficient number of qualified interpreters" (29). Niemi (2006, 437) summarizes the critique expressed by another CoE monitoring committee, the Advisory Committee for the Framework Convention (see earlier discussion): "The committee's report praises the Norwegian investment in the Saami indigenous people, but . . . notes that little has been accomplished to date for the groups that are now defined as national."[22] "National" in this context refers to "national minorities" (e.g., the Kven and Roma), as opposed to "indigenous people" (the Saami).

The Norwegian and Swedish Ratifications in a Wider European Context

The Nordic ratifications of the Charter and also the Framework Convention are part of a new trend that has been visible in Europe since the 1990s. The CoE initiated this trend by creating the two minority rights instruments that triggered new developments in a number of countries. Sia Spiliopoulou Åkermark, lawyer and Swedish member of the Advisory Committee for the Framework Convention, assesses the process as follows:

> International organisations serve many different functions. They do not simply offer a forum for state interaction, common production, and management—or even the elaboration of new norms. They offer a forum for the implementation of the treaties, which in the case of the Framework Convention and the Language Charter entails a combination of political discussion by the Committee of Ministers and expert examination by the Advisory Committee and the Committee of Experts. Those organs become "normative intermediaries" and interpret as well as disseminate the adopted treaties nationally and internationally. (Spiliopoulou Åkermark et al. 2006, 28)

By attaching a detailed monitoring system to the treaties (see earlier discussion), the CoE has provided the minorities with a new means of language protection. The minorities now also have enhanced opportunities to cooperate on a larger European level and to follow how various governments implement the obligations of the Charter. As of November 2006, the Charter has been ratified by twenty states (Armenia, Austria, Croatia, Cyprus, Denmark, Finland, Germany, Hungary, Liechtenstein, Luxembourg, The Netherlands, Norway, Serbia and Montenegro, Slovakia, Slovenia, Spain, Sweden, Switzerland, Ukraine, and the United Kingdom). In addition, twelve states have signed the Charter, and some of them are expected to ratify soon. The latest developments in different countries as well as the effectiveness of the Charter and its monitoring system in the ratifying countries are continuously discussed in reports and international follow-up conferences (e.g., Council of Europe 1998, 1999, 2003, 2004; Woehrling 2006).

Conclusion

As shown earlier, the northern minorities and their revitalization movements currently find themselves in a political and social environment that in many ways appears to be more favorable to their revitalization efforts than ever before. Not only are the governments obliged to protect and promote minority languages, but also there is a growing pressure from outside, from the CoE, to enhance the status of minority languages and to secure their survival in the long run.

So far, we can see that international treaties have actually led to clear improvements in the field of minority language protection and revitalization. In the Nordic countries, the cases of Kven and Meänkieli may be the most obvious examples. Without language status, they would have been much weaker than they are today, and the renaissance of the Kven and Tornedalian cultures that we are witnessing today would probably not have come into being. But even the other languages have benefited from the Charter in various ways, as I have demonstrated. In the wake of the ratifications, a new interest and engagement in language policies and revitalization efforts can be found among all minorities. Of course, this is far from enough to secure the long-term survival of the northern minority languages. What is important is that the presence and value of minority cultures has been recognized, at least at the official level, and that the governments are now expected to enhance the level of minority language protection in line with the obligations they have subscribed to—a fact that has given the minorities new hope. It is still unclear, however, whether this trend will be sufficient to curb a further decline of the smaller languages and to inspire minority communities to engage in even stronger efforts in favor of their languages and cultures. There are indeed signs of an increase in school instruction in Saami (especially in Sweden), Meänkieli, and Kven as well as an increasing interest among adults in taking courses to learn or relearn these languages.

However, there are no studies or other indications pointing to an increased use of these languages at home, between parents and children. As argued by Joshua Fishman (1991) and others, intergenerational language transmission is crucial for long-term language maintenance and language shift reversal. What is certainly needed now is reinstating and maintaining the northern minority languages, at least to a higher degree than today, as mother tongues spoken in the home rather than as mere second languages learnt at school or through courses. Parental language choices might very well turn out to be decisive for the long-term outcome of the northern revitalization movements.

NOTES

1. See www.coe.int/T/E/Human_Rights/Minorities/.
2. European Charter for Regional or Minority Languages, Article 1 (see http://conventions.coe.int/treaty/en/Treaties/html/148.htm).
3. Ibid., Article 7 (see http://conventions.coe.int/treaty/en/Treaties/html/148.htm).

4. Ibid.
5. The Committee of Ministers is the CoE's decision-making body, comprised of the foreign affairs ministers of all member states (or their permanent diplomatic representatives in Strasbourg). See www.coe.int/t/cm/aboutCM_en.asp.
6. See www.kautokeino.kommune.no and www.karasjok.kommune.no.
7. Lov om Sametinget og andre samiske rettsforhold [Law on the Saami Parliament and other Saami rights issues]; see www.lovdata.no/all/hl-19870612-056.html.
8. See Regeringens proposition [Government Bill] 1998/99:143 Nationella minoriteter i Sverige [National minorities in Sweden]. Stockholm: Ministry of Industry, Employment and Communications.
9. Niemi (2006.423) quotes a government representative saying in 1994 at a seminar at the University of Tromsø that "he did not care if the Kvens had arrived 'in the 19th or the 17th century'; they were immigrants 'because that was what the Norwegian government had decided.'" This kind of attitude toward the Kven might have contributed to the fact that the Kven language was included in part II of the Charter, together with Romani, and not in part III like the Saami language.
10. The authors here refer to the fact that Swedish is an official language within the European Union according to the wishes of the Swedish government. Another reason for this is the fact that Swedish is one of the two (legally based) "national languages" of Finland and therefore also eligible for official status in the European Union.
11. An English summary titled "Speech: Draft Action Programme for the Swedish Language. Committee on the Swedish Language" (SOU 2002:27, Summary) can be found on the website of the Swedish Government: www.regeringen.se.
12. See www.sprakrad.no/Aktuelt/Norsk_i_hundre_Strategiar/.
13. Björn Melander, personal communication, September 2005.
14. The Government Bill (2005–6:2), *Bästa språket: En samlad svensk språkpolitik* (The Best Language: A Comprehensive Swedish Language Policy), is, as the translation of the Swedish title shows, the basis for the current language policies of Sweden.
15. The meaning of the term "language cultivation" is explained on the website of the Language Council of Sweden as follows: "What is language cultivation? The Swedish word 'språkvård' is a loan translation of the German word 'Sprachpflege.' Literally, språkvård means 'language care,' but is often translated as language cultivation or language planning. This involves the making of handbooks, giving lectures and linguistic guidance and raising people's linguistic awareness, but also entails longer-term efforts to influence the language situation in the country." www.sprakradet.se/about_us.
16. See www.sprakradet.se/about_us.
17. For information on the Swedish Saami Parliament, see www.sametinget.se.
18. "Yhtäkkiä oon myötätuuli!" *Met-Aviisi,* 2001, no. 3.
19. The second periodical report from the Norwegian government included a fourth Saami language, Eastern Saami (also called Skolt Saami) not mentioned in the initial periodical report, even though its existence had long been known to Norwegian authorities. Eastern Saami was possibly left out of the initial report because it is apparently quite small, with as few as only two or three elderly speakers remaining in Norway.
20. For information on the Norwegian Saami Parliament, see http://www.samediggi.no.
21. These examples are based on notes taken during 2000–2004 when the author was a member of the Committee of Experts for the Charter in Strasbourg.
22. The Saami in Norway did not want to be included in the Norwegian ratification of the Framework Convention for the Protection of National Minorities because they consider themselves an indigenous people and not a minority group. The Swedish Saami opted otherwise and are therefore included in the Swedish ratification of the same Convention.

REFERENCES
Boyd, Sally, and Leena Huss, eds. 2001. *Managing multilingualism in a European nation-state: Challenges for Sweden.* Clevedon, UK: Multilingual Matters
Council of Europe. 1998. International Conference on the European Charter for Regional or Minority Languages. Regional or Minority Languages No. 1. Strasbourg: Council of Europe.

————. 1999. Implementation of the European Charter for Regional or Minority Languages. *Regional or Minority Languages* No. 2. Strasbourg: Council of Europe.

————. 2003. From theory to practice: The European Charter for regional or minority languages—Noordwijkerhout, November 2001. *Regional or minority languages* No. 3. Strasbourg: Council of Europe.

————. 2004. The European Charter for regional or minority languages: Working together—NGOs and regional or minority languages. Strasbourg: Council of Europe.

ECRML. 2001. Application of the Charter [in] Norway. November 22. Report 6. Strasbourg: Council of Europe.

————. 2003:1. Application of the Charter [in] Sweden. June 19. Strasbourg: Council of Europe.

Elenius, Lars. 2005. Ett uthålligt språk: Genomförande av lagarna om användning av minoritetsspråk i förvaltningsområdena i Norrbottens län åren 2000–2004. [A sustainable language: The implementation of the laws on the use of minority languages in the administrative areas of the county of Norrbotten in 2000–2004]. 2004/05: RFR3 *Nationella minoriteter och minoritetsspråk* [National minorities and minority languages]. Stockhom: Committee on the Constitution.

Fishman, Joshua. 1991. *Reversing language shift: Theoretical and empirical foundations of assistance to threatened languages*. Clevedon: Multilingual Matters.

Government Bill. 1998–99. *Nationella minoriteter i Sverige* [National minorities in Sweden]. Report 143. Stockholm: Ministry of Industry, Employment and Communications.

————. 2005–6. *Bästa språket: En samlad svensk språkpolitik*. [The best language: A comprehensive Swedish language policy]. Report 2. Stockholm: Ministry of Education and Culture.

Hyltenstam, Kenneth. 1996. *Begreppen språk och dialekt: Om meänkielis utveckling till eget språk. Utredning för minoritetsspråkskommittén* [The concepts of language and dialect: The development of Meänkieli into a language in its own right. Commission report to the Minority Language Committee]. Stockholm: Centre for Research on Bilingualism.

————.1999. *Sveriges sju inhemska språk: Ett minoritetsspråksperspektiv*. [The seven domestic languages of Sweden: A minority language perspective]. Lund: Studentlitteratur.

Hyltenstam, Kenneth, and Tommaso Milani. 2003. *Kvenskans status. Rapport för Kommunal-og regionaldepartementet och Kultur-og kirkedepartementet i Norge, oktober 2003.* [The status of the Kven language. Report to the Ministry of Local Government and Regional Development, and the Ministry of Culture and Church Affairs, in October 2003]. Stockholm: Centre for Research on Bilingualism.

————. 2005. Nationella minoriteter och minoritetsspråk. Uppföljning av Sveriges efterlevnad av Europarådets konventioner på nationell nivå: Ett minoritetsspråksperspektiv [National minorities and minority languages. A follow-up study on the implementation of the Council of Europe conventions in Sweden on a national level: A minority language perspective]. 2004–5. RFR3 *Nationella minoriteter och minoritetsspråk*. [National minorities and minority language]. Stockholm: Committee on the Constitution.

KU. 2004–5. RFR3 *Nationella minoriteter och minoritetsspråk*. [National minorities and minority languages]. Stockholm: Committee on the Constitution.

MINLANG/PR. 1999. Norway. Initial Periodical Report presented to the Secretary General of the Council of Europe in accordance with Article 15 of the Charter. Report 5. Strasbourg, 31 May 1999.

————. 2005. Norway. Third Periodical Report presented to the Secretary General of the Council of Europe in accordance with Article 15 of the Charter. Report 3. Strasbourg, 2 May 2005.

Niemi, Einar. 2006. National minorities and minority policy in Norway. In *International obligations and national debates: Minorities around the Baltic Sea,* ed. Sia Spiliopoulou Åkermark, Leena Huss, Stefan Oeter, and Alastair Walker, 397–451. Mariehamn, Finland: The Åland Islands Peace Institute.

Norsk i hundre! [One hundred years of Norwegian in motion]. 2005. Norsk som nasjonalspråk i globaliseringens tidsalder: Et forslag til strategi. [Norwegian as a national language in the era of globalization: A strategy proposal]. Oslo: Norwegian Language Council.

Samisk er tøft! [Saami is cool!]. 2004. Sametingsrådets medling om samisk språk, 18.03.2004 [Report on the Saami language by the Board of the Norwegian Saami Parliament, March 18, 2004]. Karasjok: Board of the Norwegian Saami Parliament.

SFS. 1999a. Lag om rätt att använda samiska hos förvaltningsmyndigheter och domstolar [Law on the right to use Saami with administrative authorities and courts]. Report 1175.

————. 1999b. Lag om rätt att använda finska och meänkieli hos förvaltningsmyndigheter och domstolar [Law on the right to use Finnish and Meänkieli with administrative authorities and courts]. Report 1176.

SOU. 2002. *Mål i mun: Förslag till handlingsprogram för svenska språket* [Speech. Draft Action Programme for the Swedish Language]. Report 27. Stockholm: Ministry of Education and Culture.

————. 2006. *Att återta mitt språk: Åtgärder för att stärka det samiska språket. Slutbetänkande från Utredningen om finska och sydsamiska språken* [Taking back my language: Measures to strengthen the Saami language. Final report from the Committee on the Finnish and Saami languages]. Report 19. Stockholm: Government Offices of Sweden.

Spiliopoulou Åkermark, Sia, Leena Huss, Stefan Oeter, and Alastair Walker, eds. 2006. *International obligations and national debates: Minorities around the Baltic Sea.* Mariehamn, Finland: Åland Islands Peace Institute.

Teilus, Mikael. 2004. *Start för en offensiv samisk språkpolitik* [Launching a strong Saami language policy effort]. Kiruna: Swedish Saami Parliament.

Woehrling, Jean-Marie. 2006. *The European Charter for Regional or Minority Languages: A critical commentary.* Strasbourg: Council of Europe.

10

Language Development in Eritrea
The Case of Blin

PAUL D. FALLON
University of Mary Washington

The Blin People and Language
Background of Blin

Blin, also called Bilin or Bilen, is a Central Cushitic (or Agaw) language of Eritrea with approximately ninety thousand speakers. The Blin are located in the 'Anseba Administrative Zone, centered around Keren, which is ninety-one kilometers north-west of the national capital, Asmara. Most Blin are agriculturalists, conducting mixed farming and breeding of goats, sheep, and cattle (Abbebe 2001; Smidt 2003). The Blin comprise only 2.1 percent of the national population, and even in Keren they form no more than 20 percent of the population. Their nearest linguistic rela-tives (Xamtaŋa, Kemantney) are in Ethiopia. The Blin are surrounded by a sea of Ethiosemitic speakers, primarily Tigre to the north, spoken by more than 31 percent of the national population, and Tigrinya to the south, spoken by 50 percent (U.S. Dept. of State 2007). Further, they are divided along religious lines, with roughly half or more of the population being Muslim, and the other half Christian, primarily Eritrean Catholic. Because of a fairly large degree of intermarriage, there are very few monolingual Blin; most are bi- or trilingual in Tigrinya and/or Tigre, and many also know such languages as Arabic, English, Amharic, and Italian. Abbebe (2001) reports that at least in urban areas, many Blin are Tigrinya- or Tigre-dominant and use Blin as a second language in limited domains. The language, he notes, "is there-fore particularly threatened" (77).

Although Blin was first recorded in the 1850s by the Italian missionary Sapeto, and the first publication in Blin was in 1882 (Reinisch 1882b), Blin has primarily been an oral language with relatively few publications (Kiflemariam 1986, 1996). With the independence of the newest African nation, Eritrea, in 1991, however, Blin has had a certain measure of equality conferred upon it by the Eritrean Constitution, which guarantees mother-tongue education in the primary grades (Chefena, Kroon, and Walters 1999). This chapter examines language development efforts of the Blin language using the framework of Wolff (2000) and archival sources, as well as inter-views with Blin speakers during fieldwork conducted for one month in Asmara and Keren, Eritrea, in the summer of 2002.

Language Planning

Language planning is a huge field with a variety of competing classifications and accompanying terminologies (Clyne 1997; Dadoust 1997; Ferguson 1968; Fishman, Ferguson, and Das Gupta 1968; Haugen 1966; Ricento 2005). Wolff (2000), following Haugen (1966), distinguishes between two major sets of problems and activities: status planning and corpus planning. Status planning establishes and develops the "functional usage of a particular language or languages within a state" (Wolff 2000, 333) and concerns the official language(s), and the educational, cultural, and religious uses of language (Cooper 1989; Ferguson 1968; Fishman 1974; Spolsky 1977; see Bloor and Tamrat 1996; Chefena, Kroon, and Walters 1999, for status planning and policy in Eritrea). The second division of language planning, which is the focus of this chapter, is corpus planning, which is "geared at establishing and developing spelling norms, setting norms of grammar and expanding the lexicon" (Wolff 2000, 333). By language standardization, Wolff means:

1. an approved and accepted *norm* above all vernacular, colloquial and dialectal varieties for *generalized* and *normative* usage in certain domains such as literature, science, higher education, the media, the churches and all public sectors; and

2. a *regularized* and *codified* normative *system of reference* supported by a standard orthography, standard reference grammars and (preferably monolingual) standard dictionaries. (2000, 332)

Language standardization may be broken into several different phases, which will serve as the basis of the analysis of Blin corpus planning. For an overview, see Hornberger (2005). Here, I follow the outline in Wolff (2000).

1. *Determination* "of language status and the norm within a chosen language, which is to serve as [a] standard frame of reference."

2. *Codification* "of languages or language variants with no writing tradition at all, or choice among or unification of, competing systems already existing in the area."

3. *Elaboration* "of vocabulary (*modernisation*) and grammar (*normalisation*) to serve as sources for reference and basic tools for the development of pedagogical materials for all levels of formal education."

4. *Implementation* "of both language status and the norms of standardisation, that is creating and enhancing acceptance in the speech communities."

5. *Cultivation* "of the so created standard languages by language authorities to ensure continued observance of the norms and control implementation. In Africa in particular, language cultivation would also be concerned with the creation and continuous production of post-literacy materials" (Wolff 2000, 334).

A sixth category, *harmonization,* the unification of mutually nonintelligible dialects, need not concern us. We turn next to the application and analysis of these principles in Blin corpus planning.

Blin Corpus Planning
Determination

The Eritrean Constitution guarantees the equality of all languages in Article 4 but declines to name an official language; rather, there are three working languages of the country (Simeone-Senelle 2000): English, the language of secondary and higher education as well as an international language of business and diplomacy; Arabic, although spoken natively by fewer than 1 percent of the population, is the religious language of Islam and plays an important role in commercial transactions and regional diplomacy; and Tigrinya, spoken natively by half the population, serves as a unifying national language (Chefena, Kroon, and Walters 1999). Estimates for the degree of bilingualism in Tigrinya cannot be stated "with any confidence" (Chefena, Kroon, and Walters 1999), but according to Tekle (2003), 68 percent of all schools teach in Tigrinya. In a 1997 Eritrean government survey of twelve major towns, 77 percent of the population was Tigrinya speaking, and the language has also become a "symbolic official language" (Chefena, Kroon, and Walters 1999). There remain several other minority languages: Arabic of the Rashaida (0.5 percent), Ethiosemitic Tigre (31.4 percent), the Nilo-Saharan Kunama (2 percent) and Nara (1.5 percent), North Cushitic Beja (2.5 percent), Lowland East Cushitic Saho (5 percent) and Afar (5 percent), and Central Cushitic Blin (2.1 percent). Each of these languages has been guaranteed mother-tongue education. In the case of Blin, determination therefore refers to which norm is to be the basis of literacy materials.

Since Reinisch (1882a), scholars have generally recognized two main dialects of Blin, Bet Taqʷe (or Tawque) and Bet Tarqe (or Senhit; Daniel and Sullus 1997; Hetzron 1976; Kiflemariam 1986)[1]. However, it was not until Eritrean independence, in preparation for implementation of the constitutional guarantee of mother-tongue education, that actual research was carried out by Daniel and Beyed (1997). Using several instruments of their own creation, they surveyed six sites, three in each dialect zone; for the Tawque dialect, they surveyed Halhal, Jengeren, Sit'ur (Brekentya), and for the Senhit dialect, Ashera, Bambi, and Feledarb.

In Daniel and Sullus's (1997) survey of language attitudes of a total of thirty-five parents, with five to seven from each of the six sites, 79 percent of the Senhit dialect speakers thought that their dialect was "easily understood by the majority of Blin speakers," as opposed to 94 percent of Tawque speakers; the rest thought that both dialects were easily understood. When asked about the utility of each dialect, 74 percent of Senhit Blin speakers and 75 percent of Tawque speakers replied that their own dialect "gave more/wider service," and the remainder responded that both dialects did. Finally, when asked which dialect they preferred the textbooks to be prepared in, 58 percent of the Senhit speakers replied in favor of their own language, while 63 percent of Tawque speakers desired their own dialect to be the model; the remainder believed that the Ministry of Education should "find out the best and make the choice."

One instrument, a list of 320 words known to vary between dialects, was given to five to seven parents and ten students at each site. Results indicated that 93 percent of the items were familiar to speakers of both dialect areas, even if they did not use the term. In a test of lexical, morphological, and phonological differences, they found that "dialect intelligibility is no problem for Blin speakers" (Daniel and Sullus 1997, 11). Most of the problems in a test of listening comprehension involved only names of nonlocal or unfamiliar "trees, people, places, or clans" (13). In a test in which six teachers (four Tawque and two Senhit) were asked to make corrections to a story for a primer by Blin language teachers, there were no syntactic differences, a few had minor grammatical differences involving a verbal suffix, and there were a few vocabulary differences.

Daniel and Sullus (1997) conclude that despite certain phonological and lexical differences, "each dialect is easily understood by, and entirely familiar to, the speakers of the other dialect" (17). The curricular materials are written in the Senhit dialect of Blin but contain a large number of words from Tawque Blin. The authors observed that because of the high degree of awareness among both dialects of "typical Senhit" or "typical Tawque" vocabulary, the choice of words did not affect intelligibility. However, they proposed that the textbook writers should choose synonyms from both dialects "to avoid appearing biased or partial" (11).

Most written Blin has been in the Senhit dialect. In the survey by Daniel and Sullus (1997), most parents who had seen written Blin found it in the Senhit dialect, while most of those who had not seen written Blin were from the Tawque area.

Codification
Blin codification posed an interesting sociolinguistic dilemma in that there were no competing writing systems, yet the existing one was replaced with a government-mandated Roman script. The earliest known writings in Blin are from the work of foreign scholars such as Leo Reinisch, who wrote the first grammar (1882a), transcribed texts (1883), compiled a dictionary of Blin (1887), and who supervised a translation of the Gospel of Mark (1882b). While the more academic work contains a phonetic transcription, the Gospel translation, and several subsequent collections of tales (e.g., Capomazza 1911; Conti Rossini 1907), use the Ethiopic script, or *abugida*. An abugida is a script reminiscent of a syllabary in that it usually transcribes consonant–vowel (CV) sequences, but the basic shape contains an inherent vowel, and other vowels (or "orders") contain relatively consistent modifications of the basic shape. An example of some of the abugida, given in traditional order, is shown in table 10.1.

The sixth order is ambiguous in transcribing either a coda consonant alone or an onset plus the high central vowel /ɨ/. It is thus inadequate to show geminate consonants or long vowels, and it does not show phonological prominence (either stress or pitch accent). Nevertheless, because the abugida has a long history as the liturgical language of Geʻez and is used to write Amharic and Tigrinya, the major Ethiosemitic languages of the area, it was natural to use it as the basis of writing for Blin, especially because its phonology is similar to that of Tigrinya (Palmer 1960). The script needed only three additional basic graphemes for sounds not found in Geʻez (/xʷ, ŋ, ŋʷ/), which used diacritic modifications of similar symbols.

The second stage of writing in Blin was led by native Blin-speaking clergymen (e.g., Wolde-Yohannes 1939), who translated catechisms, service books, and the

▓ Table 10.1
Partial Sample of the Ethiopic *Abugida,* in Traditional Order

	ə	u	i	a	e	C/Cɨ	o
h	ሀ	ሁ	ሂ	ሃ	ሄ	ህ	ሆ
l	ለ	ሉ	ሊ	ላ	ሌ	ል	ሎ
ħ	ሐ	ሑ	ሒ	ሓ	ሔ	ሕ	ሖ
m	መ	ሙ	ሚ	ማ	ሜ	ም	ሞ
s	ሰ	ሱ	ሲ	ሳ	ሴ	ስ	ሶ
r	ረ	ሩ	ሪ	ራ	ሬ	ር	ሮ
ʃ	ሸ	ሹ	ሺ	ሻ	ሼ	ሽ	ሾ

other gospels. The third stage occurred when a critical mass of Blin students and intellectuals began serious language planning efforts, creating grammatical terms, and refining the orthography. Foremost among these is Kiflemariam Hamdé (1986), who also wrote an excellent overview of developments in Blin orthography (1996). Among the greatest achievements of this movement is Kiflemariam and Zememariam (1992), the first monolingual dictionary of five thousand words (with English glosses), and the book *Gerbesha* (Committee for Developing Blin Language and Culture in Keren 1997). This movement has continued into the twenty-first century with the acceptance of the extra symbols into the Unicode 4.1.0 standard (Yacob's 2004 proposal, in consultation with Tekie Alibeket; changes documented at www.unicode.org/versions/ Unicode4.1.0/#NotableChanges). The abugida is still the only script used among Blin in the diaspora (e.g., Mowes 2003) and is used to help integrate Blin into the larger Eritrean diaspora.

Beginning in 1985, however, the Eritrean People's Liberation Front began a policy of promoting non-Ethiosemitic minority languages in Roman-based scripts, along with their use of Tigrinya, Arabic, and English as working languages. When Eritrea's war of independence from Ethiopia ended in 1991, Eritrea's provisional constitution guaranteed mother-tongue education in primary school in each of the nine ethnic languages. Due to lack of sufficient training and teachers, the Blin Language Panel of the National Curriculum of the Ministry of Education did not begin until the survey by Daniel and Sullus (1997).

To the disappointment of many of those backing a modified form of abugida, government policy chose to write Blin in Roman letters. Since the abugida was first used to write Ge'ez, the liturgical language, and because most speakers of Tigrinya, one of the official working languages of the country (and spoken by half the population), are Eritrean Orthodox Christian, many of the Muslim Blin (about 50 percent of ethnic Blin) associated the script with the Christian religion. Conversely, the Arabic script is intimately bound with Islam. The choice of Roman script was therefore seen by the government as a unifying compromise and as an aid in learning English, the language of secondary and higher education (Tekle 2003; Zeraghiorghis 1999). For an assessment of each script, see Fallon (2006).

The Roman-based alphabet for Blin uses a combination of diacritics, digraphs, and trigraphs. A mapping between grapheme (in angled brackets) and phoneme (in slashes) is shown in (1) below, with single graphemes shown in (1a) and digraphs in (1b):

(1) a. <a, b, c, d, e, f, g, h, i, j, k, l, m, n, ñ, o, q, r, s,
        / a, b, ʕ, d, ə, f, g, h, i, dʒ, k, l, m, n, ŋ, o, k', r, s,

        t, u, w, x, y, é>
        t, u, w, ħ, j, ɨ /

    b. <ñw,   kw, qw, gw   ch, qh, th   kh, sh,
        / ŋʷ,   kʷ, kʷ', gʷ   tʃ', k', t'   x, ʃ,

       ee   khw, qhw>
       e   xʷ, kʷ' /

In the codification of the writing system, the alphabetical order has undergone several shifts. A chart published by the Eritrean Ministry of Education (1997a) titled "The Alphabets" contains the Blin alphabetical order, along with a basic Geʻez form and a modified IPA (International Phonetic Alphabet) form. With the exception of the labialized velar nasal, it follows standard alphabetical order, then letters with diacritics, then digraphs in groups, and then trigraphs, though the digraphic labialized voiced velar stop is inexplicably last. The order is shown in (2):

(2) Ministry of Education Chart "The Alphabets"

    a, b, c, d, e, f, g, h, i, j, k, l, m, n, ñw, o, q, r, s, t, u, w, x, y, é, ñ, ch, kh, qh, sh, th, kw, qw, khw, qhw, gw.

The order of the Blin alphabet ("Blina Xaleget") in the first grade primer (Eritrean Ministry of Education 1997b) gives the vowels first, in traditional abugida order, and then the consonants. It includes consonants for borrowed letters such as <p> and <z>, and then gives the digraphs in fairly random order and excludes trigraphs. The order is shown in (3):

(3) "Blina Xaleget"

    vowels: e, u, i, a, é, o

    consonants: b, c, d, f, g, h, j, k, l, m, n, p, q, r, s, t, v, w, x, y, z, ñ, ñw, th, ch, sh, kh, kw, hw, qw, gw.

Since 2002 (Sulus personal communication), the revised alphabetical order is strictly alphabetical, with quasi-ligature status (Rogers 2005, 12) for digraphs or trigraphs, as in traditional Spanish. The quasi-ligatures are treated as separate letters and placed after the basic letter. The two letters with diacritics, é and ñ, are alphabetized after their graphically simpler counterparts. A sample of the revised order may be seen in (4):

(4) Revised Alphabetical Order

a, b, c, ch, d, e, é, f, g, gw, etc.

One unfortunate gap is that there is not yet a dictionary of the new Romanized Blin orthography; for more on this, see the conclusion.

In addition to flux in alphabetical order, certain lexical items have had their spelling changed as teachers become used to the system and as Blin educators get more experience. Differences in spelling usually involve different speaker perceptions of vowel or consonant length and different ideas concerning shallow or deep orthography, that is, whether the orthography should be closer to surface phonemics or whether it should more closely reflect underlying representations. For example, should the underlying vowel /i / next to a labialized consonant be represented as /i / or as /u/, its surface pronunciation?

For now, there is a relatively bumpy transition during this period of sequential digraphia, "the use of two or more different systems of writing the same language" (DeFrancis 1984). For example, Blin speakers in their twenties and older, unless they are teachers, are generally unfamiliar with the newer writing system. Thus some of the radio announcers must have their scripts retranscribed into abugida. Many of those involved in the creation of a dictionary still use the abugida. The transition to the new orthography will clearly be a fairly lengthy process, unlike the transition to the Roman-based Somali orthography. The reason for this is that relatively little is at stake outside the domain of education, as the language is not a full-fledged standard. Little is written in the Roman orthography, and no standards have been published yet.

Elaboration

As we saw from the survey by Daniel and Beyed (1997), there is substantial agreement in the grammar between the two dialects; there is, therefore, no real need for normalization. There is, however, a desperate need for the elaboration (or modernization, to use Ferguson's 1968 term) of the language. As noted earlier, the Blin are mostly agriculturalists, with a historic background in cattle breeding. However, their language must be modernized or elaborated in order to talk about the current needs of the twenty-first century nation-state (Sulus 1999).

There are a number of ways in which the vocabulary has been elaborated: derivation, derivation with semantic extension, compounding, reintroduction of obsolescent vocabulary, calques, borrowing, and semantic extension (Sulus 2003). These will be discussed in turn, using examples drawn mostly from Sulus (2003). The author is unaware of any particular preference hierarchy of the following strategies, except that there is a general avoidance of borrowed terms. Although there is a Committee for Developing Bilin Language and Culture (discussed under implementation later), the head of the Blin language curriculum has direct influence on these neologisms, along with the radio announcers.

Derivation. Derivation is a common way of increasing the vocabulary in a language, and Blin is no exception. In many cases, deverbal nouns are formed through the addition of a suffix. The suffix -na is both an infinitival marker and a deverbal nominal

suffix, in some cases (such as "conclusion" below) yielding what appears to be
zero-derivation.

(5)

la-	"one"	*laréñ*	"unit"
lakhw	"one" (adj.)	*lakhunnar*	"unity"
kémna	"to own; contain"	*kémana*	"content"
déñwna	"to finish, conclude"	*déñwna*	"conclusion"

Derivation with Semantic Extension.   It is also common for new derivations to contain some
semantic extension, as shown in (6) (data from Sulus 2003):

(6)

geb-na	"resist"	*geb-ana*	"defence or military force"
jéléw-na	"to rotate, move around"	*jéléw-ana*	"circumference"
berhéd-na	"to illuminate"	*berhéd-isena*	"explanation"
tekken-na	"to stick together"	*ték-na*	"appendix"
sid-na	"to separate"	*sid-a*	"characteristic; feature"
wellem-na	"to talk much"	*wellam-a*	"journalist"
ékéb-na	"to gather s.t."	*ékb-o*	"meeting"

Compounding.   Compounding is the combination of two independent elements into a
complex word. Blin makes use of a variety of compounds, though most contain a
nominal head, modified by either an adjective or participle or by a noun. Examples
are in (7):

(7)

gab	"speech"	+	*terrebew*	"mocking"	*gab terrebew*	"fiction"
kida	"good"	+	*teeyas*	"accomplishment"	*kida teeyas*	"efficiency"
yegna	"best"	+	*deréb*	"way"	*yegna deréb*	"skillful"
luwér	"knowledge"	+	*deréb*	"way"	*luwér deréb*	"science"
kewa	"people"	+	*dibba*	"group"	*kewa dibba*	"community"
kwara	"sun"	+	*leb*	"setting"	*kwara leb*	"west"
baxar	"sea"	+	*gena*	"mother"	*bexargena*	"ocean"
tika	"exact"	+	*ketaba*	"writer"	*tikerketaba*	"secretary"

The last two examples are from Zeraghiorghis (1999, 11).

Revival of Forgotten Words.   Through language planning efforts, the Blin language planners discovered many words used by elders that had not been transmitted to a younger generation who had experienced thirty years of civil war, life in refugee camps,
exile, and disruption. It became conscious policy to attempt to revive these authentic
Blin words that had fallen into disuse.

(8)

héjjam	"history"	*gula*	"south"
sexe	"north"	*tantarwa*	"town"
fered	"natural"	*ébéd qur*	"foreigners"
fédi gudi	"discussion"	*qurtha*	"drama"
falay	"imitation"	*shéngareeb*	"criticism"
méb	"grade"		

Calques (Loan Translation). Calques involve the use of native vocabulary elements to encode the meaning of foreign words or phrases. Examples are given in (9):

(9)

cado téttax	"antibiotics"	"against" + "tiny creatures"
késakhw	"administrator"	"be in service of; spend the night" cf. Tigrinya *amahadari,* Amharic *astedadaí*
gikh afriqikhw	"Horn of Africa"	"horn" + "African"
selfa ella	"first aid"	"first" + "aid"
séqwa séffet	"infrastructure"	"below" + "something which can hold any material"
seqeer kédemukhw	"network"	"net" + word derived from a material that is used to handle traditional basket of water
shur gérés	"self-reliance"	"self" + "ability"

Borrowing. If a language does not use native morphemes to express a concept, it may simply use the morphemes or words of another language, often adapting the loan to fit its phonology. Zeraghiorghis provides several examples of borrowing, shown in (10):

(10)

Loanword	Gloss	Source
hikumet	government	Arabic
kortelora	small knife	Italian
metro kubo	cubic meter	Italian
boletika	politics	English

Semantic Extension. Perhaps the most interesting of word formation processes are those that involve metaphoric extension of meaning to expand native vocabulary. Recent Blin words display a playful creativity of language in their application to novel referents or concepts, as shown in (11) (from Sulus 2003):

(11)

gésset baxarukhw	"style of children's haircut in which the sides of the head are shaved and a small tuft of hair is left on the crown of the head" + "of the sea"	>	"island"
wesheqdenta	"one who makes his bed or who makes smooth pavements"	>	"minister, coordinator"
bejjakhdéna	"to increase in quantity"	>	"multiplication"
keleeb	"round pen for cattle or goats"	>	"circle" (in math)
wechem	"group of something"	>	"set"
gaba gug	"road to a language"	>	"grammar"
fikhwen mekettey	"sign of a pause"	>	"punctuation"
chercherna	"to make smooth the thatched leaves of the hut"	>	"to calculate mathematical problems"

Processes common in English that have not (yet) been recorded in Blin include blending and acronymy. In short, Blin displays a variety of word formation processes to form new words to expand, modernize, and codify its native vocabulary to meet new semantic demands.

Implementation

There are several entities to implement Blin language planning. Foremost among these is the thirty-member Committee for Developing Bilin Language and Culture. The committee contains some members in the national capital, Asmara, while others are in or around the Blin cultural capital (and capital of 'Anseba region), Keren, some 91 kilometers to the northwest. Some members focus on language, while others focus on artistic and cultural events. There is, of course, close contact between the Ministry of Education's Blin Language Panel and members of the aforementioned committee. In addition, there are close ties between the Blin Language Panel and the daily radio program, *Dehai Gebaylakh,* "Voice of the Masses" (Zeraghiorghis 1999).

In its first broadcast, the radio program stated three main objectives:

1. To provide for Blin speakers current, truthful, and clear information in their mother tongue.
2. To provide a suitable atmosphere for Blin people for knowing and developing their culture, language, and its people in particular and the nation at large.
3. To make the people active participants in the process of developing Eritrea politically, economically, and socially (after Zeraghiorghis's translation, 1999, 10).

The radio program, broadcast for thirty minutes daily, is the primary means for dissemination and explanation of neologisms. It has been well received (Abbebe

2001, 86) and, based on observations during the author's fieldwork, it was often listened to by members of the community. Zeraghiorghis's (1999) survey of one hundred Blin found that 38 percent "always" listened, 35 percent listened "once a week," and 27 percent listened less frequently. However, at present, there is no documentation for how successful the transmission of neologisms to the public has been, though according to Zeraghiorghis's survey, 80 percent of the listeners liked the new words used on the program, and only 10 percent didn't like them.

Cultivation

The Eritrean government has cultivated the use of Blin primarily through its support of mother-tongue education in elementary grades. The Blin Language Panel has created primary school materials in Blin language, mathematics, science, and history/geography. Furthermore, it conducts periodic teacher training and has trained more than three hundred teachers in twenty-seven schools.

As mentioned earlier, the government also supports the daily radio program, which many Blin listen to. Materials include news, interviews, songs, and other cultural information. In addition, the Committee for Developing Bilin Language and Culture (1997) has published (in abugida) a highly regarded volume, *Gerbesha*. Furthermore, this committee organizes popular and well-attended oral poetry competitions and tests of cultural knowledge.

Conclusion

Eritrea has supported minority languages in many concrete ways. However, it is unfortunate that just after Blin mother-tongue education began in 1997, a terrible border war between Ethiopia and Eritrea broke out from 1998 to 2000. Although hostilities have ceased and the United Nations has recommended border demarcation, Ethiopia does not accept the United Nations' terms, thus raising tensions. In response to these tensions, the Eritrean government has suspended scheduled presidential and parliamentary elections, which would have formally implemented the constitution, and has prohibited the publication of private newspapers (U.S. Dept. of State 2007). Blin speakers reported to the author that Blin-language newspapers had been published previously (confirmed independently in Abbebe 2001, 86), but he never saw any during the course of fieldwork and archival research in the University of Asmara library in Eritrea in 2002.

The biggest need for language planning is the creation of a standard dictionary in the new orthography. Members of the Committee for Developing Bilin Language and Culture told the author that plans for such a dictionary were under way and that twenty thousand words had been collected but that they were on thousands of different scraps of paper. Clearly, resources must be dedicated to recording and collecting the standard vocabulary and the neologisms that have been coined. Such a dictionary might also be a multilingual dictionary, covering Tigre and Tigrinya, either or both of which languages the Blin people are also fluent in, and possibly also English, the language of secondary and higher education. Furthermore, as an aid to those in the diaspora and to those who did not have the benefit of mother-tongue education in the Roman script, such a dictionary might include the abugida orthography.

If Blin is to thrive, there should also be a number of postliteracy materials. Once a Blin speaker graduates from fifth grade, there is literally nothing else to read in the language. In the abugida script, aside from various grammars, there is only a book of love poems published abroad (Bogos 1992) and the *Gerbesha* volume. Elders should be encouraged to tell their stories, which literate speakers could transcribe and collect in published volumes. The poetry contests of the young should be recorded, transcribed, and published. Literate speakers have a rich history and life stories full of dramatic and traumatic events, the raw materials for the development of a promising literature. For example, one Blin whom the author interviewed desired to write a play about the wartime period but was frustrated by a lack of time, training, and literary models.

In the assessment of Eritrean anthropologist Abbebe (2001), "Bilin is . . . a symbol of the persistence of a 'small' people against all odds in a world which seems to favour 'big' peoples, cultural standardization and linguistic hegemonization." Yet he believes that Bilin has "enough positive symbolism to justify [a] lot of optimism for its survival" based on mother-tongue education in Blin, institutional support such as the radio program and literary competitions, and the "nostalgic reintroduction of traditional Bilin customs, belief systems, herbal medicinal practices, and aesthetic estates" (86). Mother-tongue education will certainly be crucial for reestablishing the language after a generation and a half was disrupted and displaced into refugee camps by thirty years of upheaval during the war of independence. But even after independence, the tensions between Ethiopia and Eritrea divert resources from nation building into national defense, from cultural flourishing to daily survival.

Unlike the situation of many endangered languages with very small numbers of elderly speakers (see, e.g., the studies in Brenzinger 2002), Blin does not face immediate obsolescence. With speakers numbering around ninety thousand, the number of Blin speakers is one of its strengths. But the study by Abbebe (2001), confirmed by the author's own field observations, shows that many young speakers are "opting out of their native speech community" (74), drifting to Tigre in rural areas and Tigrinya in urban areas. They are unable to use Blin in a wide range of domains, and they do not interact with the oldest generation of speakers and are not familiar with traditional Blin greetings, blessings, or even counting. These are clearly threatening signs to the language's vitality. The future lies with the 44 percent of the population that is under the age of fifteen (CIA 2007), a generation now receiving its primary education in Blin. What they do with their language after primary school and whether they will develop the language, create literature, and pass Blin on to their children will determine if language drift becomes language shift.

ACKNOWLEDGMENTS

The author acknowledges the assistance of a faculty supplemental grant from the University of Mary Washington to present this paper at GURT. Research in Eritrea was made possible through a New Faculty grant to the author by Howard University. Difficult to obtain materials were kindly provided through the cooperation of the Eritrean Ministry of Education, especially Daniel Teclemariam and Sulus Beyed, as well as Kiflemariam Hamde. The author is also grateful for judicious comments by the editors of this volume, as well as by two anonymous reviewers. Of course the opinions expressed here (and any errors) remain my own.

NOTE

1. In keeping with Eritrean and Ethiopian custom, authors are cited by their given name. In the references, they are cited by given name followed by their patronymic, with no comma separating them. This practice is used by Bender et al. (1976) and Unseth (1990) among others.

REFERENCES

Abbebe Kifleyesus. 2001. Bilin: Speaker status strength and weakness. *Africa* 56:69–89.

Bender, Marvin L., J. D. Bowen, R. L. Cooper, and Charles A. Ferguson. 1976. *Language in Ethiopia.* London: Oxford University Press.

Bloor, Thomas, and Wondwosen Tamrat. 1996. Issues in Ethiopian language policy and education. *Journal of Multilingual and Multicultural Development* 17:321–38.

Bogos, Goitom. 1992. *Enkeli! [Love Poems!].* Uppsala: Nyna Tryckeri.

Brenzinger, Matthias, ed. 2002. *Endangered languages in Africa.* Köln: Rüdiger Köppe.

Capomazza, Ilario. 1911. Un testo bileno. *Revista degli studi orientali* 4:1049–56.

Chefena Hailemariam, Sjaak Kroon, and Joel Walters. 1999. Multilingualism and nation building: Language and education in Eritrea. *Journal of Multilingual and Multicultural Development* 20:475–93.

CIA. 2007. Eritrea. The World Factbook. www.cia.gov/library/publications/the-world-factbook/geos/er.html (accessed October 1, 2007).

Clyne, Michael, ed. 1997. *Undoing and redoing corpus planning.* Berlin: Mouton de Gruyter.

Committee for Developing Blin Language and Culture in Keren. 1997. *Gerbesha: On Blin and culture.* Asmara: Sabur Printing House.

Conti Rossini, Carlo. 1907. Racconti e canti bileni. *Actes du XIVᵉ Congrès International des Orientalistes, Alger 1905,* vol. 2, 331–94. Paris: Ernest Leroux.

Cooper, Robert L. 1989. *Language planning and social change.* Cambridge: Cambridge University Press.

Dadoust, Denise. 1997. Language planning and language reform. In *The handbook of sociolinguistics,* ed. Florian Coulmas, 436–52. Oxford: Blackwell.

Daniel, Teclemariam, and Sullus Beyed. 1997. *Blin dialect survey April/May 1997.* Report by the Blin Language Panel submitted to the Ministry of Education, Asmara, Eritrea.

DeFrancis, John. 1984. Digraphia. *Word* 35:59–66.

Eritrean Ministry of Education. 1997a. The alphabets. Asmara: n.p.

———. 1997b. *Blina gab selfa mé-ébéd. Xétam selfukhw. [Bilin language, First grade.* 1st ed.] Asmara: Publishing Unit of the Department of General Education.

Fallon, Paul D. 2006. Blin orthography: A history and an assessment. In *Selected proceedings of the 36th Annual Conference on African Linguistics: Shifting the center of Africanism in language politics and economic globalization,* ed. Olaoba F. Arasanyin and Michael A. Pemberton, 93–98. Somerville, MA: Cascadilla Proceedings Project. Also available online at www.lingref.com/cpp/acal/36/paper1411.pdf.

Ferguson, Charles. 1968. Language development. In *Language problems of developing nations,* ed. Joshua Fishman, Charles Ferguson, and Jyotirindra Das Gupta, 27–35. New York: Wiley.

Fishman, Joshua, ed. 1974. *Advances in language planning.* The Hague: Mouton.

Fishman, Joshua, Charles Ferguson, and Jyotirindra Das Gupta, eds. 1968. *Language problems of developing nations.* New York: Wiley.

Haugen, Einar. 1966. *Language conflict and language planning.* Cambridge, MA: Harvard University Press.

Hetzron, Robert. 1976. The Agaw languages. *Afroasiatic Linguistics* 3:31–75.

Hornberger, Nancy H. 2005. Frameworks and models in language policy and planning. In *An introduction to language policy: Theory and method,* ed. Thomas Ricento, 24–41. Malden, MA: Blackwell.

Kiflemariam Hamdé. 1986. *Bilin language project: The origin and development of Bilin.* Unpublished Research Paper, Institute of African Studies, Asmara University.

———. 1996. Recent developments in Blin writing. *Adveniat Regnum Tuum* 64(2): 80–84.

Kiflemariam Hamde, and Paulos Zeremariam, eds. 1992. *Blina k'olata ʔendiba (ʔenglisedi diwisite).* Uppsala: Nina Tryckeri for the Blin Language Research Group.

Mowes, Ghebre Adem. 2003. *Blin mähärsina.* [Learning Blin. Book 1]. London: self-published.

Palmer, Frank. 1960. An outline of Bilin phonology. In *Atti del Convegno Internazionale di Studi Etiopici (Roma 2–4 April 1959)*, 109–16. Rome: Accademia Nazionale dei Lincei.

Reinisch, Leo. 1882a. *Die Bilin-Sprache in Nordost-Afrika.* Sitzungsberichte der Kaiserlichen Akademie der Wissenschaft, Philosophisch-historisch Klasse, 94 (2): 583–718. Vienna: Gerold Sohn.

———, ed. 1882b. *Wengel Marqos: Gospel of Mark in Bilin or Bogos language.* Vienna: Adolf Holzhausen for the British and Foreign Bible Society.

———. 1883. Texte der Bilin-Sprache. Leipzig: Griebens.

———. 1887. Wörterbuch der Bilin-Sprache. Vienna: A. Hölder.

Ricento, Thomas, ed. 2005. *An introduction to language policy: Theory and method.* Malden, MA: Blackwell.

Rogers, Henry. 2005. *Writing systems: A linguistic approach.* Malden, MA: Blackwell.

Simeone-Senelle, Marie-Claude. 2000. Les langues en Erythrée. *Chroniques yéménites* 8. http://cy.revues.org/document39.html (accessed October 1, 2007)

Smidt, Wolbert. 2003. Blin ethnography. In *Encyclopaedia Aethiopica, Vol. 1,* ed. Siegbert Uhling, 585–86. Wiesbaden: Otto Harrassowitz.

Spolsky, Bernard. 1977. The establishment of language education policy in multilingual societies. In *Frontiers of bilingual education,* ed. Bernard Spolsky and Robert Cooper, 1–21. Rowley, MA: Newbury House.

Sullus Beyed Awed. 1999. The Blin language: Prospects and challenges in introducing Blin as a medium of instruction. MA thesis, University of London.

———. 2003. Neologism in Bilin language. Paper presented at the Fourth International Conference of Cushitic and Omotic Languages, Leiden, April 10–12.

Tekle M. Woldemikael. 2003. Language, education, and public policy in Eritrea. *African Studies Review* 46 (1): 117–36.

United States Department of State. 2007. Background note: Eritrea (updated August 2007). www.state.gov/r/pa/ei/bgn/2854.htm (accessed October 1, 2007).

Unseth, Peter. 1990. *Linguistic bibliography of the non-Semitic languages of Ethiopia.* (Ethiopian Series Monograph No. 20). East Lansing, MI: African Studies Center, Michigan State University.

Wolde-Yohannes Habtemariam. 1939. *Awi mehedxwna?* [Who created us?]. Vatican City: n.p.

Wolff, H. Ekkehard. 2000. Language and society. In *African languages: An introduction,* ed. Bernd Heine and Derek Nurse, 298–347. Cambridge: Cambridge University Press.

Yacob, Daniel. 2004. Revision of the N1846 proposal to add extended Ethiopic to the BMP of the UCS. http://std.dkuug.dk/jtc1/sc2/WG2/docs/n2747.pdf (accessed October 1, 2007).

Zeraghiorghis Mengistu. 1999. Blin language development in vocabulary and orthography: Case study of the Blin radio program and adoption of the Latin script. Senior BA thesis, University of Asmara.

11

Indigenous Language Policies in Social Practice
The Case of Navajo

TERESA L. McCARTY
MARY EUNICE ROMERO-LITTLE
Arizona State University

OFELIA ZEPEDA
University of Arizona

INDIGENOUS PEOPLES represent 4 percent of the world's population, yet they speak 60 percent of the world's languages (Nettle and Romaine 2000, ix, 12). The contexts in which Indigenous languages are spoken are as diverse as humankind itself, spanning language situations such as that of Quechua, spoken by 8 to 12 million people in six South American countries (and nonetheless an endangered language; see Hornberger and Coronel-Molina 2004; King 2001; King and Hornberger 2004); to that of Aotearoa/New Zealand, where a single Indigenous language, Māori, shares co-official status with English and New Zealand Sign Language (May 2005); to the extraordinary linguistic diversity of Papua New Guinea, where 760 distinct languages, most spoken by fewer than one thousand people, coexist in an area the size of the American state of California; to the state of California itself, where fifty Native American languages are still spoken, none as a first language by children. With some exceptions—Guaraní in Paraguay, for example—the viability of Indigenous languages is severely threatened by legacies of language repression and the myriad contemporary forces that privilege languages of wider communication and marginalize "local" languages. Thus, for Indigenous peoples, language revitalization, maintenance, and reversal of language shift are key language planning and policy (LPP) goals.

The subaltern status of Indigenous languages positions Indigenous LPP as a de facto expression of identity, sovereignty, and human rights. There is an abundance of promising educational, social, and political activity under way by and for Indigenous peoples vis-à-vis those rights. A recent Web search on Indigenous LPP, for example, reveals more than a million sources!

In this chapter we focus on one "telling case" (cf. Hornberger 1997) of Indigenous language shift and maintenance: Navajo in the U.S. Southwest. Benally and Viri (2005) describe the Navajo language as at a "crossroads": "On several levels, extinction seems to be looming . . . , but on other levels, the language appears to remain strong and viable" (107). Navajo has also been described as a "test case" for stemming the tide of language shift in Native North America (Slate 1993). If something can be done to shore up the utility and status of Navajo, particularly among youth and young parents, these efforts hold real hope for other endangered Indigenous languages.

With an eye toward supporting these efforts, we are currently engaged in a large-scale study of language shift and retention in several Native American communities. Our purpose is to examine language shift "on the ground" as experienced by Native children and adults. We come to this work as educators, anthropologists, linguists, and activists in Indigenous education. Ofelia Zepeda is a linguist and native speaker of O'odham, the language of the Tohono O'odham or Desert People Indigenous to what is now southern Arizona and northern Sonora. Mary Eunice Romero-Little is a Keresan language educator from the Pueblo of Cochiti, New Mexico. Teresa McCarty is a non-Indian educational anthropologist who works with Navajo and in the field of Native American bilingual-bicultural education. In the more than twenty-five years of our individual professional involvement with Native American communities and schools, we have been witness to an alarmingly accelerating pace of Native language shift. Our goal in this study is to better understand language shift across a range of social, linguistic, and educational contexts and to use this knowledge to inform Indigenous LPP efforts, educational reform, and future research.

In the sections that follow we draw on ethnographic interviews from our Navajo site to illustrate the ways in which tacit and official language policies play out in everyday social practice. These language policies-in-practice are embodied in complex and contradictory language ideologies that simultaneously valorize and stigmatize Navajo and its speakers. As we show, these processes have a profound impact on language choices, particularly among youth.

We begin with a brief discussion of our theoretical and methodological approach. We then position the Navajo case within the broader context of Native American language vitality and shift. We go on to provide an overview of the research project, showing where the Navajo case fits within a larger data set. We then examine two prominent "thematic strands" that thread through the interview data— recurrent and interweaving discourse pairings that are indicative of language choices and practices. We conclude with a discussion of the challenges and possibilities these data raise for Native American language revitalization and maintenance.

A Sociocultural, Ethnographic Approach to Language Planning and Policy

Research and scholarship on language planning and policy have tended to emphasize government action or its lack (e.g., Ricento and Burnaby 1998, 33). Although government-backed initiatives are, of course, important, we do not want to privilege *only* official acts and policies, as this tends to obscure the complex human dynamics these official acts represent. Bernard Spolsky reminds us that language policy "exists even where it has not been made explicit or established by authority" (2004, 8). We therefore view language policy as a complex sociocultural process—as "modes of human interaction, negotiation, and production mediated by relations of power" (McCarty

2004, 72). A sociocultural approach to the study of LPP enables us to scrutinize these processes as de facto and de jure, covert and overt, bottom up and top down—and thereby to more closely examine the everyday, ever-present social practices that normalize some languages and language choices and marginalize others. "After all," Levinson and Sutton point out, "policy is a kind of normative decision making, and such decision making comprises an integral part of everyday life" (2001, 3). This includes the regulation of language use. For example, when a bilingual Navajo child hears a request from a parent in Navajo and chooses to respond in English, that child is also responding to a wider policy discourse; both child and parent are negotiating the language policy of the home.

With its "underlying concern with cultural interpretation" (Wolcott 1999, 68), ethnography is uniquely suited to study these processes. Participant observation and in-depth interviews are the mainstays of the ethnographic toolkit; in the study discussed here, we supplement these methods with document analysis, sociolinguistic questionnaires, and analysis of school achievement data. This combination of methods helps create "locally informed, comparatively astute, ethnographically rich account[s] of how people make, interpret, and otherwise engage in the policy process" (Levinson and Sutton 2001, 4). Throughout this work, we are also informed by a critical perspective and a concomitant commitment to use ethnographic knowledge to support Indigenous self-determination and linguistic human rights.

The Present Status of Navajo

The present situation of Navajo is part of a larger process of language shift engulfing all Native American communities. According to the linguist Michael Krauss (1998), of 175 Indigenous languages still spoken in the United States, only 20 are being acquired as a first language by children. The causes of language shift in Native American communities include a history of genocide, the seizure by whites of Indigenous lands, and explicit federal policies designed to eradicate Indigenous languages and to "remake American Indian children into brown White citizens" (Benally and Viri 2005, 89). Like other minoritized languages, Native American languages have not fallen into disuse due to "natural" causes; "they have been 'helped' on their way" (Skutnabb-Kangas 2000, 222).

Navajo is among the most vital Native American languages, with "more children speaking [it] than children speaking all other Indigenous U.S. languages combined" (Krauss 1998, 14–15). An Athabaskan language, Navajo claims more than 178,000 speakers (Benally and Viri 2005, 88). Most speakers reside within the 27,000-square-mile Navajo reservation (the largest reservation and the second most populous Native nation in the United States), but recent census data place speakers of Navajo in every U.S. state as well as in Puerto Rico and the District of Columbia (Benally and Viri 2005).

On Fishman's (1991) Graded Intergenerational Disruption Scale (GIDS), Navajo falls within stages 1–6: Intergenerational transmission still occurs within many families (stage 6); there is a significant (although not uniformly distributed) level of Navajo literacy (stage 5); education is carried out in Navajo in some public and most community-controlled schools (stage 4); some tribal-level and many local-level government activities are conducted in Navajo, the tribe has its own college, and a Navajo-language radio station broadcasts throughout the region, including in adjacent nonreservation towns (stages 1, 2, and 3). Despite these conditions, fewer children enter school speaking Navajo each year (McCarty 2002). As Spolsky (2002) reports: "Whereas in 1970 some 90 percent of the Navajo children in boarding schools had no preschool experience of English, by 1990 the situation had reversed, with six-year-old Navajo children beginning [preschool] or kindergarten suspected to have little if any knowledge of the language of their people" (140).

Even as more Navajo children come to school speaking English, they nevertheless tend to be stigmatized as limited English proficient (LEP) and to fare poorly in school. This paradox of language shift is widespread among Native American children and youth and is of growing national concern. More than 10 percent of all Native pupils enrolled in U.S. public schools are identified as LEP. In federal schools overseen by the Bureau of Indian Education, nearly 60 percent of all Native pupils are so identified (Tippeconnic and Faircloth 2002, 1). Understanding this paradox and its implications for Native American students is the focus of our study.

The Native Language Shift and Retention Study

The goal of the Native Language Shift and Retention Study is to examine the nature and impact of language shift and retention on American Indian students' language learning and academic achievement across a range of tribal-community contexts. Where are Native languages and English spoken in these communities, by whom, and for what purposes? What language attitudes and ideologies prevail in these settings? What is the nature of youth language proficiencies? What are the relationships among children's language proficiencies, their language attitudes and ideologies, and their school achievement? What are schools doing, if anything, to promote the Native language and culture—and to what effect? Finally, what are the implications for tribal, state, and national language education policies?

To address these questions, the research team identified five Native communities and seven school sites as research partners. All are located in the U.S. Southwest, a region that is representative of a wide range of Native American communities and language situations. The sites represent a cross section of tribes, rural and urban settings, language families, language vitality, and school types (federally funded community schools, urban public schools, and an urban charter school). At each site, we have negotiated research protocols according to school, community, tribal, university, and federal norms. This has been a labor-intensive process, but it has resulted in a high degree of local participation in the work. A key component of the study is the involvement of Native coresearchers identified as community research collaborators or CRCs. The CRCs have been instrumental to all phases of the research, facilitating entrée and access to sites, helping to design and validate research protocols, assisting in the conduct of interviews and the administration of questionnaires, and participating in university-based classes on language planning, heritage-language immersion, and ethnographic and sociolinguistic research methods. The CRCs are the critical change agents positioned to apply research findings to local and tribal language education planning once the study ends.

From 2001 to 2006, we conducted hundreds of hours of observation of language use and teaching in these school-community settings, collected student achievement data, and administered six hundred sociolinguistic questionnaires designed to elicit (1) perceptions of language proficiencies; (2) domains for English and Native-language use; (3) language attitudes and ideologies; and (4) normative assessments of the effectiveness of school language programs and the role of the school, community, and tribe in promoting Native-language maintenance. In addition, we conducted 205 individual ethnographic interviews and 7 focus group interviews with a total of 168 adults and 62 students in grades 3 through 12. Interviews were semistructured and included (1) a focused life history, including language learning inside and outside of school; (2) participants' observations of language use at home, in the school, and in the community; and (3) normative assessments of the role of families, community members, tribal leaders, and the school in supporting Native language maintenance. All interviews were audiotaped and transcribed. Most were conducted in English, although some Navajo participants preferred to be interviewed in Navajo. In that case, we relied on the expertise of native Navajo-speaking CRCs and a Navajo member of the research team, Gilbert Brown. Interviews conducted in Navajo were transcribed and translated by bilingual, biliterate native speakers with expertise in Navajo linguistics.[1]

Data analysis is ongoing. Qualitative data, including those reported here, are being analyzed using NVivo 7, a software tool for organizing, coding, and retrieving text data that facilitates analysis of fine detail and determination of patterns or themes. Quantitative analysis involves correlation and regression analyses to determine relationships between language proficiency and school performance. For the total data set, we are conducting both within-case and cross-case analyses.

In this chapter, we concentrate on a select corpus of data from interviews with Navajo youth and adults. We have been drawn to a closer inspection of these data because they are especially revelatory of the individual, family, and community-wide influences on language "tip" (Dorian 1981, 1989). We identify two key "thematic strands"—recurrent patterns that weave throughout the interviews. The first thematic strand juxtaposes language identity with language endangerment; the second juxtaposes language pride with language shame. Each strand is distinguishable in and of itself, but the two strands also interweave and overlap to construct a discernable, holistic configuration of the "language–policies–in–practice" in this setting that influence language choices.

All data are from a community we call Beautiful Mountain (all names are pseudonyms). Beautiful Mountain is a reservation-interior community with a population of about thirteen hundred; approximately six hundred students are served by the local pre-K–12 school. Wage labor at the school, in other government services, and in mining and construction is a primary source of income. Family incomes are well below national poverty levels, giving continuing economic and symbolic importance to the traditional economic pursuits of ranching, small-scale farming, and sheep and goat herding. In this setting, children's language socialization occurs across a wide range of contexts: in the nuclear family, often physically situated in federal and tribal housing near the school's two main campuses; in extended family gatherings (where Navajo is likely to predominate, particularly among older adults); in school (where English predominates, sometimes even in Navajo language and culture classes); in reservation-based commercial centers and tourist industries; in English-dominant off-reservation commercial centers; and, perhaps most importantly, through English-dominant mass media and technology.

Thematic Strand 1: Language Identity and Language Endangerment

Language shift in Native American communities has been attributed to a pattern of "denial" about the endangered state of these languages (Krauss 1998) and to "collective ignorance and apathy" (Benally and Viri 2005, 98). Our study paints a very different picture—one of widespread concern about language attrition. Moreover, talk about language endangerment regularly intertwines with claims of Indigenous identity. "We're Navajo. That's our language. We need to keep on talking [Navajo]," a young father of four told us when we interviewed him in 2004. The following statements were typical of many adults whom we interviewed:

> Your child some day . . . she is going to look back and say, . . . "I am Navajo and I don't know anything. I can't speak my language. I don't know who is related to me. I don't know my community." (Interview with Navajo educator, 3/27/03)

> I wish for us not to lose the language for our children's sake. . . .We are made up with our language. . . .Who will we be when we have lost our language? (Interview with Navajo parent and school staff member, 1/23/03)

The themes of "language as key to identity" and "language as carrier of culture and worldview" are common in discussions of language shift. As Hinton (2002, 152) points out, these are among the most prevalent reasons given for why language revitalization is important (see also Fishman 1991; Hornberger 1996; May 1999). What has not been well studied is whether or how these themes resonate with Native youth. We have found young people to be remarkably conscientious, articulate, and even passionate in addressing these issues. A twenty-year-old, for example, described knowledge of Navajo language and culture as the "foundation to go on for better things in life": "It gives you strength . . . to know where you're coming from and to know your self-identity and your culture . . . you will always come through obstacles with your foundation being there to back you up" (Interview, 12/12/02). Asked to speculate on the future of Navajo, he added, "We [Navajo people, Diné] have survived a lot of hard things. . . . I think it will go on."

Samuel represents a case in point. A tall, upbeat young man with a ready smile, Samuel was a seventeen-year-old high school senior when we interviewed him in 2004. He had learned to speak Navajo and Apache (a closely related Athabaskan language) from birth but considered Navajo his primary language. By his own and his teachers' accounts, Samuel liked school and was excelling in his studies. He aspired to become a medical doctor and to return to the Navajo reservation to treat his people. Asked whether "knowing and keeping Navajo" was important to him, Samuel replied, "Very important":

INTERVIEWER: Why?

SAMUEL: Because I get the best of both worlds. . . . [To become a medical doctor], I have to know how to communicate with patients in Navajo and . . . English. And not just because I want to go into medicine, it's important because the language is dying out—not slowly, as it used to be, but it's going very vigorously now. (Interview, 5/5/04)

In this interview excerpt, Samuel clearly signals his concern with the future of his native language. He also ties Navajo proficiency to both instrumental ends (anticipating the need to communicate with patients with different language abilities) and intra- and intercultural participation ("the best of both worlds"). Asked whether he would feel "less Navajo" if he could not speak the language, Samuel said that "no matter if you speak it or not, you're Navajo," but "traditionally, if you're not speaking Navajo, you [aren't] a Navajo." Samuel insisted that Navajo "is supposed to be spoken at all times in the house, . . . and . . . parents, they're Navajo, and they should be speaking Navajo."

Sixteen-year-old Jonathan presented a more pensive demeanor but expressed similar sentiments. At the beginning of each interview, we asked participants to identify the language or languages they understand, speak, read, and write and which language they considered their primary language. Jonathan initially reported that he was "learning" Navajo in school. However, in the course of a two-hour interview, he revealed that his first language was, in fact, Navajo. Jonathan had been ridiculed by his first teachers for his lack of proficiency in English, and for years, he said, he was "caught up in the confusion of learning English, having to form those words in my head." Despite these negative school experiences, Jonathan viewed Navajo as integral to his identity and his ability "to bring about some change in the world": "Having [Navajo] as my first language . . . it helps separate the side . . . of where all these [traditional] Navajo teachings come in. That helps me not . . . lose the identity of who I am, of where I come from. . . . It's a search for who you are . . . your outlook, you know." (Interview, 5/5/04)

Asked what would happen "if there is no Navajo language anymore," Jonathan responded: "It's like taking away the spirit; it's like taking away a real big part of who you are."

In these and other youth interviews, sentimental and even sacred attachments to the Navajo language are recurring themes. For Jonathan, retaining Navajo in the foreseeable future meant that "we can go about living with the sacredness a little longer." Samuel viewed the future viability of Navajo as necessary to maintaining mental and spiritual balance as well as cultural values such as proper stewardship of the land. Some youth situated Navajo speaking ability within origin accounts of the Diné (The People Navajos), which refer to being "created with" the language, which entails a lasting bond. A thirteen-year-old girl said simply, "Tell the parents to let the kids speak Navajo when they're born." (Interview, 5/5/04)

The juxtaposition of language identity with language endangerment also appears regularly in our interviews with Beautiful Mountain adults. One educator described the ability to speak Navajo as a "gift" (again, a reference to Navajo origin accounts): "That's what makes you a Navajo" (Interview, 2/13/03). "Our Holy People gave [the language] to us," another educator explained. "We were blessed with that" (Interview, 9/19/02). The future of Navajo, the first educator maintained, depends upon youth "getting back down to roots, . . . being able to say, 'Yes, . . . I'm proud to say I'm Navajo.'" "The language," he added, "it needs more takers, somebody to hold it up high." In these utterances, we see the interweaving of discursive themes: language identity ("getting . . . down to roots"), language endangerment ("it needs more takers"), and language pride ("being . . . proud to say 'I'm Navajo'"). Latent in these utterances is also the theme of language shame—a discourse illuminated further in the following section.

Thematic Strand 2: Language Pride and Language Shame

Many youth at Beautiful Mountain did, in fact, hold the Navajo language "up high." "I'm proud that I can read and write Navajo," a young woman told us (Interview, 2/13/03). A recent graduate of Beautiful Mountain School stated that his ability to speak Navajo enabled him to be "a role model for the kids." Like many youth, this young man equated knowledge of Navajo language and culture with school and life success: "I think to be a successful person in life you have to have both sides . . . , English and Navajo together. So that would make you a successful person in both worlds—Navajo and English" (Interview, 12/12/02). Katie, a petite female senior with a ponytail, said that knowing Navajo helped her in school "because you can compare the two different languages." Asked to name a person she most admired, Katie chose her school principal "because he's a Navajo and he talks Navajo on the intercom" (Interview, 5/5/04). Samuel maintained that although "English is important because it's spoken a lot in America, . . . you have to know your own language to succeed" (Interview, 5/5/04). When asked on project questionnaires whether they believed "it is important for you to speak your tribal language," 162 of 182 Beautiful Mountain secondary school students (89 percent) responded that knowing Navajo is "very important."

Not all youth shared these language attitudes, however. Jamie was eighteen years old when he was interviewed in May 2004. Having grown up in a reservation border town, his primary language was English. Asked whether knowing Navajo was important, Jamie claimed that the language was "just the past." He distanced himself from his Navajo-ness, referring to Navajo as "*their* [Navajo people's] culture" (emphasis added). Asked if he believed there had been a decline in the use of Navajo among youth, he replied: "Yes, because kids don't really care any more" (Interview, 5/5/04). At the same time, Jamie was trying to learn Navajo in school.

Discourses such as this reveal contradictory ideological currents that run throughout our interviews with youth and adults. A teacher assistant reported that a few of her students had insisted, "I'm not going to learn [Navajo]. Navajo's nothing. I hate it" (Interview, 3/27/03). These discourses were further illuminated in interview segments in which individuals were asked to estimate the proportion of Beautiful Mountain students who were proficient Navajo speakers. With a few exceptions, adults uniformly placed the number at about 30 percent. One bilingual educator maintained that "no one speaks Navajo. They only speak English now" (Interview, 1/23/03). Adolescents, conversely, expressed a very different view, uniformly placing the number of their peers who were fluent in Navajo at 75 to 80 percent. In contrast to adults, one youth stated emphatically that "everybody knows Navajo out here" (Interview, 5/6/07).

To the surprise of some school staff, formal tests of secondary school students' Navajo language abilities showed the youth's self- and peer-assessments to be on target, with 85 percent of students tested demonstrating age-appropriate proficiency on a local assessment administered in the spring of 2004. The divergent youth-adult responses in interviews nonetheless signify local perceptions of language vitality that have important implications for language choices. A bilingual adult who believes that the child to whom she or he is speaking has little knowledge of or is indifferent to the Native language is likely to address the child in English. For their part, youth may possess greater Native language proficiency than they manifest, "hiding" it out of shame or embarrassment. The net effect is to curtail opportunities for rich, natural, child-adult interaction in the heritage language and to reproduce a de facto language policy: "No Navajo spoken here."

The divergent youth-adult responses led us to question participants more closely as to the reasons for the differences. Samuel explained that for some of his peers, speaking Navajo stigmatized one as "uneducated, and they haven't experienced anything in the world": "Well, . . . a lot of [youth] tend to hide [their Native language ability]. . . . They put a façade on, and they . . . try to make teachers believe that they speak primarily [English] and weren't exposed to Navajo. . . . They probably think [Navajo] is important, but . . . they're judged by other people that speak English more clear than they do and they just kind of feel dirty about the whole thing, and that's why they put on the fake" (Interview, 5/5/04).

Jonathan provided this thoughtful, if troubling, analysis: "Many of these kids [have] that kind of self-hate. It's been pumped into them. It's not something natural. It's being told Navajo is stupid . . . to speak Indian is the way of the devil, . . . and many times, the older people will encourage English so [their children] can make it in the White man's world" (Interview, 5/5/04). Youth feelings of language shame were confirmed in interviews with adults: "A lot of them [young people] fake not [speaking] Navajo. I knew. They're ashamed. I caught a few students who claim they only speak English [but] there are hundreds who are fluent Navajo speakers" (Interview with Navajo educator, 2/13/03). A bilingual teaching assistant offered this poignant testimony: "Seeing children not speaking Navajo is a very emotional thing. I wonder why do they speak English more? None were born by Bilagáanas (Whites). Why don't they want to speak Navajo . . .? Are they ashamed of it? I don't know. How can our children come to understand us [through our language] again?" (Interview, 9/19/02).

These psychosocial dynamics have been documented for minoritized speech communities around the world. Writing of language shame among Garifuna children in Belize, Donna Bonner points out that the cause is not language per se, but rather the marginalization of Garifuna and "the association of Garifuna ethnic identity with poverty and low social status" (Bonner 2001, 86). King (1999, 2001) describes shame and insecurity about Quichua among Saraguros in Ecuador; Reese and

Goldenberg (2006) describe similar processes for Spanish speakers in southern California; and Baugh (2000, 103) critiques the "false burdens of linguistic shame through historical circumstances" for speakers of Ebonics (African American Vernacular English). In a collection of life histories reflecting the multiple "face[t]s" of heritage language loss, Sandra Kouritzin further demonstrates the complicity of racism and linguicism: "I grew up feeling ashamed to be Chinese, and . . . to speak Cantonese," a young woman of Canadian-born Cantonese parents told Kouritzin, recalling racist taunts by her classmates (1999, 43). "You shame people away from their language," a Cree speaker stated: "You deal with it by speaking English, and that way you don't have to face the hurt of the loss. . . . It's better because now you're white, right?" (Kouritzin 1999, 66–67).

"Being Navajo in Navajo": What Might the Future Hold?

Writing more than a decade ago, language educator and activist (and biliterate Navajo-as-a-second-language speaker) Clay Slate observed that "a society that allows people to be Navajo in Navajo is worth maintaining" (1993, 10). Data from the Native Language Shift and Retention Study illuminate the language ideologies forged in everyday practice that influence whether and how such a societal language policy might be sustained. We have highlighted two overlapping discursive themes that appear prominently in our data and have shown the ways in which these discourses juxtapose complicated and contradictory language ideologies (identity/endangerment; pride/shame). These discourses implicate a complex array of ideological forces underpinning language allegiances and choices, particularly among youth. On the one hand, many youth express pride in their heritage language, fusing it solidly to their senses of self. For these youth, the Native language is a tool for negotiating multiple cultural worlds—as one young man put it, a foundation "to go on for better things in life." Further, youth are keenly aware of language shift mechanisms and consequences. They recognize, as Samuel pointed out, that "the [Native] language is . . . [declining] very vigorously now," and, as Jonathan described, the colonial antecedents of the shift. On the other hand, youth are not immune to dominant, racialized ideologies that link Navajo with "backwardness" and English with modernity, opportunity, and success. For some youth, these associations render Navajo-ness and the Navajo language as useless, or worse, as emblems of shame.

Although the sociolinguistic dynamics underlying the Navajo case are in many ways unique—as previously indicated, Navajo is distinct among Native American languages in that it still has a relatively large number of child speakers—the discursive themes raised by this case have been reported for other endangered-language communities (e.g., Bonner 2001; Kouritzin 1999). Similar themes are also apparent in the late-shift communities in our study (Romero-Little et al. 2007).

What can we learn from these discourses on language ideologies and practices? We find it useful to frame this discussion in terms of Ruiz's (1984) language-as-a-resource approach. Our data suggest that Navajo youth may possess greater heritage-language proficiency than they demonstrate or than adults credit. Further, youth are well aware that their heritage language is at a "crossroads" (Benally and Viri 2005); many are searching for ways to counter the forces of language shift. The latent and manifest Native-language proficiencies of these youth, and the sentimental and instrumental value they place on the language constitute critical resources for Native language maintenance.

The next step, we believe, is to marshal those resources. With the CRCs we have begun school-community dialogues around study findings and local LPP issues, and a fledgling Navajo immersion effort has taken root. Community- and reservation-wide youth forums, in which youth take a leadership role, might follow. The research process itself has heightened intergenerational awareness of language shift and retention; the involvement of community members as coresearchers has been central to this. As Samuel told us: "This research you guys are doing, . . . It's trying to find a way to bring the Navajo language . . . back to the Navajo Tribe. And you're supposed to keep your language alive. . . . And that research can hopefully do a lot to bring all of that back" (Interview, 5/5/04).

We are heartened by several important new LPP developments at the tribal and national levels. In August 2005, the Navajo Nation Tribal Council approved the Navajo Sovereignty in Education Act, an unprecedented policy that places supervisory authority over schools on Navajo lands under tribal control. The act also establishes a Navajo Nation-wide board of education, elevates the Division of Diné (Navajo) Education to operate much like a state educational agency, and creates the position of Navajo superintendent of schools (www.navajocourts.org/Resolutions/CJY-37-05.pdf). Although the policy is being contested in English-only Arizona, it is both a concrete and symbolic source of support for tribal sovereignty and pan-Native LPP efforts. "We can never forget who we are," Navajo President Joe Shirley Jr. declared in signing the act into law. "We are a sovereign nation and . . . these changes now head us in that direction" (Norrell 2005, 1).

Just as important is a growing national Indigenous LPP movement. This movement is represented by the many successful Native-language immersion programs under way (for examples of these programs, see Hinton and Hale 2001); the annual Stabilizing Indigenous Languages Conference, now in its thirteenth year (for sample reports from the conference, see Burnaby and Reyhner 2002; Cantoni 1996; McCarty and Zepeda 2006; Reyhner et al. 1999); the policy and programmatic leadership of the American Indian Language Development Institute (AILDI), now in its thirtieth year (for a discussion, see McCarty et al. 2001; www.u.arizona.edu/~aildi); and the 1990/1992 Native American Languages Act (NALA). Drafted by Indigenous and non-Indigenous educators, linguists, and activists associated with AILDI, NALA reverses more than two centuries of federal language policy by vowing to "preserve, protect, and promote the rights and freedom of Native Americans to use, practice, and develop Native American languages" (NALA 1990, Sec. 104[1]). The legislation further makes it federal policy to "use the Native American languages as a medium of instruction" in all schools funded by the federal government (NALA 1990, Sec. 104[5]). In 2006, NALA was augmented by the Esther Martinez Native American Languages Preservation Act (NALPA). Named to honor a Tewa language educator and activist, NALPA supports additional Native American language programs for young children and their families as well as Native American language survival schools. While it is too early to determine whether these recent policy initiatives will bear fruit, the fact that they are under way at all is a sign of growing language policy activism.

Youth discourses are particularly helpful in illuminating the pressures and tensions inherent in maintaining a minoritized language. As Wyman notes in her (2005) study of language ideologies and Yup'ik youth culture, "Attending to young people's experiences has much to teach us about where we need to work harder to counteract growing pressures and contradictions in early shift settings" (8; see also Bielenberg 2002; Lee 1999, 2007; Nicholas 2005, 2007). Carefully listening to youth discourses opens up new understandings of language shift dynamics and new possibilities for language education programs and practices. We are hopeful that these possibilities will continue to unfold and that they will actively involve youth and the generation of young parents, not only as language learners but as language planners, researchers, and educators in their own right.   ▨

ACKNOWLEDGMENTS

We wish to acknowledge the U.S. Department of Education Institute of Education Sciences for its financial support of the research reported here. Part of the lead author's work for the project was supported by the Alice Wiley Snell Endowment for Education Policy Studies at Arizona State University. We express our deep appreciation to the Beautiful Mountain Community Research Collaborators: Sally Begay, Mary Benally, Leroy Morgan, Twylah Morris, Darlene Redhair, Delrey Redhair, Treva Yazzie, and Marvin Yellowhair. We are also indebted for the essential contributions of the graduate research assistants who have worked on the project over the years: Sherilyn Analla, Luis Barrigan, Victor Begay, AnCita Benally (now Dr. Benally), RoseMary Big, Gilbert Brown, Terri Edwards, Jaime Eyrich, Fernando Londoño, Lynn Mascarelli, Mildred Walters, Larisa Warhol, and Yuriko C. Wellington (now Dr. Wellington). The statements, opinions, conclusions, or implications that may be drawn from the data presented in this chapter solely reflect the view of the authors and do not necessarily reflect the views of the funding agency, the university sponsors (Arizona State University, the University of Arizona, and the Arizona Board of Regents), or the tribes or tribal councils who approved the research. Parts of this chapter are adapted from McCarty, Romero, and Zepeda (2006a, 2006b). Data here were collected from 2001 to 2004.

NOTE

1. Dr. AnCita Benally and Mildred Walters transcribed the Navajo interviews. We wish to especially recognize their painstaking, excellent, and essential contributions to this research.

REFERENCES

Baugh, John. 2000. *Beyond Ebonics: Linguistic pride and racial prejudice.* New York: Oxford University Press.

Benally, AnCita, and Denis Viri. 2005. *Diné bizaad* (Navajo language) at a crossroads: Extinction or renewal? *Bilingual Research Journal* 29:85–108.

Bielenberg, Brian T. 2002. "Who will sing the songs?" Language renewal among Puebloan adolescents. Ph.D. diss., Graduate School of Education, University of California Berkeley.

Bonner, Donna. 2001. Garifuna children's language shame: Ethnic stereotypes, national affiliation, and transnational immigration as factors in language choice in southern Belize. *Language in Society* 30:81–96.

Burnaby, Barbara, and Jon Reyhner, eds. 2002. *Indigenous languages across the community.* Flagstaff: Northern Arizona University College of Education. http://jan.ucc.nau.edu/~jar/TIL_Pub_Info .html#2 (accessed November 26, 2006).

Cantoni, Gina, ed. 1996. *Stabilizing Indigenous languages.* Flagstaff: Northern Arizona University Center for Excellence in Education.

Dorian, Nancy C. 1981. *Language death: The life cycle of a Scottish Gaelic dialect.* Philadelphia: University of Pennsylvania Press.

———. 1989. *Investigating obsolescence: Studies in language contraction and death.* Cambridge, UK: Cambridge University Press.

Fishman, Joshua A. 1991. *Reversing language shift: Theoretical and empirical foundations of assistance to threatened languages.* Clevedon, UK: Multilingual Matters.

Hinton, Leanne. 2002. Commentary: Internal and external language advocacy. *Journal of Linguistic Anthropology* 12:150–56.

Hinton, Leanne, and Ken Hale, eds. 2001. *The green book of language revitalization in practice.* San Diego, CA: Academic Press.

Hornberger, Nancy H., ed. 1996. *Indigenous literacies in the Americas: Language planning from the bottom up.* Berlin: Mouton de Gruyter.

———. 1997. Literacy, language maintenance, and linguistic human rights: Three telling cases. *International Journal of the Sociology of Language* 127:87–103.

Hornberger, Nancy H., and Serafin Coronel-Molina. 2004. Quechua language shift, maintenance, and revitalization in the Andes: The case for language planning. *International Journal of the Sociology of Language* 167:9–67.

King, Kendall A. 1999. Language ideologies and heritage language education. *International Journal of Bilingual Education and Bilingualism* 3:167–84.

———. 2001. *Language revitalization processes and prospects: Quichua in the Ecuadorian Andes.* Clevedon, UK: Multilingual Matters.

King, Kendall A., and Nancy H. Hornberger, eds. 2004. *Quechua sociolinguistics.* Theme issue, *International Journal of the Sociology of Language* 167:1–168.

Kouritzin, Sandra. 1999. *Face[t]s of first language loss.* Mahwah, NJ: Lawrence Erlbaum Associates.

Krauss, Michael. 1998. The condition of Native North American languages: The need for realistic assessment and action. *International Journal of the Sociology of Language* 132:9–21.

Lee, Tiffany. 1999. Sources of influence over Navajo adolescent language attitudes and behavior. PhD. diss., Graduate School of Education, Stanford University.

———. 2007. "If they want Navajo to be learned, then they should require it in all schools": Navajo teenagers' experiences, choices, and demands regarding Navajo language. *Wicazo Sa Review* 22:7–33.

Levinson, Bradley A. U., and Margaret Sutton. 2001. Introduction: Policy as/in practice: A sociocultural approach to the study of educational policy. In *Policy as practice: Toward a comparative sociocultural analysis of educational policy,* ed. Margaret Sutton and Bradley A. U. Levinson, 1–21. Westport, CT: Ablex.

May, Stephen, ed. 1999. *Indigenous community-based education.* Clevedon, UK: Multilingual Matters.

———. 2005. *Bilingual/immersion education in Aotearoa/New Zealand.* Theme issue, *International Journal of Bilingual Education and Bilingualism* 8:365–503.

McCarty, Teresa L. 2002. *A place to be Navajo: Rough Rock and the struggle for self-determination in Indigenous schooling.* Mahwah, NJ: Lawrence Erlbaum Associates.

———. 2004. Dangerous difference: A critical-historical analysis of language education policies in the United States. In *Medium of instruction policies: Which agenda? Whose agenda?* ed. James W. Tollefson and Amy M. B. Tsui, 71–93. Mahwah, NJ: Lawrence Erlbaum Associates.

McCarty, Teresa L., Mary Eunice Romero, and Ofelia Zepeda. 2006a. Reclaiming multilingual America: Lessons from Native American youth. In *Imagining multilingual schools: Languages in education,* ed. Ofelia García, Tove Skutnabb-Kangas, and María Torres-Guzmán, 91–110. Clevedon, UK: Multilingual Matters.

———. 2006b. Reclaiming the gift: Indigenous youth counter-narratives on Native language loss and revitalization. *American Indian Quarterly* 30:28–48.

McCarty, Teresa L., Mary Eunice Romero-Little, and Ofelia Zepeda. 2006. Native American youth discourses on language shift and retention: Ideological cross-currents and their implications for language planning. *International Journal of Bilingual Education and Bilingualism* 9:659–77.

McCarty, Teresa L., Lucille J. Watahomigie, Akira Y. Yamamoto, and Ofelia Zepeda. 2001. Indigenous educators as change agents: Case studies of two language institutes. In *The green book of language revitalization in practice,* ed. Leanne Hinton and Ken Hale, 371–83. San Diego, CA: Academic Press.

McCarty, Teresa L., and Ofelia Zepeda, eds., with Victor H. Begay, Stephanie Charging Eagle, Sarah C. Moore, Larisa Warhol, and Tracy M. K. Williams. 2006. *One voice, many voices: Recreating Indigenous language communities.* Tempe: Arizona State University Center for Indian Education.

Native American Languages Act of 1990 (NALA) 1990. P.L. 101–477. Washington, DC: United States Congress. http://nable.org/documents/policy_legislation/NALanguagesAct.pdf (accessed March 9, 2006).

Nettle, Daniel, and Suzanne Romaine. 2000. *Vanishing voices: The extinction of the world's languages.* Oxford, UK: Oxford University Press.

Nicholas, Sheilah. 2005. Negotiating for the Hopi way of life through literacy and schooling. In *Language, literacy, and power in schooling,* ed. Teresa L. McCarty, 29–46. Mahwah, NJ: Lawrence Erlbaum Associates.

———. 2007. Becoming "fully" Hopi: The role of the Hopi language in the contemporary lives of Hopi youth—A Hopi case study of language shift and vitality. PhD diss., American Indian Studies Program, University of Arizona.

Norrell, Brenda. 2005. Education reform elevates status of Navajo-controlled education. *Indian Country Today,* August 12. www.indiancountry.com/content.cfm?id=1096411394 (accessed November 25, 2006).

Reese, Leslie, and Claude Goldenberg. 2006. Community contexts for literacy development of Latina/o children: Contrasting case studies. *Anthropology and Education Quarterly* 37:42–61.

Reyhner, Jon, Gina Cantoni, Robert N. St. Clair, and Evangeline Parsons Yazzie, eds. 1999. *Revitalizing Indigenous languages.* Flagstaff: Northern Arizona University Center for Excellence in Education.

Ricento, Thomas, and Barbara Burnaby, eds. 1998. *Language and politics in the United States and Canada: Myths and realities.* Mahwah, NJ: Lawrence Erlbaum Associates.

Romero-Little, Mary Eunice, Teresa L. McCarty, Larisa Warhol, and Ofelia Zepeda. 2007. Language policies in practice: Implications from a large-scale study of Native American language shift. *TESOL Quarterly* special topic issue: *Language policies and TESOL: Perspectives from practice* 41:607–18.

Ruiz, Richard. 1984. Orientations in language planning. *NABE Journal* 8:15–34.

Skutnabb-Kangas, Tove. 2000. *Linguistic genocide in education—Or worldwide diversity and human rights?* Mahwah, NJ: Lawrence Erlbaum Associates.

Slate, Clay. 1993. Finding a place for Navajo. *Tribal College Journal* 4:10–14.

Spolsky, Bernard. 2002. Prospects for the survival of the Navajo language: A reconsideration. *Anthropology and Education Quarterly* 33:139–62.

———. 2004. *Language policy.* Cambridge, UK: Cambridge University Press.

Tippeconnic, John W., III, and Susan C. Faircloth. 2002. Using culturally and linguistically appropriate assessments to ensure that American Indian and Alaska Native students receive the special education programs and services they need. *ERIC Digest,* EDO-RC-02-9. Charleston, WV: ERIC Clearinghouse on Rural Education and Small Schools.

Wolcott, Harry F. 1999. *Ethnography: A way of seeing.* Walnut Creek, CA: AltaMira Press.

Wyman, Leisy. 2005. Language ideologies, youth culture, and Indigenous language education: Lessons from a Central Alaskan Yup'ik example. Paper presented at the 104th Annual Meeting of the American Anthropological Association, Washington, DC, December 3.

12

Heritage Language Education in the United States

A Need to Reconceptualize and Restructure

JOY KREEFT PEYTON
Center for Applied Linguistics

MARIA CARREIRA
California State University, Long Beach

SHUHAN WANG
Delaware Department of Education

TERRENCE G. WILEY
Arizona State University

IN RECENT YEARS interest in the language proficiency of the U.S. population has increased significantly. Calls for individuals with professional-level proficiency in languages other than English have come from several quarters, and new initiatives and legislative actions focus on proficiency in languages considered critical to U.S. security and economic success. The good news is that there is a large population of individuals who live in the United States and speak many different languages, including those languages considered critical to U.S. national interests. Including this population in efforts to develop a language proficient society (Marcos and Peyton 2000) presents both opportunities and challenges. If we are to take seriously the language proficiency and cultural knowledge that many individuals in this country already have, we need to restructure the language education field in a number of ways. In this chapter we first describe the current need for language proficiency in the United States. We then call for a shift in our understandings and action on several fronts. We need to understand and articulate the benefits to individuals and to society of proficiency in languages other than English; create and document excellent programs to develop, to professional levels, the language proficiency of those who speak languages other than English; develop systematic methods for deciding which languages to focus on; and create networks of stakeholders who will work together to build effective programs and approaches.

Need for Language Proficiency in the United States

Calls for a focus on developing a language-proficient society are pervasive and increasing. According to Edwards (2006) the United States is experiencing attention on and support for language education at a level that we have not seen since the late 1950s and early 1960s days of the Cold War and Space Race. Brecht and Rivers (2000), for example, argue that globalization and increased international trade, democratization, the emergence of local languages in many countries, and the desire of the United States to remain a world superpower are powerful forces driving the perceived need for greater language proficiency. The attacks on the World Trade Center in September 2001, the launch of the "war on terrorism," U.S. presence in Afghanistan and Iraq, and China's recent economic growth have resulted in an increased sense of urgency among policymakers and government officials. Studies, reports, and hearings have noted our nation's serious language shortages and called for improvement of our language capabilities through scholarships and fellowships for students to study overseas, investment in international and foreign language study, and the creation of a "language pipeline to address the paucity of Americans fluent in foreign languages, especially critical, less commonly taught languages" (Committee for Economic Development 2006; see also Edwards 2006 and Government Accounting Office 2002 for discussion).

These calls, and the advocacy of the language community, have resulted in new and increased federal policies and funding for language and international study. For example, recent funding includes the National Security Language Initiative (NSLI), launched by President Bush on January 5, 2006, which may provide up to $114 million to "further strengthen national security and prosperity through education, especially in developing foreign language skills." NSLI outlines a coordinated national vision to expand the number of Americans mastering "critical need languages," increase the number of advanced-level speakers of foreign languages, and increase the number of foreign language teachers and resources for them. Initially languages identified as critical include Arabic, Chinese, Hindi, Japanese, Korean, Russian, and Central Asian languages that incorporate languages in the Indic, Iranian, and Turkic families. NSLI funding includes increased support for the Foreign Language Assistance Program (FLAP) for K–12 programs; fellowships and scholarships for study abroad; domestic summer programs for teachers and students (STAR TALK); and flagship programs to develop "language pipelines," opportunities for long, articulated sequences of language study from the early grades to advanced levels, grades K–16. (Three such programs have been funded, two Chinese and one Arabic.) Many current initiatives require Congress to authorize new or amended legislation and appropriate funds, and the 109th Congress considered more than forty bills dealing with languages and international education.

Lists of critical need languages are, of course, always changing. In 1985, the U.S. Department of Education published a list of 169 "critical" foreign languages, considered critical because they were spoken in different parts of the world and because proficiency in them would enable U.S. citizens to be involved in global issues (Crystal 1987). Current emphasis on critical languages focuses on national security and economic interests. Many educators argue for an expanded view, focused on individual and societal communicative competencies as part of the core twenty-first-century skills that global citizens in an interconnected world must possess, which goes beyond political and economic interests of a nation (Partnership for 21st Century Skills 2003; Pratt 2003; Sandrock and Wang 2005).

Language Proficiencies of Heritage Language Speakers

As can be seen from the previous discussion, various sectors of the U.S. government recognize the importance of proficiency in languages other than English and are seeking to build programs to develop proficiency in these languages. What is still unclear is the extent to which we will be able to build on the language proficiencies of a large portion of the U.S population, those who already speak the languages of interest.

In 2005, the foreign-born population reached more than 35 million, slightly over 12 percent of the U.S. resident population (U.S. Census Bureau 2005), and the highest proportion of foreign-born residents since the early 1900s, when the percentage reached 15 percent. This represents a huge influx of recent immigrants; between 1990 and 2000, 13.3 million people, roughly 44 percent of all foreign-born residents, arrived in this country (U.S. Census Bureau 2001). Between 2000 and 2005, 7.9 million new immigrants settled in the United States, making the first half of this decade the highest five-year period of immigration in U.S. history (Camarota 2005). As a result, the percentage of residents with a language other than English in their home background has also risen dramatically. In 2005, almost 52 million individuals, over 19 percent of U.S. residents aged 5 and older, spoke a language other than English at home (U.S. Census Bureau 2005).

The number of languages spoken is on the rise as well. More than 53 percent of the foreign born are Latin Americans who speak Spanish and various indigenous languages. Another 26.7 percent are Asians, who speak a diversity of East, Southeast, and South Asian languages, among them Chinese, Hindi, Khmer, Korean, Lao, Tagalog, Urdu, and Vietnamese. Newcomers from Africa and Oceana speak Amharic, Arabic, Fijian, Hausa, Swahili, and Yoruba, among other languages (U.S. Census Bureau 2005; see figure 12.1). What is not known is the extent to which members of these language groups maintain their language skills or have opportunities to develop those skills to a point that would be considered "functional native proficiency" (Interagency Language Roundtable n.d.).

In many government and education sectors the individuals described earlier are referred to as "heritage language speakers," and language researchers and educators are focusing on what a heritage language is and who heritage language speakers are.

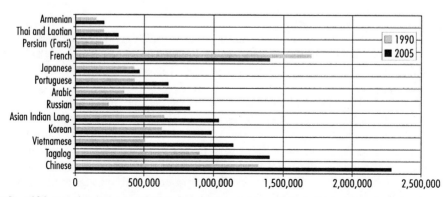

Figure 12.1 Growth in Languages Other than English and Spanish in the United States
Source: U.S. Census Bureau 2005.

Heritage Language

Within the language research and practice community, there is considerable discussion of the question of what a "heritage language" is. Although the term has been used in the United States only recently, it was used in Canada in the 1970s with the inception of the Ontario Heritage Languages Programs (Cummins 2005). Fishman (2001) has argued that heritage languages include indigenous languages, American Indian (Amerindian) languages spoken before the arrival of Europeans; immigrant and refugee languages, spoken by the many groups who have come to live in this country for a variety of reasons, both voluntary and involuntary; and colonial languages, spoken here before the United States of America became a nation (e.g., Dutch, French, German, Spanish). As Wiley (2005b) points out, Spanish, spoken by the largest number of people in the United States after English, can be considered all of these—an indigenous language (spoken by those living here before their land was annexed into the United States), an immigrant language (spoken by those who have come from Mexico, Central and South America, the Caribbean, Spain, and the Philippines), a refugee language (spoken by refugees from Cuba and Central America), and a colonial language (the language of the former Spanish Empire and the national language of the areas of Mexico that became part of the continental United States).

Baker and Jones (1998), Corson (1999), and Wiley (2001, 2005b) have pointed out that "heritage language" may not be the most effective term to use to describe these populations because it evokes images of the past and tradition rather than of contemporary reality. They have argued that "community language" may be a better term, because it focuses on the immediate reality of individuals and their desire to shape their lives in their communities. This term does not, however, convey the sense of individuals participating in professional endeavors with a global perspective. In this chapter we use the term "heritage language" because it is still used widely in the United States, including in the recent legislation described earlier and specific projects described later, and does not limit language proficiency to community concerns. However, the groups concerned about language development and involved in language education, as well as individual heritage language speakers, will use the terms that best describe their realities and goals and with which they choose to be identified (Hornberger and Wang forthcoming).

Heritage Language Speakers

A number of scholars have outlined who should be included in the population of heritage language speakers (also referred to as heritage language learners). Valdés (2000, 2001, 2005), speaking from the perspective of an educator, includes individuals who have "actually developed functional proficiencies in the heritage language" (2005, 412), who speak or at least understand and are to some degree bilingual in the language and in English. Fishman (2001), taking a sociological perspective, focuses on one's identity and historical and personal connections. For Fishman, one's heritage language is the language of one's parents, grandparents, ancestors, and members of the community, no matter what one's level of proficiency. Many educators use the term to refer to students who have had exposure to the language at home and in the community but are not fully fluent or literate in it and distinguish among heritage, fluent, and native speakers (see also Carreira 2004; Hornberger and Wang forthcoming; Van Deusen-Scholl 2003; Wiley 2001 for discussion of various perspectives on a definition).

Whatever one's perspective or definition, there is a need to understand, value, and document the language proficiencies and cultural knowledge of heritage language speakers in the United States and to create opportunities for them to develop that knowledge and proficiency. Efforts to develop the English language proficiency of students in schools are strong, as reflected in state-based English for the Children initiatives (e.g., Proposition 227 in California, Proposition 203 in Arizona, and Question 2 in Massachusetts) and in federal education policy (e.g., No Child Left Behind). Inherent in some of these efforts is a view of languages other than English as a problem (Ruiz 1984) and a repudiation of the societal and individual benefits of bilingualism. With an exclusive focus on English, we are neglecting and devaluing the languages other than English that students already speak (Evans and Hornberger 2005). The "squandering of personal, community, and national linguistic and intellectual resources within the mainstream classroom" (Cummins 2005, 585) is pervasive, because the language ability and cultural knowledge that children bring to school is often considered irrelevant or even an impediment to their English language and academic achievement (Cummins 2005). As a result, students continue to lose the native languages that they come to school speaking. Our focus on English needs to be broadened to include interest in developing in students high levels of proficiency in their heritage languages as well as in English (Malone et al. 2005). In addition, there needs to be a concerted effort in the education field to meet the urgent linguistic requirements of U.S. security and economic interests that goes beyond the confines of federal legislation and is carried out by schools, universities, communities, and national education organizations themselves.

Heritage Language Programs

As Wiley (1998, 2005b), Fishman (2001), and Toth (1990) have pointed out, heritage language education is not new in this country. Formal heritage and community language education have been taking place in what has become the United States for well over three centuries, and communities of speakers of dozens of different languages have maintained and developed their languages and cultures in community-based schools. The scope of this activity was documented by Fishman (1966) when he raised "the first modern call to conserve and foster our nation's heritage language resources by developing capacity in the various heritage languages before they were assimilated out of existence" (Fishman 2001, 88–89) and documented 1,885 ethnic community schools operating in dozens of languages. Twenty years later he identified 6,553 heritage language schools involving 145 languages, a growth of 228 percent (Fishman 1985), and proclaimed that "heritage language schools were a more self-confident breed . . . maintained by a younger generation of advocates who were more secure in their own ethno-American identities" (Fishman 2001, 88). As Valdés (2005) points out, some minority language communities have been deeply committed to maintaining their community languages in spite of strong pressures to assimilate.

Although Fishman made his data available for distribution in the hope that information on heritage language programs would be maintained and developed further, unfortunately this has not been the case. No similar study is in the works, and no up-to-date, national database of heritage language programs exists. On a smaller scale, Valdés and others (2006) are documenting heritage Spanish programs in secondary schools and universities, and the Alliance for the Advancement of Heritage Languages is collecting profiles of heritage language programs in community-based and K–12 public and private school settings (www.cal.org/heritage). More funding and effort need to be devoted to documenting the heritage language programs in all sectors of the U.S. education system.

Benefits of Language Proficiency

Many calls to increase the language proficiency of the United States include arguments that language proficiency is a "resource." This began with Fishman (1966) and was followed by Brecht and Walton (1994) in their call for the development of the "language capacity" of heritage language speakers (see also Brecht and Ingold 2002). Ricento, however, questions this "commodification orientation" (Ricento 2005, 358), a focus on the language proficiencies of individuals as an instrument that is tied to dominant sociopolitical agendas of national security, international trade, and law enforcement. Similarly, Wiley (forthcoming) critiques the alignment of heritage language development with national security issues. Wang (2004) argues that we should focus instead on language as capital, a benefit that belongs to an individual or group and benefits that individual or group as well as society. In addition to national security and economic competitiveness interests, language as human capital includes noninstrumental benefits of language proficiency and cultural knowledge. These can include personal capital, with psychological, aesthetic, and professional or career benefits; cultural capital, connections with one's own family and cultural heritage and space for one's language and culture in mainstream society; and social capital, use of the language to accomplish one's own and others' social, economic, and political goals. A focus on language as capital in our national discourse would broaden our understanding of the benefits of language proficiency and place value on linguistic and cultural knowledge in their own right.

Development of Language Programs

Two trends in the U.S. education system inhibit development of language proficiency—the squandering of the language proficiencies of U.S. residents, discussed earlier, and the lack of foresight in strategically selecting languages to be taught in schools, developing and documenting excellent language programs that are appropriate for the students involved, and determining the levels of language proficiency to be reached. In addition to teaching the languages traditionally taught in the U.S. public and private school systems grades K–16 (Spanish, French, and German; see Rhodes and Branaman 1997; Welles 2004), there is a need to focus attention and resources on the specific languages that are spoken by large segments of the U.S. population; those considered important around the world because of demographic, economic, and political factors (figure 12.2); and those called for in the federal initiatives and legislation described earlier.

Sectors of the education system, beginning in elementary school and community-based programs and continuing through university, need to work together to develop criteria for selecting the languages to be taught and the language education efforts to be

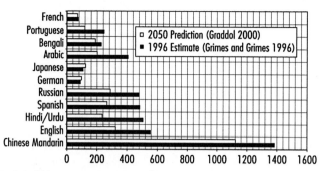

Figure 12.2 Major World Languages in 1996 and 2050
Source: Ulrich 2003.

supported so that language development efforts are responsive and responsible. At a minimum the following criteria should guide decisions:

- Importance of the language to specific communities
- Demographic importance of the language within the United States
- Transnational uses of the language
- Importance of the language in global contexts

Importance of the Language to Specific Communities

We are seeing a revival in the learning of some Native American languages, with community-based programs growing in enrollments and resources, and in learning languages of interest to specific communities, such as French, German, Polish, and Yiddish (Olsen et al. 2001). Likewise, because of national interests discussed earlier and efforts of specific language communities, there is growing interest in the study of languages formerly considered "less commonly taught" (e.g., Chinese, Hindi, Japanese, Korean, Tagalog, and Vietnamese), with new programs being established across the country and university enrollments growing (Brod and Welles 2000). A few of these languages are now receiving considerable attention and resources and are experiencing significant increase in class enrollments along with their importance (e.g., Chinese, discussed later). At the same time, others, the "truly less commonly taught languages" (e.g., Bengali, Hindi, Hmong, Kashmiri, Pashto, Punjabi, Sinhala, and Zulu; Brod and Welles 2000; Gambhir 2001) are experiencing a "struggle for legitimacy and public presence" (Byrnes 2005, 584). However, these languages often represent a "core value" (Smolicz 1980, 1992) for the groups that want to maintain them—a way for these groups to understand the world, interact in specific communities and settings, create communities of purpose (McNulty 2004), and open up a language and cultural space of their own in the dominant society.

Efforts to develop programs to teach languages that have formerly been less commonly taught need to be supported by trained teachers, materials, and communications with other programs in similar situations. Gambhir (2001, 224–26) profiles two such programs, one that teaches Armenian (the Rose and Alex Pilibos Armenian School in Los Angeles, California) and one that teaches Khmer (Long Beach, California), and the Alliance for the Advancement of Heritage Languages is creating a collection of profiles of programs (www.cal.org/heritage). Efforts to provide materials for the instruction of these languages include the collection of materials for the teaching of hundreds of languages maintained by the University of California, Los Angeles (UCLA), and the Center for Applied Linguistics (www.lmp.ucla.edu), and the LangNet website, sponsored by the National Foreign Language Center at the University of Maryland, College Park (www.nflc.org). Finally, the area-focused National Language Resource Centers (http://nflrc.msu.edu) collect and archive information on language teaching materials, and the National Heritage Language Resource Center at UCLA (www.nhlrc.ucla.edu) is collecting materials and conducting research on heritage language learners. However, the majority of the materials available are for adult learners. Along with decisions about what languages should be taught in schools, we need a process for developing materials that are appropriate for the learners involved and are articulated across levels.

Demographic Importance of the Language within the United States

If there are sizable communities of speakers of a language and the language is an important part of U.S. culture, we will benefit from developing skills in that language. Spanish is an example. The Spanish-speaking population is the fastest-growing language group in the United States. According to the 2005 American Community Survey, almost 42 million Latinos lived in the country (14.5 percent of the population), and more than 32 million people said they spoke Spanish at home (U.S. Census Bureau 2005). Hispanics/Latinos accounted for 49 percent of the country's growth from 2004 to 2005, and 70 percent of that growth is in children younger than five years old (U.S. Census Bureau 2005). The number of Spanish language radio stations, television programs, and newspapers has grown significantly, with 673 Spanish radio stations and 543 Spanish language newspapers counted in 2000. We have made important progress in our public and private school systems in the teaching of Spanish. Teacher training programs and summer institutes are held for teachers of Spanish and for Spanish speakers, classes for heritage/fluent/native/Spanish speakers (the name varies by program) have been established across the country, and many materials for instruction in these classes are commercially available.

Russian is another language with a significant number of speakers, with a nearly 191 percent increase in speakers from 1990 to 2000 (Wiley 2005a), and efforts are under way at the university level to promote the teaching of Russian to Russian speakers (Kagan 2005). Hmong and Korean also have significant numbers of speakers and a strong tradition of community-based schools, organizations, and publications (Olsen et al. 2001). Programs in these languages with a long tradition and strong base need to be improved to better serve the students in them. These programs also need to be studied and documented so they can serve as models for the development of heritage language programs in other languages.

Transnational Uses of the Language

There is a critical need for development in the United States of languages that are used broadly for international diplomacy and trade. Chinese is an example. The number of Chinese speakers in the world is projected to reach 1.4 billion by 2020 (National

Intelligence Council 2004). China is rising as an economic power (with the fifth largest economy in the world, recently overtaking France), and Chinese is a major world language (see figure 12.2). In the United States, Chinese is the third most commonly spoken language (after English and Spanish). In 2005, almost 2.3 million individuals in the United States spoke varieties of Chinese, and one-fourth were under eighteen. This represents a remarkable increase since 1960, when there were 89,609 speakers (U.S. Census Bureau 1999, 2005).

As McGinnis (2005) points out, our nation's supply of those who are fluent in the Chinese language and have cultural knowledge may have the potential to meet our needs for Chinese language proficiency. Enrollments in community-based Chinese language programs number more than 150,000 students. At the same time, K–12 institutions are reporting having 25,000 students, and colleges and universities, 34,000 students studying Chinese. (See Shuhan Wang 1996, 1999 and Xueying Wang 1996 for documentation of the organization and challenges of community-based Chinese heritage language schools in the United States.) However, while there is a strong community-based school system, the infrastructure to meet current needs for high-quality programs, curricula, materials, and teachers is still woefully inadequate and needs to be developed (Asia Society 2005).

Importance of the Language in Global Contexts
As discussed earlier, many claim that proficiency in specific, "critical need languages" is needed for the United States to maintain our economic, political, and national security positions in the world. Arabic, one of the fastest-growing languages of study at U.S. colleges and universities (with a 92 percent increase in students studying Arabic from 1998 to 2002; Welles 2004), is one such language. While the study of Arabic is still dwarfed by students learning Spanish, French, and Chinese, efforts are under way to develop high-quality Arabic language programs, primarily in universities. At the same time, a network of K–12 Arabic teachers has been formed by the National Capital Language Resource Center (www.arabick12.org), and the *Standards for Foreign Language Learning* (ACTFL 2006) now includes standards for the teaching and learning of Arabic. As with Spanish and Chinese, there is a critical need for well-trained teachers, credentialing programs for teachers, and programs that are appropriate for Arabic-speaking as well as English-speaking students that include effective curricula, instructional materials, and assessments.

Increasingly the movement of peoples, the interconnectedness of international business, and advances in communication technology and travel are enabling an unprecedented degree of connectivity around the world. In the United States, the more than 32 million speakers of Spanish have access to Spanish media on an unprecedented scale through numerous radio stations and television networks. Univisión commands the sixth largest television network in the United States, and Little Saigon Radio in Orange County, California, reaches an audience of approximately 1 million listeners in California and Texas. Friends and relatives can keep in frequent communication via the Internet and telephone communication, and global travelers frequent ancestral and adopted homes. Opportunities to maintain heritage languages and cultural ties across nations are abundant, and they need to be recognized and built on in our efforts to increase high levels of language proficiency.

Goals and Structure of Language Programs

If policymakers and educators are serious about developing the language proficiency of heritage language speakers and being responsive to demographic realities in the United States and to global developments that have an impact on language use, significant work needs to be done to transform language programs and instructional practices. Historically, "foreign" language programs (that teach languages other than English) have served native English speakers (without personal or family background in the language) and have assumed that students have similar language backgrounds and experiences, prior course work, language learning goals, and abilities in the language. Curricula and materials have followed a sequential approach that moves learners through predetermined levels, content, and materials, with set outcomes based on assumed prior course work rather than on students' characteristics and proficiencies.

However, heritage language learners represent a wide range of linguistic profiles (Valdés 2005). Some have attended school for a few years in their country of origin and may therefore be able to read and write the language, albeit with errors. Others have oral fluency in the language but limited reading and writing abilities, having used the language only at home and in the community. Others have well-developed receptive skills but limited productive skills, having had limited opportunities to use the language during their formative years. What heritage language students know about their native language is more closely aligned with their life experiences—where they were born, what they speak at home, and their reading habits—than their course work history within a foreign language department.

To respond to the needs of a diverse student population that includes heritage language learners, we need to implement a learner-centered philosophy (McGinnis 2005) and instruction that is based on students' actual backgrounds and needs (Tomlinson 1999). One possible approach is "differentiated instruction," in which knowledge of student differences helps shape the curriculum; ongoing assessment of students is built into the curriculum; multiple types of learning materials are available; pacing of learning and grading criteria are varied depending on student needs; and work is assigned according to students' proficiency levels, needs, and interests (Tomlinson 1999, 2). Differentiated instruction can accommodate a variety of purposes for learning the language, which might include communicating and connecting with family and the community, who may speak nonstandard varieties of the language; and pursuing various professional, occupational, recreational, and personal goals that require proficiency in standard forms of the language at high levels or specialized vocabulary and expressions for use in specific fields such as medicine, law enforcement, or technical careers. Differentiated courses can also have a variety of instructional formats, which might include learning opportunities not only in classes and face-to-face settings but also in mentoring relationships, internships in occupational settings, and varied uses of technology in and out of class.

Specific examples of differentiated instruction include content-based and theme-based approaches that focus on course content as well as on language forms (Brinton, Snow, and Wesche 2003); task-based, experiential learning, in which students work together to carry out projects in the school or community (Rosebery,

Warren, and Conant 1992); and multilevel instruction, in which teachers know the different language proficiency levels, educational backgrounds, and learning goals and needs of their students and adjust instruction accordingly. Instructional strategies in multilevel classes include use of learning contracts and portfolios with individual students, learning stations and centers, and peer support for learning (Hess 2001; Shank and Terrill 1995).

Differentiated instruction and courses for specific groups of learners can be labor intensive, particularly for new teachers. However, this challenge must be balanced against its many benefits, which include greater independence for students, a classroom climate that respects and capitalizes on student backgrounds and differences, and instruction that addresses the needs of a diverse student body. A critical need is for teachers in heritage language programs—K–12, university, community-based, and after-school—to receive training and support in effective instructional approaches and materials selection.

Conclusion

The United States needs more individuals who are comfortable with and proficient in more than one language and culture. To accomplish this, there is a need to restructure the ways that languages other than English are developed in this country. First, we need to understand the value, to individuals and groups and to society, of proficiency in more than one language. We then need to develop systematic methods for selecting languages to be taught; effective instructional programs, materials, curricula, and placement and progress assessments appropriate to the population of learners in our programs and to our national needs; systems for awarding credit for language study within and outside the education system; logically sequenced, articulated courses that move students from heritage community to K–12 to college and university programs; goals for high levels of proficiency for multiple purposes; and credentialing of and professional development for both native speakers of English and heritage language speakers as language educators. Finally, there is a need for greater collaboration among business and industry; government and nongovernmental agencies; and community-based, K–12, and university partners committed to building national language capacity. Through joint collaboration across all sectors of the nation, we have a historic opportunity to advance language maintenance and learning in the United States.

ACKNOWLEDGMENTS
The authors wish to thank the editors of this volume and two anonymous reviewers for their helpful comments on earlier drafts of this chapter and Emily Becketti and Dora Johnson of the Center for Applied Linguistics in Washington, D.C., for their review of and contributions to the chapter.

REFERENCES
American Council on the Teaching of Foreign Languages (ACTFL). 2006. *Standards for foreign language learning: Preparing for the 21st century.* 3rd ed. Yonkers, NY: National Standards in Education Project.
Asia Society. 2005. *Expanding Chinese language capacity in the United States.* Washington, DC. www.asiasociety.org/ (accessed September 25, 2007).

Baker, Colin, and Sylvia Prys Jones. 1998. *Encyclopedia of bilingual education and bilingualism.* Clevedon, UK: Multilingual Matters.

Brecht, Richard D., and Catherine W. Ingold. 2002. *Tapping a national resource: Heritage languages in the United States.* Center for Applied Linguistics: Washington, DC. www.cal.org/resources/digest/0202brecht.html (accessed September 25, 2007).

Brecht, Richard D., and William P. Rivers. 2000. *Language and national security in the 21st century: The role of Title VI/Fulbright-Hays in supporting national language capacity.* Dubuque, IA: Kendall/Hunt.

Brecht, Richard D., and A. Ronald Walton. 1994. National strategic planning in the less commonly taught languages. *Annals of the American Academy of Political and Social Science* 532:190–212.

Brinton, Donna M., Marguerite Ann Snow, and Marjorie Wesche. 2003. *Content-based second language instruction.* Ann Arbor: University of Michigan.

Brod, Richard, and Elizabeth B. Welles. 2000. Foreign language enrollments in United States institutions of higher education, Fall 1998. *Association of Departments of Foreign Languages Bulletin* 31:2.22–29.

Byrnes, Heidi. 2005. Introduction to special issue. *Modern Language Journal* 89:582–85.

Camarota, Steven A. 2005. *Immigrants at mid-decade: A snapshot of America's foreign-born population in 2005.* Washington, DC: Center for Immigration Studies. www.cis.org/articles/2005/back/405.html (accessed September 25, 2007).

Carreira, Maria. 2004. Seeking explanatory adequacy: A dual approach to understanding the term "heritage language learner." *Heritage Language Journal* 2:1. www.heritagelanguages.org/ (accessed September 25, 2007).

Committee for Economic Development. 2006. *Education for global leadership: The importance of international studies and foreign language education for U.S. economic and national security.* www.ced.org (accessed September 25, 2007).

Corson, David. 1999. Community-based education for indigenous cultures. In *Indigenous community-based education,* ed. Stephen May, 8–19. Clevedon, UK: Multilingual Matters.

Crystal, David, ed. 1987. *The Cambridge encyclopedia of language.* Cambridge, UK: Cambridge University Press.

Cummins, Jim. 2005. A proposal for action: Strategies for recognizing heritage language competence as a learning resource within the mainstream classroom. *Modern Language Journal* 89:585–92.

Edwards, J. David. 2006. *A new era for foreign languages.* Washington, DC: Joint National Committee for Languages/National Council for Languages and International Studies. www.languagepolicy.org (accessed September 25, 2007).

Evans, Bruce, and Nancy Hornberger. 2005. No Child Left Behind: Repealing and unpeeling federal language education policy in the United States. *Language Policy* 4:87–106.

Fishman, Joshua A. 1966. *Language loyalty in the United States.* The Hague, Netherlands: Mouton.

———. 1985. *The rise and fall of the ethnic revival.* Berlin: Mouton de Gruyter.

———. 2001. 300-plus years of heritage language education in the United States. In *Heritage languages in America: Blueprint for the future,* ed. Joy K. Peyton, Donald A. Ranard, and Scott McGinnis, 81–97. Washington, DC: Center for Applied Linguistics and Delta Systems.

Gambhir, Surendra. 2001. Truly less commonly taught languages and heritage language learners in the United States. In *Heritage languages in America: Blueprint for the future,* ed. Joy K. Peyton, Donald A. Ranard, and Scott McGinnis, 81–97. Washington, DC: Center for Applied Linguistics and Delta Systems.

Government Accounting Office. 2002. *Foreign languages: Human capital approach needed to correct staffing and proficiency shortfalls.* GAO-02-375. Washington, DC: Government Accounting Office.

Graddol, David. 2000. *The future of English?* London: British Council.

Grimes, Barbara F., and Joseph E. Grimes. 1996. *Ethnologue: Languages of the world.* 13th ed. Dallas, TX: SIL International.

Hess, Natalie. 2001. *Teaching large multilevel classes.* Cambridge, UK: Cambridge University Press.

Hornberger, Nancy H., and Shuhan C. Wang. Forthcoming. Who are our heritage language learners? Identity and biliteracy in heritage language education in the United States. In *Heritage language education: A new field emerging,* ed. Donna M. Brinton, Olga Kagan, and Susan Baukus. New York: Rutledge.

Interagency Language Roundtable. n.d. *ILR language skill level descriptions.* www.govt.ilr.org (September 26, 2007).

Kagan, Olga. 2005. In support of a proficiency-based definition of heritage language learners: The case for Russian. *International Journal of Bilingual Education and Bilingualism* 8:196–221.

Malone, Meg E., Benjamin Rifkin, Donna Christian, and Dora E. Johnson. 2005. *Attaining high levels of proficiency: Challenges for foreign language education in the United States.* CAL Digest. Washington, DC: Center for Applied Linguistics. www.cal.org/resources/digest/attain.html (accessed September 25, 2007).

Marcos, Kathleen M., and Joy Kreeft Peyton. 2000. *Promoting a language proficient society: What you can do.* Washington, DC: Center for Applied Linguistics. www.cal.org/resources/digest/0001 promoting.html (accessed September 25, 2007).

McGinnis, Scott. 2005. More than a silver bullet: The role of Chinese as a heritage language in the United States. *Modern Language Journal* 89:592–94.

McNulty, B. A. 2004. *McRel's balanced leadership framework: School leadership that works.* Paper presented at the Second Annual Delaware Policy and Practice Institute for School Leaders, Dover, June 29.

National Intelligence Council. 2004, December. *Mapping the global future: Report of the National Intelligence Council's 2020 project.* Author.

Olsen, Laurie, Jhumpa Bhattacharya, Mamie Chow, Ann Jaramillo, Dora Pulido, and Jesus Solorio. 2001. *And still we speak: The story of communities sustaining and reclaiming their languages and cultures.* San Francisco: California Tomorrow.

Partnership for 21st Century Skills. 2003. *Learning for the 21st century.* www.21stcenturyskills.org (accessed September 25, 2007)

Pratt, Mary Louise. 2003. Building a new public idea about language. *ADFL Bulletin* 34:509.

Rhodes, Nancy C., and Lucinda Branaman. 1997. *Foreign language instruction in the United States: A national survey of elementary and secondary schools.* Washington, DC: Center for Applied Linguistics.

Ricento, Thomas. 2005. Problems with the "language-as-resource" discourse in the promotion of heritage languages in the U.S.A. *Journal of Sociolinguistics* 9:348–68.

Rosebery, Ann, Beth Warren, and Faith Conant. 1992. Appropriating scientific discourse: Findings from language minority classrooms. *Journal of the Learning Sciences* 2:61–94.

Ruiz, Richard. 1984. Orientations in language planning. *NABE Journal* 8:2.15–34.

Sandrock, Paul, and Shuhan C. Wang. 2005. Building an infrastructure to meet the language needs of all children. *State Education Standard.* Journal of the National Association of State Boards of Education, 24–31.

Shank, Cathy, and Lynda Terrill. 1995. *Teaching multilevel adult ESL classes.* Washington, DC: Center for Applied Linguistics. www.cal.org/caela/esl_resources/digests/SHANK.html (accessed September 25, 2007).

Smolicz, Jerzy J. 1980. Personal cultural systems in a plural society. *Polish Sociological Bulletin* 50:2.21–34.

———. 1992. Minority languages as core values of ethnic cultures: A study of maintenance and erosion of Polish, Welsh, and Chinese languages in Australia. In *Maintenance and loss of minority languages,* ed. Willem Fase, Koen Jaspaert, and Sjaak Kroon. Amsterdam: John Benjamins.

Tomlinson, Carol Ann. 1999. *The differentiated classroom: Responding to the needs of all learners.* Alexandria, VA: Association for Supervision and Curriculum Development.

Toth, Carolyn R. 1990. *German-English bilingual schools in America: The Cincinnati tradition in historical context.* New York: Longman.

Ulrich, Amman. 2003. The international standing of German as an international language. In *Languages in a globalizing world,* ed. Jacques Maurais, and Michael A. Morris, 231–49. Cambridge, UK: Cambridge University Press.

U.S. Census Bureau. 1999. Mother tongue of the foreign-born population: 1910 to 1940, 1960, and 1970. www.census.gov/population/www/documentation/twps0029/tab06.html (accessed September 25, 2007).

———. 2001. *Census 2000 supplementary survey: Profile of selected social characteristics.* http://factfinder.census.gov/home/en/c2ss.html (accessed September 25, 2007).

———. 2005. *American Community Survey: Selected characteristics in the United States.* http://factfinder.census.gov/servlet/ADPTable?.html (accessed September 26, 2007).

Valdés, Guadalupe. 2000. Introduction. In *AATSP professional development series handbook for teachers K–16: Vol. 1. Spanish for native speakers,* 1–20. Orlando, FL: Harcourt College.

———. 2001. Heritage language students: Profiles and possibilities. In *Heritage languages in America: Blueprint for the future,* ed. Joy K. Peyton, Donald A. Ranard, and Scott McGinnis, 81–97. Washington, DC: Center for Applied Linguistics and Delta Systems.

———. 2005. Bilingualism, heritage language learners, and SLA. Opportunities lost or seized? *Modern Language Journal* 89:410–26.

Valdés, Guadalupe, Joshua Fishman, Rebecca Chávez, and Davis William Pérez. 2006. *Developing minority language resources: The case of Spanish in California.* Clevedon, UK: Multilingual Matters.

Van Deusen-Scholl, Nelleke. 2003. Toward a definition of heritage language: Sociopolitical and pedagogical considerations. *Journal of Language, Identity, and Education,* 2:211–30.

Wang, Shuhan C. 1996. Improving Chinese language schools: Issues and recommendations. In *A view from within: A case study of Chinese heritage community language schools in the United States,* ed. Xueying Wang, 63–67. Washington, DC: The National Foreign Language Center at the University of Maryland.

———. 1999. Crossing the bridge: A Chinese case from mother tongue maintenance to foreign language education. In *Mapping the course of the Chinese language field,* ed. Madeline Chu, 271–312. Monograph Series, Vol. 3. Kalamazoo, MI: Chinese Language Teachers Association.

———. 2004. *Biliteracy resource eco-system of intergenerational transmission of heritage language and culture: An ethnographic study of a Chinese community in the United States.* Ph. D. diss., University of Pennsylvania.

Wang, Xueying, ed. 1996. *A view from within: A case study of Chinese heritage community language schools in the United States.* Washington, DC: The National Foreign Language Center at the University of Maryland.

Welles, Elizabeth B. 2004. Foreign language enrollments in United States institutions of higher education, 2002. *ADFL Bulletin* 35:2–3.8–22.

Wiley, Terrence G. 1998. The imposition of World War I era English-only policies and the fate of German in North America. In *Language and politics in the United States and Canada,* ed. Tom Ricento and Barbara Burnaby, 211–41. Mahwah, NJ: Lawrence Erlbaum Associates.

———. 2001. On defining heritage languages and their speakers. In *Heritage languages in America: Blueprint for the future,* ed. Joy K. Peyton, Donald A. Ranard, and Scott McGinnis, 29–36. Washington, DC: Center for Applied Linguistics and Delta Systems.

———. 2005a. *Literacy and language diversity in the United States.* 2nd ed. Washington, DC: Center for Applied Linguistics.

———. 2005b. The reemergence of heritage and community language policy in the U.S. national spotlight. *Modern Language Journal* 89:594–601.

———. 2007. Beyond the foreign language crisis: Toward alternatives to xenophobia and national security as bases for U.S. language policies. *Modern Language Journal* 91:2.252–55.

———. Forthcoming. The foreign language "crisis" in the U.S.: Are heritage and community languages the remedy? *Critical Inquiry in Language Studies, 4:2.*

13

Language Diversity and the Public Interest

WALT WOLFRAM
North Carolina State University

> That's the good thing about dialects; anybody can do it as a hobby.
> —Taxi cab driver, Albuquerque, NM, January 5, 2006

THE CASUAL COMMENT of a chatty taxi cab driver to a van full of passengers attending the annual meeting of the Linguistic Society of America encapsulates the popular perception of dialect diversity in American society. On the one hand, language variation is so transparent that it can be assumed that most speakers of English, particularly native speakers but also speakers of English as a second language (Damann 2006), will readily notice these differences. On the other hand, the remark exposes the presumption common among nonlinguists that all language users can make accurate and informed observations about language diversity without any specialized expertise or formal training in the study of language. Not only do people notice language diversity, but also they feel free to make pronouncements about the status of these language differences, thus creating a good news–bad news scenario in which natural observations about language diversity are often accompanied by uninformed opinions espoused as fact.

Language ideology is among the most entrenched belief systems in society, rivaling religion, morality, and nationalism in terms of partisanship. In the United States, public controversies ranging from the so-called Ebonics controversy of a decade ago (Baugh 2000; Rickford 1999; Wolfram 1998) to the recent passage of Senate measures to make English the official language of the United States, a "common and unifying" tongue (Associated Press 2006), confirm the intensity of people's beliefs and opinions about the symbolic status of language diversity. Of course, such debates about language are hardly new; they have erupted periodically in the United States since the early attempts of John Adams to establish a national language academy for the new nation more than two centuries ago. At the same time, these debates affirm the pervasive level of public misunderstanding about language diversity. As a number of sociolinguists have now pointed out, this misinformation is not simply innocent folklore; its consequences extend from linguistic prejudice and legal discrimination against speakers of minority languages and dialects (Baugh 2003; Lippi-Green 1997) to the systematic educational misdiagnosis of speakers of dialects and languages other than the standard as "deficient" rather than legitimately "different" (Adger, Wolfram, and Christian 2007; Labov 1976).

It is difficult to imagine a period in the history of human development when issues of language diversity, linguistic subordination, and language loss have been more evident. Just a half-century ago, small, physically remote communities and socially subordinate groups were relatively invisible and inaudible within the dominant, mainstream society. Accordingly, the sociolinguistic status of these communities was unrecognized and their voices unheard. Language varieties often developed, lived, and died without extensive public attention. Today, images and voices can be beamed globally within milliseconds, and the naturalness of diversity is readily transparent. One of the obvious implications of the heightened awareness of language diversity is, of course, the increased need for education about the nature and implications of linguistic diversity.

Despite the significance of language in all spheres of public life and at least twelve years of compulsory education in English and/or language arts in U.S. public schools, there is still no tradition of English language studies that regularly includes the examination of language diversity as a regular part of this education. The need for informed knowledge about language diversity and the dissemination of essential knowledge to the public thus remains an imposing challenge for sociolinguists.

The Challenge of Public Education
Though many sociolinguists assume the social and educational relevance of knowledge about language diversity on some level, this position is certainly not a given in the field of linguistics. In fact, no less a figure than Noam Chomsky, well known for both his groundbreaking linguistic theories and his political activism, obviously compartmentalizes his professional life and his social life when he observes, "You're a human being, and your time as a human should be socially useful. It does not mean that your choices about helping other people have to be within the context of your professional training as a linguist. Maybe your training just doesn't help you to be useful to other people. In fact, it doesn't" (Olson, Faigley, and Chomsky 1991, 30). Chomsky's stance on the (ir)relevance of linguistics to public life is, of course, quite contrary to the position articulated in Labov's (1982, 172–73) principles of linguistic involvement where he maintains that linguists have an obligation to use their linguistic knowledge to address language-related social issues, including both the "principle of error correction" and the "principle of debt incurred." My personal position is that our professional training as sociolinguists should, in fact, be used to address language-related social and educational inequality. Language can be used as a tool of social oppression, and linguists can apply their knowledge to address some of the linguistic manifestations of social subordination.

In formal education, very few linguists and classroom teachers have been engaged in programs related to dialect diversity despite the fact that a number of national and state educational agencies affirm the importance of this educational practice. The standards of the National Council of Teachers of English (NCTE) specify that students are to "show a respect for and an understanding of diversity in language use, patterns, and dialects across cultures, ethnic groups, geographic regions, and social roles" (NCTE/NCATE 2003, Section 3.1.4) and the NCTE/NCATE (National Council for Accreditation of Teacher Education; 2003) standards for teacher training programs include objectives for the preparation of secondary teachers specifically related to language diversity. A couple of these are illustrated in table 13.1.

Despite the admirable NCTE/NCATE ideals, systematic educational curricula and teacher-training programs in compliance with the "acceptable" and "target" standards for learning outcomes related to knowledge about language diversity are virtually nonexistent in formal public education programs for students and are rarely incorporated into training programs for teachers.

Programs targeting language diversity are also conspicuously absent from informal public education, apart from the sporadic language controversies that afford linguists their proverbial fifteen minutes of media exposure for a "teachable moment." In the past two decades, only two national public TV documentaries related to language diversity have aired, *American Tongues* in 1986 (Alvarez and Kolker 1986) and *Do You Speak American?* in 2005 (MacNeil/Lehrer Productions 2005). The lack of public discussion about language diversity does not appear to be a simple matter of oversight. Instead, it affirms Fairclough's observations that beliefs about language need not be made explicit and that language ideology is most effective when its workings are least visible (Fairclough 1989, 85). The application of the correctionist model still dominates the public interpretation of language, and most public discussions of English dialect differences are still consumed by the discussion of the right and wrong way to use the English language. The sustained application of descriptive labels such as "correct," "proper," "right," and "grammatical" when speaking of language differences is hardly accidental; it directly reflects the underlying belief that nonmainstream and minority varieties of English are simply unworthy approximations of the standard variety. Indeed, the most persistent sociolinguistic challenge in all venues of public education continues to be the widespread application of the so-called principle of linguistic subordination (Lippi-Green 1997), in which the language of socially subordinate groups will be interpreted as linguistically inadequate and deficient by comparison with the language of socially dominant groups.

Socialized public opinion about the nature of language differences is only one side of the challenge of public education for linguists. The other side of the challenge is rooted in the entrenched value system within the professional academy. As with practically all academic disciplines, there is a clear-cut status hierarchy in which abstract, theory-driven research is most prestigious and applied research and public engagement have little academic capital. The research–application dichotomy is instantiated in professional valuation that extends from definitions of core and marginal areas of linguistic study in general to the establishment of criteria for promotion and tenure decisions on a local university level. In the traditional dichotomy between realms of professional responsibility designated as "research" and "service," service tends to be trivialized in faculty evaluations vis-à-vis research. The road to professional acclaim is rarely paved with public education activities, and it is unlikely to change in the immediate future. This reality brings us back to the fundamental rationale for considering sociolinguistic engagement. At the heart of the concern for public education about language diversity is a commitment to sociolinguistic equality

NCTE/NCATE Standards for the Initial Preparation of Teachers in Secondary English Language Arts

Section	Not Acceptable	Acceptable	Target
3.1.4	Show a lack of respect for, and little knowledge of, diversity in language use, patterns, and dialects across cultures, ethnic groups, geographic regional, and social roles	Know and respect diversity in language use, patterns, and dialects across cultures, ethnic groups, geographic regions, and social roles and show attention to such diversity in their teaching	Show extensive knowledge of how and why language varies and changes in different regions, across different cultural groups, and across different time periods and incorporate that knowledge into instruction and assessment that acknowledge and show respect for language
4.4	Show limited ability to create learning environments that promote respect for, and support of, individual differences of ethnicity, race, language, culture, gender, and ability	Create and sustain learning environments that promote respect for, and support of, ethnicity, race, language, culture, gender, and ability	Create opportunities for students to analyze how social context affects language and to monitor their own language use and behavior in terms of demonstrating respect for individual differences of ethnicity, race, language, culture, gender, and ability

rather than professional advancement and status. Some opportunities and obligations simply cannot be measured by their academic capital. I must confess that the blend of intellectual inquiry and social engagement has always been one of the most attractive aspects of sociolinguistics, and one of the reasons that language variation studies appealed to me decades ago. Nothing has changed in that regard. On a personal level, I fully agree with Chomsky's proclamation that "your time as a human should be socially useful," but I find his dissociation of language from public usefulness to be an ironically obscurantist position on language and life. Further, commitment to applying sociolinguistic knowledge in no way precludes the energetic scholar/teacher from academic success, as evidenced by the fact that some of the most respected research scholars in sociolinguistics have been dedicated to improving public understandings regarding linguistics and language diversity from the outset of their careers.

An Approach to Public Education

While sociolinguistics remains a small, chiefly invisible professional field, media presentations dominate the representation of American culture. In such a context, the public impact of sociolinguistics is severely limited if it does not effectively use a range of media venues to communicate its messages. The challenge, of course, is to present information in such a way that it is accessible to a broad-based audience of nonexperts. Though this may seem like an insurmountable challenge, Deborah Tannen's popular books (1990, 1995, 2006) and media presence on topics related to language and social interaction have taught us that it is not an unachievable ideal. There are also aspects of language variation that hold inherent intrigue for general audiences, and we need to start by connecting language diversity with this public curiosity.

My first experience with a television production executive at a public broadcasting station emphatically reinforced the value of audiovisual appeal in presentations featuring language diversity. As the executive surfed through the channels on the television in his office, he proclaimed, "You have ten to fifteen seconds to appeal to your potential audience; if you don't capture their interest during that time period, you've lost them." Five television documentaries later, I'm inclined to think that viewers enjoy seeing and hearing diverse language varieties in lively, natural settings and that they will stay tuned if language diversity is presented in a generally appealing format. The notion that media presentations about language should be entertaining may seem somewhat superficial to those of us accustomed to classroom instruction and academic presentations focused more on the transmission of knowledge than on entertainment, but language-related media productions do indeed compete with other types of entertainment, including professionally produced documentaries for educational television stations. One of the reasons that the documentary *American Tongues* (Alvarez and Kolker 1986) has been effective for two decades is due to its high entertainment value. The use of striking dialogue and humor also serves as a nonconfrontational method for opening up candid discussions about language attitudes. For more than a decade, I and my colleagues at the North Carolina Language and Life Project, housed at North Carolina State University, have produced a number of documentaries on language diversity in North Carolina. We have shown that it is quite possible to pique the public's interest in language differences if these are framed in appropriate, natural cultural settings. For example, when our documentary *Voices of North Carolina* (Hutcheson 2005) aired on the nonprofit, noncommercial Public Broadcasting Service (PBS) in North Carolina, it had a rating of 2.3 per 1,000 viewing homes, significantly higher than the regular programming in that time slot (generally less than 2). Perhaps just as importantly, viewers did not turn the program off; there was no significant drop-off in the early- and late-show audience share during the program, and the station received numerous follow-up e-mails about the viewers' fascination with the program. While a viewer rating of 2.3 may pale by comparison with the rating of a popular major network program, it does demonstrate that presentations about dialect diversity can compete at least within the restricted audience of potential viewers who watch public television.

The themes that frame our presentations of language diversity are typically related to cultural legacy and historical heritage. One can hardly study culture and history without considering the iconic role of language in the sociohistorical and sociocultural development of diverse populations. As one of our Cherokee language speakers put it in *Voices of North Carolina* (Hutcheson 2005), "Language is culture and culture is language." When language diversity is associated with other aspects of historical and cultural roots such as settlement history and traditions such as music and other folkways, a meaningful context for broader cultural and social issues is established for the presentation of language differences. As I often say to inquiring reporters and journalists in search of sound bytes for their articles on issues connected to language diversity, "It's never really about the language; it's always about cultural behaviors that are symbolically represented by language" (Associated Press 2006). Though the general public may neither understand nor value the seemingly myopic obsession of linguists with technical structural detail, it can appreciate and identify with the symbolic role that language plays in historical, regional, and cultural developments.

One of the attributes of our public outreach programs is the focus on the positive dimensions of language diversity rather than on the controversy sometimes associated with this topic. Despite deep-seated ideological differences between sociolinguistic axioms and public interpretations of language differences, we have taken the position that positively framed presentations of language differences hold a greater likelihood of being received by the public than the direct confrontation of seemingly unassailable ideologies. Some may question the ethics of what appears to be an avoidance strategy in confronting public misperceptions of language differences, but our interpretation is that the initial stage of public presentation is not the place for this discussion. Once a few fundamental sociolinguistic premises about language diversity are established inductively, such a discussion may become more meaningful. Furthermore, deductive linguistic proclamations about the legitimacy of language diversity rarely lead to the honest discussion of language differences. The most effective and permanent education always takes place when learners discover truths for themselves. Inductive, incremental education that begins with a positive, nonthreatening perspective on language diversity provides a much more effective opportunity for an authentic discussion of language issues than direct statements of opposition to deep-rooted positions. In the final analysis, we want our audiences to come to understand the truth about language diversity for themselves.

Venues of Public Education

Venues for public education extend from opportunistic-based, teachable moments that spontaneously arise from current news events involving language to planned programs that systematically target specific or broad-based public audiences. On a sporadic basis, sociolinguists are called upon by the media to provide perspectives and opinions on language-related stories. These stories may range from long-standing national debates about the adoption of English as the official language of the United States to local stories that involve comments or observations about language or dialect. The responses by linguists to such opportunities vary, from those who view these queries as a welcome opportunity for public education to those who dismiss these requests because they feel that such reporting, or news reporting in general, is superficial and unreliable. I personally think that these occasions offer public exposure that can raise public awareness of language issues if nothing else. When a prominent, nationally recognized linguist such as Deborah Tannen talks about the role of language in social interaction or when John Baugh talks about linguistic profiling on a national network news program, it paves the way for teachable moments in public education. I have, for example, effectively used the *20/20 Downtown* news program on linguistic profiling (ABC News 2002) and the subsequent U.S. Fair Housing Commission's sixty-second public advertisement (Ad Council 2003) about the role of linguistic profiling in housing discrimination as important illustrations of the subtle but significant role of language in discrimination with audiences that range from traditional classrooms to community-based civic groups.

Though news events involving language provide an opportunity for public education, such responses are typically reactive rather than proactive, and linguists have little control over the presentation format or the reduction of their input to a convenient, abbreviated sound byte. Our current proactive efforts have attempted to be more deliberate, detailed, and diverse, ranging from documentaries produced for public television to dialect awareness curricula for teachers and public school students.

Documentaries

Documentary productions of the North Carolina Language and Life Project have ranged from productions for local communities to those produced for general public television audiences, mostly for the state affiliate of PBS, or, in one case, PBS nationally. Some of our productions have focused exclusively on language (Blanton and Waters 1996; Hutcheson 2001, 2004, 2005), while others have followed local interests to the point of having little to do with language directly (Hutcheson 2006; Rowe and Grimes 2006). The documentary on Lumbee English titled *Indian by Birth: The Lumbee Dialect* (Hutcheson 2001) illustrates a documentary specifically focused on language, though it naturally frames this discussion within a cultural milieu, a regional setting, and a sociohistorical background. It includes a vignette on the ancestral language background of the Lumbee Indians and the English roots of Lumbee English, a sociocultural section about the symbolic cultural role of language in community life, a cognitive component that depicts some of the linguistic structures of the dialect, and an affective section about the attitudes, stereotypes, and misconceptions that often characterize the public perception of this ethnolinguistic variety. The objective is to educate the general public, including local community members, about the role of language in its community setting and the emblematic function of Lumbee English as a marker of socioethnic identity. The sociohistorical and sociocultural legacy of language is of particular significance on a local, community level as well as for outsiders who know little about the Lumbee as a Native American tribe. Language differences are presented in terms of cultural identity and historical heritage rather than language ideology, though issues of linguistic subordination are addressed in indirect ways.

One of our most successful documentaries on public television in North Carolina, *Voices of North Carolina,* provides an overview of a number of different language situations in the state. These include the status of the Cherokee language, an endangered Native American language, and the varieties of Spanish brought to North Carolina with the recent wave of Latino immigrants to the state in the last decade. Different regional dialects of English are also featured, including Outer Banks English and Appalachian English, along with ethnic varieties such as Lumbee English and African American English. It further features a vignette on language change in metropolitan areas of the South by comparing older, lifetime residents of Charlotte, North Carolina, with younger residents and outsiders who are now predominant in the city's population. As the promotional blurb reads, "Voices of North Carolina is a unique journey through the dialects and language of this diverse Southern state, from Hoi Toider speech on the Outer Banks to the Highland Speech of the Smoky Mountains" (Hutcheson 2005). In a strategic decision to provide credibility to the presentation, we enlisted William C. Friday, president emeritus of the University of North Carolina University system and arguably the most highly respected public figure in North Carolina, to narrate the documentary. The public television station, the state affiliate of PBS, was so impressed by the interest in the program that they offered a DVD of *Voices of North Carolina* as an incentive give-away item in their annual fund-raising campaign, a symbolic recognition of the public appeal of our documentary. To my knowledge, this is the only language documentary ever used in this way.

Although the North Carolina Language and Life Project has had the good fortune of having a highly creative, full-time videographer (Neal Hutcheson) to direct the production of our documentaries, it should be noted that some projects can be done on a modest budget by students who are interested in filmmaking and/or documentary production. In fact, the first documentary ever produced under the aegis of the North Carolina Language and Life Project was done by a couple of undergraduate students in a linguistics class who were more interested in documentary production than in linguistic analysis. They had no prior experience in filmmaking and production, no equipment, and no budget to carry out the project. We set up an independent study, borrowed equipment from the laboratory of the Communication Department at the university, and operated on a shoestring budget of less than fifteen hundred dollars, mostly for travel and supplies. Almost a decade later, their twenty-three-minute production, *The Ocracoke Brogue* (Blanton and Waters 1996), about the dialect spoken on Ocracoke Island, in the North Carolina Outer Banks islands, remains one of the most well-known and economically successful documentaries we have ever produced.[1] Furthermore, it has become a staple feature in the Ocracoke Preservation Society's museum, where it runs continuously whenever the museum is open to the public. Current digital video technology available at most universities makes these types of low-budget, public education projects even more accessible for student production.

Language Exhibits

The museum exhibit is another venue for the public presentation of language diversity. With the cooperation of community-based museums and preservation societies, we have now constructed three permanent museum exhibits that highlight language diversity in North Carolina. The exhibition at the museum of the Ocracoke Preservation Society includes panels on the history and development of the dialect, its current moribund status, and an illustrative list of some distinctive lexical items of the variety, along with the continuously playing documentary that is the center of the so-called Dialect Room at the museum.

We also constructed a permanent exhibit on Lumbee language for the Museum of the Native American Resource Center in Pembroke, North Carolina.[2] The exhibit, funded by a grant from the Informal Science Education program of the U.S. National Science Foundation, features four panels highlighting the ancestral Native American language heritage of the Lumbee, the development of their unique Lumbee English dialect, the representation of Lumbee identity through dialect, and the presentation of some distinctive lexical items of Lumbee English. The exhibit also includes an interactive, touch-screen monitor that allows visitors to select from a menu of two-minute video vignettes that range from segments on the development and status of Lumbee language to an interactive vocabulary quiz. In addition to visitors and community residents, each year thousands of schoolchildren in Robeson County visit the museum to view the exhibition.

A third exhibit was recently constructed in the gallery of the Outer Banks History Center located at the Lost Colony Festival Park on Roanoke Island, one of the most popular tourist attractions in North Carolina. This exhibit, titled "Freedom's Voice: Celebrating the Black Experience on the Outer Banks," is by far the most inclusive and extensive of our exhibitions, extending far beyond language variation on the Outer Banks. It includes images, a documentary (Sellers 2006), interactive audiovisuals, and artifacts and panels that highlight the Freedmen's Colony on Roanoke Island during the Civil War, African Americans' involvement in the maritime industry, and African Americans' role in education, religion, and community life on the Outer Banks. A half-dozen different listening stations feature the voices of local residents who were a part of our research study on language variation and change in Roanoke Island (Carpenter 2004, 2005). In an important sense, this exhibition combines history, culture, and language in narrating the story of the "other lost colony" on Roanoke Island. Exhibits such as these offer a permanent venue for public education that can be used in both formal and informal education. Such presentations can also be adapted or designed as virtual museums so that their education potential extends well beyond their local, physical community site.

Dialect Awareness Curricula

One of our most ambitious programs in public education involves the development of formal curricular materials on language diversity in the public schools. We have experimented with curricular programs in a number of communities throughout North Carolina and taught a program annually for more than a decade in the public school in Ocracoke. Unfortunately, formal education about dialect variation is still a relatively novel, and in some cases controversial, idea. Our pilot program has focused on a middle-school curriculum in social studies that connects with language arts study (Reaser 2006; Reaser and Wolfram 2006a, 2006b), but similar units might be designed for other levels of K–12 education as well. The curriculum is based on humanistic, scientific, and social science rationales and engages students on a number of different participatory levels. In the process, students learn about dialect study as a kind of scientific inquiry and as a form of social science research. The examination of dialect differences offers great potential for students to investigate the interrelation between linguistic and social diversity, including diversity grounded in geography, history, and cultural beliefs and practices. There are a number of creative ways in which students can examine how language and culture go hand-in-hand as they address language diversity. For example, in one of our lessons, we consider issues of language variation related to Native American groups. Students are shown two eight- to ten-minute video vignettes, one of the Cherokee Indians whose native language is currently endangered, and one of the Lumbee Indians whose native language has been lost for generations. As noted earlier, though their native language has been extinct since at least the 1800s, the Lumbee developed a unique variety of English that symbolically differentiates them from neighboring European American and African American populations. Through this curricular unit, students consider the loss and endangered status of many Native American languages, the symbolic culture-language connection, language revitalization efforts, and linguistic stereotyping. In the following reflective exercise from Reaser and Wolfram (2006b), students are asked to compare and contrast the different sociolinguistic and sociohistorical situations affecting the Cherokee and Lumbee tribes.

1. How have the histories of the Lumbee Native Americans and the Cherokee Native Americans been similar?
2. How have they differed?
3. Why have the Cherokee been able to preserve their native language whereas the Lumbee have lost theirs?
4. How does speaking a unique dialect of English differ from speaking a different language like Cherokee?
5. What role does language play in these two communities?

A comparable video vignette on African American English sets the stage for considering issues of language accommodation and style shifting, language and identity, and even the issue of regionality in African American English. In the following exercise, the students in the Ocracoke School start by considering their own speech, then consider the speech of African Americans in different situations based on a vignette extracted from the documentary *Voices of North Carolina* (from Reaser and Wolfram 2006a).

> You will see a vignette about language experience. Before you watch the video, answer the following questions:
>
> 1. Do you feel that you have to change the way you speak? Why?
> 2. When you change your speech, is it mostly conscious or unconscious? That is, do you have to think about it or does it just happen naturally?
>
> In the following video clip, you will see some African Americans from North Carolina who are proud of their dialect but also switch their speech to Standard English when they feel it necessary. As you watch the video, think about responses to the following questions:
>
> 1. Could you hear differences in the speech of individuals in different situations?
> 2. Could you tell which African Americans lived in cities and which lived in rural areas?
> 3. Are these African Americans aware of the fact that they change their speech or not?
> 4. Why do you think that they feel that they must change their speech in different situations?

One of the greatest advantages of a curriculum on dialects is its potential for tapping the linguistic resources of students' indigenous communities. In addition to classroom lessons, students learn by going into the community to collect current dialect data. In most cases, the speech characteristics of the local community should make dialects come alive in a way that is unmatched by textbook knowledge. Educational models that treat the local community as a resource to be tapped rather than as a liability to be overcome have been shown to be quite effective in other areas of language arts education, and there is no reason why this model cannot be applied to the study of dialects. A model that builds upon community strengths in language, even when the language is different from the norm of the mainstream educational system, seems to hold much greater potential for success than one that focuses exclusively on conflicts between the community language and school language.

Though we have had great success teaching a pilot program on dialect awareness in Ocracoke, the process of implementing a local dialect awareness program taught by classroom teachers without linguistic training is a different matter. However, the formal evaluation of the pilot version of a statewide dialect awareness program taught by regular classroom teachers (Reaser 2006) shows promising results. Reaser devised a pre- and postcurricular survey measure that included items related to both language knowledge and language attitudes. The plot of the pre- and posttest change for the twenty-item test is given in figure 13.1 (from Reaser 2006, 120).

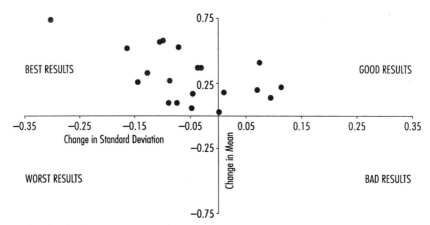

Figure 13.1 Plot of Change in Means and Standard Deviations by Statement
Source: Reaser 2006, p. 126.

All of the survey items showed change in the direction of increased tolerance toward and/or knowledge about dialect diversity, and seventeen of the twenty items indicated a significant change between pre- and postcurricular surveys. Furthermore, 98 percent of the 129 students who were involved in the pilot study reported that they learned something surprising about dialects that would change the way that they thought about language, and 88 percent of the students thought that the information in the curriculum was important for all students to study. With respect to language attitudes, 91 percent of the students found fault with people who were not aware that dialects show systematic patterning and that dialects have historical and cultural value.

We plan to continue piloting these materials with the eventual goal of providing such materials for all eighth-grade social studies students throughout the state. Our decision to target eighth-grade social studies is based in part on the fact that this level is dedicated to the study of state history and culture, a topic that dovetails neatly with the study of language variation over time and place (Reaser 2006; Reaser and Wolfram 2006a, 2006b). Our rationale for the choice is straightforward: an important component of the state's historical and cultural development is reflected in language diversity that ranges from the endangered or lost Native American languages in the state to the development of distinct regional and sociocultural varieties of English. Our program naturally fits in with the state's mandated course of study for eighth-grade social studies that includes the curricular themes of "culture and diversity," "historic perspectives," and "geographical relationships" (NC Public Schools Course of Study 2004). In addition, the dialect awareness curriculum helps fulfill social studies competency goals such as "Describe the roles and contributions of diverse groups, such as American Indians, African Americans, European immigrants, landed gentry, tradesmen, and small farmers to everyday life in colonial North Carolina" (Competency Goal 1.07) or "Assess the importance of regional diversity on the development of economic, social, and political institutions in North Carolina" (Competency Goal 8.04).

A further consideration in targeting the social studies curriculum is the fact that it tends to have more flexibility in terms of innovative materials than language arts, which is traditionally constrained by year-end standardized performance testing. The subject of language diversity may naturally merge with language arts and even science at points where the focus is on language analysis as a type of scientific inquiry. Students are not the only ones who profit from the study of dialect diversity. Teachers also find that some of their stereotypes about languages are challenged and that they become more knowledgeable and enlightened about language diversity in the process of teaching the curriculum. In fact, the classroom teachers who piloted the curriculum were among the most enthusiastic supporters of the curriculum because of the new knowledge they had received in teaching the curriculum to their students.

Popular Books and Articles

One of the most effective methods for disseminating information about language diversity is magazine articles and books for general audiences. Deborah Tannen has demonstrated that popular books about language use in social interaction can, in fact, be quite intriguing to the public and provide an effective venue for public education about the role of language in everyday life, though her popular recognition is certainly the exception rather than the rule among academics. One of the more successful popular writing ventures related to dialect diversity is *Spoken Soul: The Story of Black English* (2000), coauthored by sociolinguist John R. Rickford and his son, Russell John Rickford, then a journalist with the *Philadelphia Inquirer*. Winner of an American Book Award for outstanding literary achievement, this book demonstrates that the presentation of language diversity can, in fact, reach very broad audiences, though again it is notably the exception in sociolinguistic writing.

Our own efforts to write for general audiences have met with more modest, regional success. The book, *Hoi Toide on the Outer Banks: The Story of the Ocracoke Brogue* (Wolfram and Schilling-Estes 1997), received considerable publicity on the Outer Banks and the North Carolina mainland as well, and the first run of almost four thousand copies sold out within several months of its release. A decade after its original publication, the book is still available at tourist sites, in popular bookstores, lighthouses, and museums throughout the Outer Banks. Another trade book, *Fine in the World: Lumbee Language in Time and Place* (Wolfram et al. 2002), is distributed through the Museum of the Native American Resource Center in Pembroke and through the North Carolina State University Extension/Publications program. Though its appeal is fairly local, residents and teachers in Southeastern North Carolina have found its presentation of the role of dialect in Lumbee life informative. A more recent effort to educate the general public about the status of dialects in American society is the collection *American Voices* (Wolfram and Ward 2006), a book of brief essays for nonexperts written by linguists about both well-known and barely recognized dialects of American English that aims to demonstrate that everyone speaks a dialect and that they are all interesting and valuable. It attempts to translate the research of professional dialectologists and sociolinguists into brief, readable descriptions for those who are curious about language differences but have neither the background nor the desire to be professional linguists. The success of this attempt, coedited by a sociolinguist and career journalist, is yet to be determined, but it may ultimately have to do as much with its marketability as with its readability. Popular literary venues for the presentation of language diversity hold great potential, although the process of writing for such audiences is a formidable challenge that requires writing skills quite different from those typically exhibited by linguists. Furthermore, such ventures are probably best undertaken with professional journalists and/or by those accustomed to writing for popular audiences. Perhaps just as importantly, such literary ventures need aggressive, proactive marketing plans that ensure that they will reach their intended audience.

Dividends of Public Education

The processes and products described earlier are intended to be illustrative rather than exhaustive. Indeed, they should be complemented by other activities that range from regular radio and television shows about language diversity to other types of presentations for a wide array of public audiences. The public presentations of linguist Geoff Nunberg are exemplary in this respect; he does a regular feature on language on the NPR show "Fresh Air" and has written numerous commentaries for the Sunday *New York Times* "Week in Review" as well as for other periodicals. Nunberg has also been contributing regular letters from America to the BBC_4 series "State of the Union."

We have given presentations on the history of African American English for Black History Month and workshops on Lumbee English and the Cherokee language for Native American Heritage Month as part of human relations initiatives at organizations that extend from private corporations such as IBM and SAS to public federal and state agencies. Selecting venues for the presentation of information about language diversity is a challenge that should not be limited by past traditions or precedents of public education. In fact, it requires our most proactive and entrepreneurial endeavors. Mitigating the effects of the dominant language ideology and the widespread application of the principle of linguistic subordination involves long-term, proactive formal and informal reeducation on both local and broad-based levels.

Though it may seem like a relatively minor and incidental step, mainstreaming the discussion of language differences constitutes a major accomplishment in public education. For all of the natural interest that language naturally piques, there is little informed public discussion of language as a reflection of historical legacy, regional affiliation, and cultural background. Entire television channels are dedicated to history, geography, and the public interest, but language diversity is rarely represented despite its emblematic role in the development of peoples and cultures in time and place.

As language diversity becomes increasingly recognized in the public sector and the number of moribund language varieties increases precipitously, the sociolinguistic educational challenge increases proportionally. But education about these issues cannot be restricted to occasional, one-time, formal institutional presentations; the social and education stakes are simply too high. If, indeed, sociolinguists ever wish to change the current social order of linguistic discrimination and oppression, they must treat this challenge as central and essential to their sociolinguistic educational mission. Realistically, fundamental change in popular language ideology will take generations to effect and we must utilize the full range of formal and informal educational venues to tell the story of one of the most natural and essential manifestations of human behavioral differences.

ACKNOWLEDGMENTS
Support from NSF Grant ESI-0354711 is gratefully acknowledged for the production of the documentary *Voices of North Carolina* and NSF Grant SBR-9616331 for the construction of the exhibit on Lumbee language and the production of the documentary *Indian by Birth: The Lumbee Language.*

NOTES
1. All of the proceeds from the sale of this documentary go directly to the Ocracoke Preservation Society (OPS); in fact, the North Carolina Language and Life Project pays for the cost of production in order to maximize revenues for the OPS.
2. The exhibit on Lumbee language was originally one of thirteen exhibits selected for inclusion for the Launch Event for the Decade of Behavior displayed for the members of Congress in Washington, D.C., in 2001.

REFERENCES
ABC News. 2002. *20/20 Downtown.* February 6.

Ad Council. 2003. Accents. Washington, DC: National Fair Housing Alliance, U.S. Department of Housing and Urban Development, and Leadership Conference on Civil Rights Education Fund.

Adger, Carolyn, Walt Wolfram, and Donna Christian. 2007. *Dialects in schools and communities.* 2nd ed. Mahwah, NJ: Lawrence Erlbaum Associates.

Alvarez, Louis, and Andrew Kolker. 1986. *American tongues.* New York: Center for New American Media.

Associated Press. 2006. Debate on English has little to do with words. *Dallas Times,* May 21, 10A.

Baugh, John. 2000. *Beyond Ebonics: Linguistic pride and racial prejudice.* New York: Oxford University Press.

———. 2003. Linguistic profiling. In *Black linguistics,* ed. Cinfree Makoni, Geneva Smitherman, Arnetha F. Ball, and Arthur K. Spears, 155–68. London: Routledge.

Blanton, Phyllis, and Karen Waters. 1996. *The Ocracoke brogue.* Raleigh: North Carolina Language and Life Project.

Carpenter, Jeannine. 2004. *The lost community of the Outer Banks: African American speech on Roanoke Island.* MA thesis, North Carolina State University, Raleigh.

———. 2005. The invisible community of the lost colony: African American English on Roanoke Island. *American Speech* 80:227–55.

Damann, Melissa M. 2006. *ESL learners' perception of American dialects.* MA thesis, University of North Carolina, Chapel Hill.

Fairclough, Norman. 1989. *Language and power.* London: Longman.

Hutcheson, Neal, producer. 2001. *Indian by birth: The Lumbee dialect.* Raleigh: North Carolina Language and Life Project.

———, producer. 2004. *Mountain talk.* Raleigh: North Carolina Language and Life Project.

———, producer. 2005. *Voices of North Carolina.* Raleigh: North Carolina Language and Life Project.

———, producer. 2006. *The Queen family: Appalachian tradition and back porch music.* Raleigh: North Carolina Language and Life Project.

Labov, William. 1976. Systematically misleading data from test questions. *Urban Review* 9:146–69.

———. 1982. Objectivity and commitment in linguistic science. *Language in Society* 11:165–201.

Lippi-Green, Rosina. 1997. *English with an accent: Language, ideology, and discrimination in the United States.* London: Routledge.

MacNeil/Lehrer Productions. 2005. *Do you speak American?* Princeton, NJ: Films for the Humanities and Sciences.

NC Public Schools Standard Course of Study. 2004. Eighth-grade social studies. www.ncpublicschools
.org/curriculum/socialstudies/scos/2003-04/050eighthgrade.

NCTE/NCATE. 2003. *NCTE/NCATE program standards: Program for the initial preparation of teachers in secondary English language arts.* Urbana, IL: National Council of Teachers of English.

Olson, Gary A., Lester Faigley, and Noam Chomsky. 1991. Language, politics, and composition: A conversation with Noam Chomsky. *Journal of Advanced Composition* 11:1–35.

Reaser, Jeffrey L. 2006. *The effect of dialect awareness on adolescent knowledge and attitudes.* PhD diss., Duke University.

Reaser, Jeffrey L., and Walt Wolfram. 2006a. *Voices of North Carolina: Language and life from the Atlantic to the Appalachians, instructor's manual.* Raleigh: North Carolina Language and Life Project.

———. 2006b. *Voices of North Carolina: Language and life from the Atlantic to the Appalachians, student workbook.* Raleigh: North Carolina Language and Life Project.

Rickford, John R. 1999. *African American English: Features, evolution, and educational implications.* Malden, MA: Blackwell.

Rickford, John R., and Russell J. Rickford. 2000. *Spoken soul: The story of Black English.* New York: John Wiley & Sons.

Rowe, Ryan, and Andre Grimes. 2006. *This side of the river: Self-determination and survival in Princeville, N.C.* Raleigh: North Carolina Language and Life Project.

Sellers, James. 2006. *If they could cross the creek: The freedmen's colony of Roanoke Island.* Raleigh: North Carolina Language and Life Project.

Tannen, Deborah. 1990. *You just don't understand: Women and men in conversation.* New York: Ballantine.

———. 1995. *Talking from 9 to 5: Women and men at work.* New York: Quill.

———. 2006. *You're wearing that? Understanding mothers and daughters in conversation.* New York: Random House.

Wolfram, Walt. 1998. Language ideology and dialect: Understanding the Ebonics controversy. *Journal of English Linguistics* 26:108–21.

Wolfram, Walt, Clare Dannenberg, Stanley Knick, and Linda Oxendine. 2002. *Fine in the world: Lumbee language in time and place.* Pembroke, NC: Museum of the Native American Resource Center, UNC-Pembroke.

Wolfram, Walt, and Natalie Schilling-Estes. 1997. *Hoi toide on the outer banks: The story of the Ocracoke brogue.* Chapel Hill: University of North Carolina Press.

Wolfram, Walt, and Ben Ward, eds. 2006. *American voices: How dialects differ from coast to coast.* Oxford: Blackwell.

Afterword

14

At What Cost? Methods of Language Revival and Protection

Examples from Hebrew

ELANA SHOHAMY
Tel Aviv University

THE THEME of this volume is "sustaining linguistic diversity: endangered and minority languages and language varieties"; thus most chapters focus on how to revive and protect languages that are perceived to be "endangered." This chapter takes a different approach, discussing how such efforts can in fact entail oppressive, draconic, colonializing, and monopolizing methods. Such methods or mechanisms implicate personal rights, ethicality, morality, and freedom of speech. The act of reviving and protecting languages is deeply embedded in ideologies, beliefs, and political factors (Schieffelin, Woolard, and Kroskrity 1998); thus it can demand high costs from the individuals required to comply with the concomitant regulations, which are often in contradiction to daily practices and personal beliefs. While language revival and protection may perpetuate the goals and ideologies of a "nation" or a collective group, it may also lead to supremacy and domination of some groups while marginalizing others. Further, such language ideologies often linger long after the languages concerned are safe and well established, and oppressive acts are justified in the name of ongoing protection.

The first part of this chapter assesses the status of the Hebrew language in Israel today and is followed by a brief survey of its historical development. Next, I outline the methods and mechanisms that were employed in the process of reviving and protecting Hebrew in one Jewish town in Palestine in the late 1930s and early 1940s. The third section of the chapter raises questions about these methods in terms of their cost, ethicality, and justification and their relevance to other communities engaged in language revival.

Hebrew in Israel Today

Hebrew in Israel today is a very vital language; its status is solid and its use is broad. It is a dynamic language, as evident from its widespread use in private and public places; the large number of Hebrew books, newspapers, media, theater, and art; and its dominance as a language of instruction in most schools. It is the main language of

Israel and the one with highest prestige and status within the multilingual and multi-cultural society of 7 million people.

Most of the Arabs living in Israel (about 20 percent of the total Israeli population) use Arabic (Modern Standard and dialects) as their community languages and the language of instruction in schools but learn Hebrew from a very early age in school and beyond (Amara and Mar'i 2002). Immigrants from the former Soviet Union make up another 20 percent of the total population; they have been arriving in Israel mostly since the early 1990s and use Russian and other languages of their region of origin. Upon their arrival in Israel they are quick to acquire Hebrew (Spolsky and Shohamy 1999). Other immigrants use Amharic, Spanish, French, and a variety of other languages, and they too learn Hebrew once in Israel. The Ultra Orthodox Jews use Yiddish as their main language but have high proficiency in Hebrew. Further, the past decade has witnessed the arrival of a large number of non-Jewish foreign workers (about two hundred thousand) who use a variety of other languages such as Spanish, Tagalo, Chinese, Bulgarian, Romanian, and Polish as well as a number of African languages and acquire a basic variety of Hebrew. Hebrew in Israel today, then, is prominent, dominant, and prestigious and serves as a lingua franca for all these different language groups.

A closer examination of Israel's language policy using the three categories proposed by Spolsky (2004), *ideology, management,* and *practice,* makes it clear that ideologically speaking, Hebrew is viewed as a central language associated with the Jewish state. Thus Jewish immigrants arriving in Israel are expected to acquire Hebrew as fast as possible so that they can integrate into the Jewish state. Adults are expected to acquire Hebrew through *Ulpanim* (intensive Hebrew schools) that teach both the Hebrew language and Israel-nationalistic themes (Kuzar 2001). All immigrant children are submersed into Hebrew in schools, as all schools in Jewish areas use Hebrew as the only medium of instruction. However, there are cases where immigrants themselves get organized and offer courses for teaching Russian, mostly in after-school programs, although these are of limited scope despite an educational language policy of 1996 that encouraged the teaching of immigrant languages. Overall, then, Hebrew is viewed as the main language of Jews in Israel and as a symbol of national membership, with some declared tolerance to maintaining other languages (Spolsky and Shohamy 1999).

In terms of language management, two types of policy exist. At the national level, both Hebrew and Arabic are considered official languages. In terms of education, a new educational policy was introduced into the Israeli educational system in 1996 that requires native Hebrew-speaking Jews to learn Hebrew, English, and Arabic in public schools, as well as community, heritage, or world languages (e.g., "3+"). Immigrant children obtain help in learning Hebrew and are expected to function in the listed languages as soon as possible. The policy is similar in its application to the Arab school systems. But in different order: Arabic, Hebrew, English.

In terms of practice, Hebrew is the most dominant language, used in all domains of life and as a lingua franca for those for whom it is not the first language. While English is very popular (e.g., in academics, commerce, and the media), and Arabic and Russian are spoken by large groups, it is Hebrew that has the highest practical value and visibility. Further evidence of the vitality of Hebrew and English in relation to other languages can be drawn from a study documenting the linguistic landscape of Israel that points to the dominance of Hebrew as the main language of the public space in both Jewish and Arab locations in Israel. In Arabic-speaking communities Hebrew follows Arabic, and in Jewish areas English follows Hebrew with little representation of Arabic (Ben-Rafael et al. 2006).

Historic Development

While Hebrew is vital, vibrant, dynamic, and dominant in Israel today and its hegemony fully accepted and unchallenged, this has not always been the case. Just a hundred years ago Hebrew was considered practically a dead language. While it has always been used as a language of texts, prayer books, and the Bible, there were few native speakers, and only a few people could use Hebrew as a spoken vernacular. Thus the story of Hebrew is often referred to as a case of "successful revival" or of "Reversing Language Shift" (Fishman 1991; Harshav 1993). Multiple narratives attempt to explain both the *how* and the *why* of Hebrew revival (Harshav 1993; Karmi 1997). It has been constructed mostly in mythological terms, perceived as a "linguistic miracle" or as a case of "Jews being very stubborn." Some view it as a natural phenomenon: when people came to Palestine from many different countries and were seeking a common language, Hebrew was familiar to many as a textual language and thus a "natural" choice. Others wonder whether it is in fact a case of "language revival" or rather a "re-vernacularisation" (Ben Rafael 1994); after all, many Jews were already reading Hebrew and reciting it in prayers. Skepticism persists regarding how widespread the use of Hebrew was in different periods during the revival process, the nature of the language, the varieties, the actual levels of proficiency of those who claimed to have spoken it, and whether it was really subtractive (taking over home languages), additive (used in a bilingual way, home languages *and* Hebrew), or a hybrid (home languages along with Hebrew in mixed ways).

Historically, until the destruction of the First Temple (587 B.C.), Jews living in the land of Israel spoke mainly Hebrew. The impact of Aramaic increased during the Babylonian exile and following the Jewish exile after the Roman destruction of the Second Temple (70 A.D.), when Hebrew lost its function as a vernacular and was mainly reserved for literary-religious usage. Jews developed trilingual-multilingual patterns of some Jewish languages, territorial language(s), and reading of Hebrew texts, although this was mostly restricted to men.

Early steps of Hebrew revival as a vernacular began in Europe in the nineteenth century, as early as 1856, through the *Haskalah,* an intellectual movement that sought to expand traditional Judaism to a secular domain and to appropriate the use of Hebrew, considered a sacred language until then, for the purposes of secular and national ideologies (Ben-Rafael 1994). This movement gained force upon the arrival of waves of Jewish immigrants in Palestine, along with strong activism in the different Jewish congresses. The spoken languages of the Jews who were living in Palestine at the time were local Arabic dialects and a variety of Jewish languages— Ladino, Judeo Arabic, and Yiddish.

The revival of Hebrew in what was later to be Israel was part of a movement to create a nation for the Jews based on common history and kinship. Initially, Hebrew was rivaled by Yiddish, but the Zionist territorial ideology supported Hebrew and viewed Yiddish as a language symbolizing the past. Thus, while in the Tshernovits conference of 1906 a resolution was passed proclaiming Yiddish as a Jewish national language alongside Hebrew, in other Jewish congresses there was strong promotion of Hebrew, as in the Seventh Zionist Congress of 1905 that adopted the majority view that the educational system in Eretz-Israel should be of Hebrew character, and in the tenth and eleventh Zionist congresses (1911, 1913) that affirmed the exclusive use of Hebrew.

The term "Hebrew," rather than "Jewish" or "Zionist," was adopted to signify detachment from the past and the re-creation of a "new Jew," a "Hebrew-man" in a new homeland. Hebrew went through a period of secularization of lexical items symbolizing this new construct. Some time between 1906 and 1916 the revival of Hebrew was declared to be completed; there were claims that by 1914 it was the exclusive language of instruction, and by 1920 it was used to signify the reinvented Jewish community. The validity of these ideologically based claims remains a point of debate. For example, Chaver (2004) argues that these claims were driven by leaders of the *Yishuv* (the Jewish community living in Palestine during the British Mandate): "The Yishuv was beginning to construct a mainstream narrative that could not concede the existence of an alternative culture—or even subculture—marked by language because such an admission would cast doubt on the total success of the project" (16).

Questions also arise concerning the boundaries between language revival and language protection. For some, language revival is never completed, given ongoing immigration and a perceived need for language support. By the end of the 1930s, there seemed to be a strong feeling that aggressive measures were needed in order to protect the language, especially with the arrival of waves of German Jewish immigrants. The Yishuv had strong fears regarding the destiny and vulnerability of Hebrew.

In terms of the ideology of languages in the 1930s, Hebrew was deeply rooted within the Zionist movement. This meant that immigrants arriving in Palestine were expected to learn Hebrew and drop their home languages, as the latter were perceived as threats to the revival of Hebrew. The main targets were the German language, used by the immigrants arriving from Germany, and Yiddish, widely used by Jews coming from Eastern Europe (Segev 1999). According to Zionist ideology, Hebrew needed to be made the dominant language of the Zionist community of the Yishuv and to serve as a uniting force for creating a homogenous nation; such aims could not be reached if Jews continued to use the foreign languages (Harshav 1993; Shohamy 1994).

In terms of language management, three languages were considered official during these years: English, the language of British mandate; Hebrew, recognized as official since 1917 and accepted as one of the official languages of the Jewish community of the Yishuv; and Arabic, considered official for the Arab population residing in Palestine. Examples of the use of these three languages can be found in many official documents of the time, such as stationeries of the Mandate, as well as public signs.

In terms of language practices, a large number of languages were used in Palestine in those years, reflecting the diverse countries of origin of the Jews arriving in Palestine—Yiddish, German, Polish, Russian, among many others. However, Hebrew was the only language imposed with a strong ideological backing (Ben-Rafael 1994; Spolsky and Shohamy 1999). Young immigrants such as Shoshana Goldberg, who arrived in Palestine from New York City in 1932 at age fifteen, provide insights into the language situation at the time:

> When I was a child I was bilingual in Yiddish and English. But when I came to Israel I had trouble because nobody spoke Yiddish, it was against all the regulations and all the rules to speak another language except Hebrew. It is all from being very very stubborn. The people here were very stubborn. They did not allow anything else but Hebrew, and I think that is the reason that Hebrew took over. In school the classes were in Hebrew, Geometry was done in Hebrew, all subjects were in Hebrew. My parents got me a very good teacher, Mr. Bartov, and he taught me day after day after day.

Thus for immigrants the message was clear that they were required to switch to Hebrew and Hebrew only, as this was the language of the land and the one associated with the creation of the new nation. But how was that message delivered? What mechanisms were used? The remainder of this chapter presents a preliminary study examining the mechanisms to impose Hebrew in the example of one town in Palestine.

The Study and Setting

Shohamy (2006) introduces the notion of *mechanisms* to refer to overt and covert methods and devices used as mediators between language ideology and language practice. The view of language policy is thus expanded to being interpreted through different mechanisms used implicitly and explicitly to create de facto policies. Specifically, then, mechanisms are devices used as means for affecting, creating, and perpetuating language policies. The focus of the data discussed in this chapter is on a number of mechanisms used to perpetuate the Hebrew language ideology and turn it into practice.

The findings reported here are based on documents located in the municipal archive of Raanana, a town in the center of Israel, north of Tel Aviv. Raanana was founded in 1922 and is typical of towns founded in Palestine in the 1930s in that it consisted of Jewish immigrants arriving in Palestine mostly from Europe and the United States at the time that it was established. As documents show, residents of Raanana used Yiddish, German, Polish, Russian, English, Hungarian, Latvian, Romanian, Yemenite, and Jewish languages such as Jewish Arabic and Ladino. The documents include official letters, manifests, and instructions that pertain to the management of the Hebrew language in town. These were addressed mostly to the mayor and to other town officials associated with language planning. They include, for instance, correspondence between the mayor and other officials in the municipality (i.e., those in charge of language classes) as well as various organizations of the Yishuv who took active roles in Hebrew language management.

Key Mechanisms

The mechanisms identified in the documents include rules and regulations, the establishment of a central council for Hebrew imposition, control of public space, monitoring of language proficiency at home, and monitoring of language learning and other activities.

Strict Rules and Regulations for Hebrew Language Behaviors

One document published by The National Council (Vaad Leumi) of the Jewish Community of Palestine titled *The Directive for Linguistic and Culture Protection* (tzav hitgonenut ha-mo'atza ha-merkazit le-hashlatat ha-'ivrit ba-yishuv), dated August 22, 1939, stipulates specific language behaviors to be practiced by residents of the Yishuv. The document begins with a general statement demanding that the Yishuv commit itself to total acceptance, exclusive use, and the dominant authority of "our" Hebrew language. It states that people should be forced to speak Hebrew, and only Hebrew, at home, out of the home, and at the workplace, in private and public locations. It calls for guarding the purity of the Hebrew language in each and every forum, in sermons, lectures, and synagogues that must be carried out exclusively in Hebrew. The Hebrew language should be studied immediately after immigration so that speaking the language will become a regular habit, even in cases when the language proficiency is very elementary. The document further calls for the administration of Hebrew language tests to assess the Hebrew proficiency of all adults in order to establish the extent to which they can use the language and that these test results should be used as a requirement for employment. The document also specifies the need to change the private names of people into Hebrew names and the total eradication of foreign newspapers. It mentions the need to require the inclusion of Hebrew dates in all public announcements, to conduct all correspondence exclusively in Hebrew, to address people in Hebrew only, and to establish Hebrew courts. All the stipulations included in the document are framed within a national and patriotic justification of the need to rescue Jews and contribute to the establishment of the independence of Israel.

Establishing Central Councils for the Imposition of Hebrew

In 1941 a formalized organization was established by the Central Council for the Community of Israel (ivrit ha-va'ad ha-le'umi le-khneset yisra'el be-eretz yisre'el), the purpose of which was to impose Hebrew language use on the Yishuv. The group's name was The Central Committee for the Imposition of the Hebrew Language ('ha-mo'atza ha-merakezet le-hashlatat ha-'ivrit ba-yishuv). Three manifests were located in the municipal archive of Raanana that provide insight into the planned as well as actual activities of the group in 1941. The documents list sets of activities, stipulations, actions, and demands for specific actions required of the Jewish public regarding the use of the Hebrew language. These documents provide evidence not only of the breadth of domains but also of intended and actual activities the group was engaged in. They were sent to the mayor of the town of Raanana requesting that he become engaged in Hebrew language activism in his town.

A document dated February 2, 1941, begins with a general statement regarding the need for planned and organized actions and the urgency of upgrading the prestige of the Hebrew language in the population. It then moves to specific plans of activities—the establishment of a "Hebrew day" in each and every town; the nomination of "Hebrew agents" to be placed in industries, professional organizations, factories, hospitals, and so on; and the need to eradicate all non-Hebrew newspapers and change all the names of streets to Hebrew ones. The document then moves into very minute details such as the need to change the text on chocolate wrappers into Hebrew.

In a similar manner, a document from February 11, 1941, published by the same organization, begins with an ideological statement about the "tragic" situation that "the region is being loaded with foreign words." It then defines two main goals for the organization: to fight against the use of other languages in the Yishuv and eradicate these languages, and to engage in the teaching of Hebrew to those who do not know it. Both goals are in fact seen as complementing one another: "If we eradicate the other languages, the status of Hebrew will be raised." The document continues with specific actions for plans that the mayor needs to pursue, such as the identification of specific targets, to provide an updated report on the progress of achieving very specific language goals. Examples include the following:

- Become engaged in propaganda to create "forced" motivation: "create a situation in which people will aspire to learn Hebrew."
- Advertise Hebrew slogans to the public such as "A nation that does not speak its language lacks culture," or "Hebrew-man, speak Hebrew."
- Organize regional meetings demanding that institutions nominate Hebrew language inspectors/monitors.
- Nominate Hebrew agents, that is, people that can monitor language behavior with activities such as "to return letters written in foreign languages to the senders" or "monitor that a doctor does not use Hebrew when he is checking his patient or when he is operating on him." This is justified in the following way: "Our main issue is not whether we intrude into people's lives but how to make Hebrew a language that people know," implying that the goal justifies any means. The number of existing agents is reported: "Today, we have about 130 such agents," and it is concluded that "the fact that hospitals went along and nominated monitors indicates that they see its value."

One section of the document includes a list of all towns where violations of the Hebrew language occur, stating that the violators had received warnings from the organization and that their names were publicized. Examples include the following:

Non-Hebrew Newspapers. "The plan is to eradicate all non-Hebrew newspapers by specifying an action plan for 1 year: First 6 months, 50% German, 50% Hebrew, then 75% Hebrew, 25% German and after one year, the paper cannot be published at all." Resistance to this stipulation is described: "Yet, the German owners refuse claiming that 'why should the Yishuv impose and determine the destiny of thousands of German speakers?'"

Theater. "Since theater is still being conducted in other languages, the organization demands from the municipality of Tel Aviv not to open the doors of the halls if the shows are to be presented not in the Hebrew language."

The document continues with a list of other groups and organizations whose behavior must be changed so that they align with the Hebrew goals, as in the case of making Polish-speaking schools deny the acceptance of Jewish children.

A document from August 27, 1941, discusses more radical and aggressive plans, specifically documenting language violations in public places. The format used is (a) identifying the language violators, (b) describing the language violations, and (c) enforcing precise strategies for language repair. Examples include the following:

School Principles.   Violation: "some courses are taught via English." Repair: "He promised to stop it."

The Carmel Committee.   Violation: "conducting correspondence not in Hebrew." Repair: "You must stop"; "He said he will write to us only in Hebrew in all his letters."

The Mayor of Tel Aviv.   Violation: "holding activities without emphasizing Hebrew purity."

The National Orchestra.   Violation: "Players are not using Hebrew in rehearsals."

A Chocolate Factory.   Violation: "using 'foreign languages' during production while the language must be Hebrew only."

An Advertising Company.   Violation: "We detected one person that published a diet book for sick people not in Hebrew," and "using German in the shop windows."

The Opera.   Violation: "advertising the show in a bilingual version and even adding advertisements, half of which were in English." Repair: "They agreed not to do it any more."

A Café Owner in Jerusalem.   Violation: "saying words that offended the Hebrew language."

Controlling the Public Space

One of the arenas identified as crucial for exercising influence regarding the Hebrew language was the public space, referring mostly to the use of Hebrew on public signs, especially of shops. In the August 1941 document, there is a specific reference to a range of activities and close monitoring and documentation of the public space, describing the efforts of young people who were given the task of documenting the languages of signs on shops in all major Jewish towns in Palestine: "We recruited groups of young people in Haifa to check the number of signs that are not using Hebrew. This is what we found: 128 signs need corrections, 21 signs did not include Hebrew in the first place, on 25 signs Hebrew was not given enough space, 32 signs used 'foreign letters,' on 55 signs other languages appear (46 in German, 6 in French, 1 in Polish, 1 in Russian, 1 in Czech), in 2 signs Hebrew was written with mistakes." The document included strategies for repair: "We asked them to correct and remove all signs that had problems, but especially those in German."

There were also attempts to create laws about the use of Hebrew in the public space involving officials from the British mandate, with numerous references to such laws in other towns: "We began conducting trials for the violators according to the new 'signs' law. Lots of violations in Jerusalem. We are negotiating with the mayor the introduction of a new law like the law they established in Tel Aviv. We are involving the General Council in these negotiations. It is clear that the council is not interested in multiple languages as these make the streets and the public space look very ugly."

Monitoring Language Proficiency at Home

The level of Hebrew language proficiency was also closely monitored by conducting face-to-face oral language tests. One of the documents located in the archives, dated June 21, 1939, is an announcement posted in major newspapers in Palestine regarding the home visits to assess people's Hebrew language proficiency. People are asked to cooperate with the testers: "In Raanana: Today and tomorrow, couples of volunteers will visit you in your homes to conduct a census for the purpose of counting the number of people who know the Hebrew language. You are requested to welcome these couples using good manners." This is signed by the cultural committee of the municipality.

Monitoring Language Learning Activities through the Mayor

Teaching was a major activity for spreading and protecting the Hebrew language. Sessions were carried out with close monitoring by the central Yishuv authorities. This top-down policy meant that information on the local town activities was constantly being reported to the central authorities of the Yishuv. Thus, in the case of the town of Raanana, the mayor was expected to take an active role in the imposition of Hebrew and to act as the mediator between the central authorities and the residents of the town regarding language teaching. He was expected to report about each and every activity to the central authorities, such as Hebrew language proficiency of store owners, neighborhoods, private people, organizations, and local industries and how policies were being carried out and implemented.

In fact, many of the documents provide direct evidence of these ongoing exchanges. One document that displays the nature of the interaction is a letter dated June 2, 1941, sent by the representative of the National Council of the Jewish Community in Palestine to the mayor of Raanana, Mr. Ostrovsky. While the mayor is being complemented about the intensive activities of teaching Hebrew and culture in comparison to other towns, he is also requested to still do much more: "I am not saying that you are doing everything in order to provide cultural services, but in comparison to the apathy and carelessness of other places with regards to language and culture you are doing well. It is a great pleasure to cooperate with you, but we are asking from ourselves a much higher awareness and activities."

The tight control and monitoring by the central authorities of the teaching activities can also be gleaned from documents that were sent to the mayor demanding exact and accurate information about all language activities. This is followed by a series of letters sent by officials of the town of Raanana back to the central authorities reporting in very precise terms the language activities in the town, specifically, the number of classes, number of students, names of teachers, as well as the content covered in each course.

Violent Acts.   Additional mechanisms include the establishment of societies of Hebrew "loyalists" who assisted the various committees of the Hebrew language protection/imposition in spreading Hebrew materials and documents and disseminating language propaganda. Some of these groups had reputations for their aggressive and violent acts. Mrs. Goldberg, for instance, recalls "Jews who were beaten in the streets by other people because they spoke Yiddish, and forced to speak Hebrew."

One well-known organization was the 'Gdud Meginei Ha-safa (The Militia for the Protection of the Language), established in the 1930s and based mostly in Tel Aviv. Although no pertinent records were found so far in the Raanana municipal archives, other sources (Karmi 1997; Segev 1999) have documented the aggressive and violent activities of the group in forcing people to speak Hebrew, especially in public places.

Mr. Gabriel, one of the interviewees for this project, was a member of the 'Gdud in 1930. He was ten years old when he was recruited. In his words:

> We would get on a bus, listen to people speak, and if we heard someone not speaking Hebrew we would hang a ribbon on their shirt that reads: "Hebrew-man, speak Hebrew." And I would do other activities as well that I regret today. For example, there was a store in Tel Aviv, called Barta, so we would throw stones at the window of the store and broke the glass because they displayed names of products which were in foreign words and not in Hebrew and products which were not produced "in the land." And there were other things that it is not very pleasant to remember now. There was a concert hall, Yasha Heifetz, and they would show plays in Yiddish, so we, members of the *Gdud,* interrupted the show; we would yell and scream while the show was going on and made so much noise that we managed to "spoil" the show and they had to stop the show. The main thing was to spoil the show.

As this interview also illustrates, the imposition of the Hebrew language was part of an ideology of Zionist nationalism. Thus similar impositions were established regarding buying only "local products." One of the documents found reports about Mrs. Tishler, who was condemned for buying eggs that were not sold by Jewish producers. In the letter she is being threatened and warned not to repeat such bad acts: "If you are caught again not buying local products, you will be fined and this act will be advertised in public." Similar impositions were made concerning other products (e.g., bananas) but also for employing non-Jewish workers (i.e., Arabs).

Discussion: Hebrew Language Ideology, Zionist Ideology, and the Costs of Language Revival

These analyzed documents suggest a system of language control via a variety of mechanisms aimed at spreading and imposing Hebrew as the single language in all domains, private and public. These documents point to a subtractive ideology whereby the spread of Hebrew implied the eradication of all languages of the people of the Yishuv; these other languages were perceived as competitors, intrusions, threats, interferences, and enemies of Hebrew and therefore needed to be suppressed. There was clearly a policy of "either-or" in place that implied "Hebrew only" speech, "Hebrew only" newspapers, "Hebrew only" signs, and "Hebrew only" in the public as well as private domains. The documents reveal the mechanisms through which the "Hebrew only" policy was introduced, imposed, managed, and controlled. The goal of reviving Hebrew was so important that all means were justified, no questions asked. The documents point to the use of strategies of threats, sanctions, and insistence on actual repairs, of insults and humiliation, of blaming and shaming of acts that were perceived as a "violation" of the expected ideology and practices. These actions were not limited to the public space but entered the private and the personal, as can be gleaned from the imposition of the informal language tests at home. It is clear that the revival and protection of the Hebrew language was an integral component of a total Zionist ideology and campaign, a whole package of symbols used for collective identities, membership, patriotism, belonging, and the creation of a nation.

Hebrew is certainly a success story in terms of the revival and maintenance of a language. Yet it is difficult to prove that the mechanisms reported in this chapter in fact brought about the revival of Hebrew. Perhaps given a variety of other conditions, Hebrew would have been revived anyway, and possibly with less aggressive methods. For example, perhaps the conditions were right for a language shift given the large number and varied languages of people with a common agenda. It is also possible that Hebrew would have been revived along with the maintenance of other languages. Perhaps an additive policy would have developed whereby people continued to use home languages and acquired Hebrew as a new language in addition to the home languages. In fact, it is known that in spite of the propaganda for Hebrew only, most first-generation immigrants continued to speak home languages for a long time but tried to keep these languages from their children, so that it was the children who became monolinguals in Hebrew.

Overall, the findings reported here call attention to some major dilemmas with ramifications for language revitalization and protection efforts in any context and community. Were the measures taken in the name of Hebrew revival and protection justified? Were they needed? Were they ethical? Specifically, the present case study raises the questions of whether the goal of language protection can justify means such as the negation of other languages spoken in the territory, the nomination of language monitors, entering people's homes to test their proficiency in new languages, changing private names, enforcing the posting of signs in specific languages, eradicating foreign language newspapers, forcing anybody to speak a certain language, or requiring people to reach high proficiency in the language—especially given what is known today about the length of time and investment it takes to learn a new language at a certain age. Which means to protect a language are legitimate and which can be considered a violation of personal and human rights? And should language use be left to individual choice and not to governments?

Thus important questions need to be asked regarding the cost and ethicality of language protection activities and methods even when the goals are laudable. No doubt, as the chapters in this volume attest, there are good reasons to worry about language loss and about endangered languages—today we are all increasingly concerned about the language ecology; we all see the sad reality of languages getting lost. However, we rarely discuss the methods that will be required to bring them back—and the costs—especially for individuals.

And the costs can be high: for example, there is the cost of the elimination of other languages, especially immigrant languages—in the case of Israel, it is the loss of Yiddish, Ladino, Jewish Arabic, and a variety of territorial languages that has reduced the linguistic capacity of Israel. These languages are no longer used, with the exception of Yiddish by Ultra Orthodox communities (stories about the suppression of Yiddish are just now beginning to emerge—see, e.g., Chaver 2004). However, it may be that these Jewish languages would have disappeared even without the aggressive acts of denial and rejection.

It is in the nature of ideology that it overlooks the individual, the personal, and the sacrifices while focusing on the masses; but it is the individuals who pay the price of language ideologies. What does it mean to deny the rights of those who do not speak a given language, in terms of participation in public life and employment? What does it mean to follow the acts of private residents? How can people's identities be constructed and redefined exclusively based on their language proficiency? What does it mean to define Jews in Palestine primarily by linguistic criteria and to deny and marginalize their other identities? What does it mean to create categories based exclusively on language? How ethical is it to force a language behavior on recent immigrants?

Is it even possible to learn a new language and use it in daily functions after a certain age? What does it mean to force a language on people, especially for those who had no opportunities to learn the language and then were denied employment because of low language proficiency? How about those immigrants who did switch to Hebrew, although it was not a fully formed language for them, and consequently experienced "the tongue-tied soul" (Chaver 2004); or those who had to create double standards, promote Hebrew publicly but to use other languages at home? Such is the case, for example, of the mayor of Raanana, who promoted Hebrew publicly but privately continued to use Yiddish at home. How realistic is the demand for a total shift of language in public and at home? And what about the teachers who were forced to teach in a language they had not mastered? And what about homes where some managed to acquire Hebrew and other family members could no longer interact with them, especially older people who were not able to acquire the new language? And what about those feeling that denying one's language means denying the past? What about the experience of one's language constantly being observed, monitored, watched, and corrected in public? What about those immigrants who became silent, living in constant fear of being corrected and judged about their language—not about *what* they had to say but about *how* they said it? Many became voiceless, silent, a phenomenon well known today in research on immigration. And what about those who were threatened and degraded because of their language use, and what about their feelings of shame and embarrassment for not being able to acquire this new language in the short time they were required to accomplish it?

A myriad of such important questions arise. If it is agreed that reversing shifts and reviving, sustaining, and protecting languages are important goals, then what steps need to be taken? Can these steps even be measured in terms of their morality and ethicality? Are they all appropriate in terms of a large number of complex considerations? How moral and ethical are language policies that follow from various ideological goals? Which ideologies are legitimate? What do we mean when we talk about language rights of *all* groups? Do certain goals justify all means?

Another question relates directly to the Hebrew language data on which this chapter is based. How much can be generalized from the case of Hebrew to other cases of language revival and protection? Is Hebrew a unique case? Perhaps each language situation is unique because each is embedded in a complex set of variables, and one case is never like the other. And when does a language turn from a "minority" to a "majority," from "endangered" to "protected," from "oppressed" to "oppressive"? In other words, where is the line between revival and oppression? In the case of Hebrew, for example, similar acts as those described earlier, perhaps less overt and more subtle, continue today in the name of "unity" and "social cohesion," although, as was discussed earlier, the status of Hebrew is secure. Yet it is not perceived so by many, given that it is tied to national ideologies. Even English in the United States, clearly dominant but not the official language, is viewed by many "English Only" ideologues as endangered by Spanish and in need of special protection.

And, finally, what is the role of linguists in this debate? Should linguists support and contribute to often oppressive methods for the sake of protecting endangered languages? Even if such efforts can lead to discrimination and marginalization?

We need to consider such questions as we work to save and cultivate minority languages and language varieties on the one hand, while working to protect individuals' freedom of language choice, dignity, and personal rights on the other. Clearly, language revival costs and benefits need to be assessed within a set of contextual variables of morality, ethicality, rights, and views of success. These are all very relative terms, and we still have not clarified the real differences between them; yet there is a need to emphasize that any language policy needs to be judged in relation to the people who pay a personal price for its aggressive implementation—who may be forced to comply with a policy from which they do not benefit significantly.

The story of Hebrew as reported in this chapter is one among many, but it allows us to observe methods and mechanisms used to impose languages in order to gain insights into the cost of language ideologies and language policies. There are costs to all language policies, even those with laudable goals. Before we accept and support policies about languages, we need to ask ourselves difficult questions about acts and their outcomes—what do these acts mean, what do they lead to? This preliminary study into the mechanisms used for Hebrew revival in one town allows us a small glimpse at a phenomenon that linguists and ideologues commonly rave about: the revival of a "dead" language. However, there is a need to look more deeply into the acts, strategies, mechanisms, and consequences involved. Navigating these constitutes an important challenge that linguists and activists alike need to face and address in the coming years.

NOTE

This chapter is based on research in progress conducted by the author as part of a larger study on documenting methods of reviving Hebrew.

REFERENCES

Amara, Muhammad Hasan, and Abd Al-Rahman Mar'i. 2002. *Language education policy: The Arab minority in Israel.* Dordrect: Kluwer.

Ben-Rafael, Eliezer. 1994. *Language, identity and social division: The case of Israel.* Oxford, UK: Clarendon Press.

Ben-Rafael, Eliezer, Elana Shohamy, Muhammad Hasan Amara, and Nira Trumper-Hecht. 2006. Linguistic landscape and multiculturalism: A Jewish-Arab comparative study. *International Journal of Multilingualism* 3:1.7–30.

Chaver, Yael. 2004. *What must be forgotten: The survival of Yiddish writing in Zionist Palestine.* Syracuse, NY: Syracuse University Press.

Fishman, Joshua A. 1991. *Reversing language shift: Theoretical and empirical foundations of assistance to threatened languages.* Clevedon, UK: Multilingual Matters.

Harshav, Benjamin. 1993. *Language in time of revolution.* Berkeley: University of California Press.

Karmi, Shlomo. 1997. *One people one language: The revival of the Hebrew language in an interdisciplinary perspective.* In Hebrew. Israel: Ministry of Defense, Israel.

Kuzar, Ron. 2001. *Hebrew and Zionism: A discourse analytic cultural study.* Berlin: Mouton de Gruyter.

Schieffelin, Bambi B., Kathryn A. Woolard, and Paul Kroskrity, eds. 1998. *Language ideologies: Practice and theory.* New York: Oxford University Press.

Segev, Tom. 1999. *Yemei Hakalaniyot: Palestine under the British.* Jerusalem: Keter.

Shohamy, Elana. 1994. Issues of language planning in Israel: Language and ideology. In *Language planning around the world: Contexts and systemic change,* ed. Richard D. Lambert, 131–42. Washington, DC: National Foreign Language Center.

———. 2006. *Language policy: Hidden agendas and new approaches.* London: Routledge.

Spolsky, Bernard. 2004. *Language policy.* Cambridge, UK: Cambridge University Press.

Spolsky, Bernard, and Elana Shohamy. 1999. *The languages of Israel: Policy, ideology and practice.* Clevedon, UK: Multilingual Matters.

15

Unendangered Dialects, Endangered People

WILLIAM LABOV
University of Pennsylvania

THE TOPIC I deal with here is a difficult one, especially in a forum devoted to the struggle to save endangered languages and support endangered dialects.[1] The majority of chapters in this volume are concerned with the problem of how to preserve linguistic and cultural diversity throughout the world. Nothing that I present here should be taken to diminish or undercut the importance of these programs. But this chapter will deal with another side of diversity. I will be looking at social factors that lead dialects to diverge, develop, and flourish and at forms of cultural diversity that need no help to survive. In the conclusion I will have to say that I wish the world were otherwise.

The argument of this chapter may be outlined as follows:

- African American Vernacular English [AAVE] is not an endangered dialect; on the contrary, it is continuing to develop and diverge from other dialects.
- The primary condition for such divergence is residential segregation.
- Residential segregation, combined with increasing poverty, has led to a deterioration of many features of social life in the inner cities.
- In these conditions, a majority of children in inner-city schools are failing to learn to read, with a developing cycle of poverty, crime, and shorter life span.
- A reduction of residential segregation will lead to greater contact between speakers of AAVE and speakers of other dialects.
- If, at some future date, the social conditions that favor the divergence of AAVE are altered, AAVE in its present form may become an endangered dialect.

The Unendangered Dialect

Among all the nonstandard dialects that have been described in the history of linguistics, AAVE is the most closely and extensively studied. From the mid-1960s to the present, studies of its invariant and variable features have been published for urban speech communities throughout the United States (Columbus: Weldon 1994; Detroit: Wolfram 1969, Edwards 1992; Los Angeles: Legum et al. 1972, Baugh 1979, 1983, 1984, 1999; New York: Labov et al. 1968, Labov 1972; Philadelphia: Ash and Myhill 1986, Labov and Harris 1986; San Francisco Bay area: Mitchell-Kernan 1969, Rickford et al. 1991, Rickford and McNair-Knox 1994; Washington, D.C.:

Fasold 1972). Regional differences have appeared in only a few phonological features. (In cities with *r*-ful white vernaculars, African Americans show lower levels of
r-vocalization than in cities with *r*-less vernaculars; Myhill 1988). AAVE emerges as
a geographically uniform system with the following general characteristics.

AAVE and Sound Changes

AAVE does not participate in sound changes characteristic of surrounding white vernaculars, a fact that has been documented from the earliest sociolinguistic studies to
the most recent. In New York City, African Americans were found to be shifting the
nucleus of /ay/ in *why, wide,* and so on to the front, while in the white population, a
new and vigorous change was moving the nucleus further and further back of center
(Labov 1966, 1994). In Philadelphia, the fronting of /aw/ is an absolute differentiator
of white and black speech patterns, so that in an experimental study, the controlled
raising of the second formant of /aw/ in *out* and *house* converted the perceived identity of the speaker from black to white (Graff, Labov, and Harris 1986). At Calumet
College in Chicago, African Americans showed no tendency to participate in the
Northern Cities Shift, the rotation of five short vowels characteristic of the white
population (Gordon 2000). In cities of the North, the Midland, and the West, such
phonetic patterns immediately differentiate the speech of African Americans from
that of the local whites.

Phonological Constraints Aligned with Other
English Dialects

The alignment of AAVE with general sociolinguistic variables was first demonstrated
in the study of auxiliary and copula deletion, where deletion was found to be governed
by the same constraints as contraction in other dialects (Labov 1969). The major grammatical constraints on copula/auxiliary deletion are replicated regularly in many different geographic areas, with future tense favoring deletion over progressive over following locative/adjective over following noun phrase (e.g., Rickford et al. 1991).[2]

A similar alignment is found with the simplification of coronal clusters. The
higher quantitative level in AAVE compared to other dialects is largely due to a qualitative difference in the effect of following pause on simplification. In AAVE, following pauses favor simplification, while in other dialects this environment has a
disfavoring effect on simplification, resulting in higher overall rates of simplification
in AAVE (Guy 1980).

Several Morphosyntactic Features Not Shared

Quantitative and qualitative differences between AAVE and other dialects are illustrated in figure 15.1, based on a study of 287 elementary schoolchildren in low-income areas (Labov 2001). These children represent a random sample of recordings
of a larger group of 721 struggling readers. They were recorded in a relatively formal
situation, in a school setting, but with sociolinguistic techniques that shift speech
style toward the vernacular. For all four variables, the vertical axis represents the
percentage absence of the consonant involved. The differences among the four

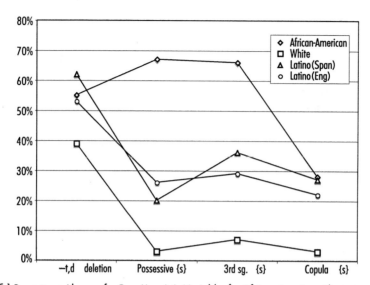

Figure 15.1 Percentage Absence for Four Linguistic Variables for African American Elementary School-children in Philadelphia, Atlanta, and California, by Language and Ethnic Group

Note: N = 287; Latino(Span) = Latinos who learned to read in Spanish first; Latino(Eng) = Latinos who learned to read in English first.

language/ethnic groups are quantitative for –t,d deletion and copula absence but qualitative for absence of attribute possessive {s} and third-singular {s}. For –t,d deletion, blacks and Latinos show 55 to 65 percent absence and whites 40 percent; for copula absence, blacks and Latinos are clustered at a much lower level, and whites are close to zero. In contrast, black children are close to 70 percent absence for attributive possessive {s} and verbal {s}, far different from Latinos and completely different from whites.

Early disagreements on the history of AAVE have been clarified by the close study of rural southern communities, particularly "Springville" in Texas (Bailey 1993, 2001; Cukor-Avila 1995) and Hyde County, North Carolina (Wolfram, Thomas, and Green 2000), as well as the examination of recordings of ex-slaves (Bailey and Cukor-Avila 1991) and expatriate communities (Poplack and Sankoff 1987; Poplack and Tagliamonte 1991/1993). It is now clear that the nineteenth-century forerunner of AAVE differed systematically from local white vernaculars, with evidence of the effects of substratum effects on inflectional morphology (Wolfram, Thomas, and Green 2000). At the same time, a number of the characteristic features of modern-day AAVE were present in a less developed form or not present at all.[3] In the twentieth century, the possessive and verbal {s} in particular show a dramatic shift toward invariant absence.

Variable Preterit Marking Reinforced by had as Past-tense Marker

The earliest studies of the 1960s detected occasional use of the past perfect as simple preterit (Labov et al. 1968). In "Springville," Cukor-Avila (1995) found an explosive growth of this feature in both apparent and real time. In all white dialects, the auxiliary *had* indicates that the event so marked occurred before the event last referenced. In current AAVE, auxiliary *had* occurs freely in semantic contexts where the marked event follows the preceding one. The speakers in Cukor-Avila's study born before World War I showed no trace of this feature, while for those in the youngest group, born after 1970, innovative *had* was the predominant form.

The ways in which AAVE is expanding and flourishing appear most clearly in the semantics of mood and aspect. The examples that I cite here have a dual import, showing on the one hand the evolution of new semantic possibilities, and on the other hand the eloquent application of these possibilities in social interaction.

New Semantic Features

Unique mood and aspect categories have developed with new semantic features, chief among which are the following:

The Rise of Habitual *be*.   The invariant form *be*, which does not alternate with *is, am,* or *are*, is one of the most widely recognized surface features of AAVE. It would appear to date back to the first half of the nineteenth century or earlier, as it has been noted in ex-slave recordings (Bailey and Cukor-Avila 1991). However, Bailey (1993) finds that the modern day "habitual" meaning is not characteristic of these early uses. Furthermore, a striking difference appeared between the use of invariant *be* by seventy-year-old men and by young children in the rural community of "Springville" that Bailey and Cukor-Avila studied over the years. Children and older speakers did not differ at all in the frequency of invariant *be* before noun phrases, locatives, adjectives, and *gonna*. But before progressive verbs with *-ing*, children showed 44 percent invariant *be*, and the older speakers only 4 percent (Cukor-Avila 1995).[4] This was the first indication that the habitual meaning of invariant *be* was a twentieth-century development.

Such a habitual meaning appears in the earliest sociolinguistic studies of AAVE, as in the speech of Larry H. of the Cobras (Labov 1972, 216):

(1) An' when they be sayin' if you good, you goin' t' heaven . . .
   and in the speech of Springville children:

(2) Sometimes them big boys be throwing [the ball]. (Bailey and Maynor 1987)

The habitual character of the construction is evident in the frequent collocation with adverbs such as *sometimes* and *always* but also directly by such semantic contrasts as (3).

(3) A: Do you know where I can find Nukey?
   B: She be here [most of the time] but she ain't here now.

Any study of AAVE will show that habitual *be* is deeply embedded in a rhetoric of everyday speech that is not easily captured in translation to other dialects. Dayton's (1996) massive archive of AAVE mood and aspect demonstrates this.

(4) [At a Gospel Choir]

A: Will everybody remember that?

B: Yeah but Angie, can we sing the chorus twice before we go into the other part? 'Cause it's like you be just about to feel Jesus then we stop.

From the stream of yearly observations made by students at the University of Pennsylvania in Philadelphia:

(5) [Penn student, observing outside of McDonald's]

Homeless: You got any change?

Me: No. Sorry.

Homeless: A'ight, maybe when you come out.

Me: Maybe.

[after I come out]

Homeless: You got any?

[hand him some change]

Homeless: Thank you man. People be tellin' me when they come out they still don't have change and I KNOW they be lyin'. Thank you.

Bailey and Maynor (1985) trace the dramatic rise in the use of habitual meaning as a percentage of all progressives with habitual meaning, from speakers born in the nineteenth century to modern times. This quantitative development has been confirmed in the study of East Palo Alto by Rickford and his colleagues (Rickford and McNair-Knox 1994).

Be as Essential and Permanent State. Despite the rapid expansion of the habitual meaning of *be,* the semantics of this invariant *be* are not fixed. New possibilities are also emerging, as first noted in Labov et al. (1968), where the meaning is not habitual but a permanent and steady state, an essential characteristic of the subject. From two observations of my own:

(6) [in a hospital emergency room, a middle-aged woman talking to a younger woman]: Her Father be your Father.

(7) [a man leaning out of a pick-up truck, to a woman on the sidewalk] Hey baby! This be Heywood!

This use, a minor pattern in everyday discourse, is efflorescing in hip-hop lyrics.

(8) We be the Funk, Four mind as one umm, Crumbs umm
he told us peace, it was against his beliefs
(The Roots, I'm Out Deah)

(9) Through the nine-six, I be that nigga that be priceless
Always blowin' up your spot, bringin more surprises

. . .

> HAH! I be the number one chosen just to keep you open
> Chill with your thoughts I got your brain frozen
> (Busta Rhymes, Do My Thing/The Coming)

Clearly this self-identification with *be* does not refer to habitual behavior but rather a permanent steady state.

The Development of *be done*.   The combination of *(will) be* with perfective/intensive *done* has been co-opted in AAVE to signal the compound tense equivalent to the future perfect (*will have*) of other dialects. Perfective *done* is well established in the southern United States and in Caribbean Creoles (Satyanath 1991; Winford 1993). It is combined with *be done* as a transparent equivalent of the future perfect.

(10) 'Cause I'll be done put—so many holes in him he'd a wish he hadn't said it.
    (Labov et al. 1968)

(11) My ice cream's gonna be done melted by the time we get there. (Dayton 1996)

Figure 15.2 shows how this *be done* marker of the future perfect is normally attached to the first of two future events, indicating that it occurs before the second, just as with the future perfect of other dialects.

Some time in the mid-twentieth century a remarkable change took place. The fused *be done* was detached from its position before the first of the two future events and attached to the second. In 1983, Baugh observed a confrontation in the Los Angeles suburb of Pacoima where an angry parent threatened a pool guard who he thought had manhandled his son:

(12) I'll be done killed that motherfucker if he tries to lay a hand on my kid again.

The change in temporal semantics from figure 15.2 is indicated in figure 15.3. But while the future perfect *be done* is a marker of tense, indicating only temporal relations between A and B, the new resultative *be done* is a marker of mood, indicating the high degree of certainty with which B follows A. The sentence (12) is not easily translated into any tense, mood, or aspect combination used in other dialects. The semantic content of this combination is not simply that B will follow A but that B will *inevitably* follow A.

They *be done* drunk up all the wine by the time we get there.

Figure 15.2 Semantics of the Future Perfect *be done*

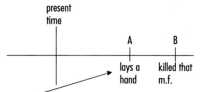

I'll *be done* killed that motherfucker if he tries to lay a hand on my kid again.

Figure 15.3 Semantics of the Resultative *be done*

This future resultative *be done* is not simply a member of the compound tense system but partakes of the semantics of mood, as it involves the degree of certainty of an event. Like many of the newly developing members of the AAVE system, the *be done* marker indicates events whose likelihood of occurrence is greater than that signaled by the indicative. While *irrealis* markers indicate lesser probabilities of occurrence, such *surrealis* markers indicate a truth that is more than *true,* a reality that is more than *real.* They are inserted in the flow of a highly interactive rhetoric, as shown by a sampling of the many examples from African American women in Dayton (1996):

(13) He [a nephew] knows best not to talk back to me 'cause I be done slapped the little knock kneed thing upside the head.

(14) The readin' of the scriptures, all that's gonna be done done.

There are many other new elements in the mood and aspect system of AAVE that add to the richness of its expressive semantics: the development of *done* as an intensifier, remote perfective *been* along with *been done* (Rickford 1973), *steady* as an intensifier of habitual *be* (Baugh 1984), and the *come* of moral indignation (Spears 1982). These often appear in rapid succession in agonistic interaction, as in (15).

(15) [Two women preparing fish at the Thriftway]
A: Marcene *been* getting those welfare checks . . .
B: Uh-uh. That a shame. How he gon come asking for somethin' like she got money?
A: Lord, he needs Jesus.

Speakers of AAVE have developed complex combinations of preverbal elements whose syntax and semantics remain to be deciphered.

(16) I'm gonna be done hafta went back and finished in eight years. (Dayton 1996)

As noted earlier, most of these emergent features are in the domain of mood and aspect rather than tense. Indeed, Dayton (1996) argues that all AAVE grammatical particles are free of tense and can be used in past, present, or future context, while Green (1994) notes a connection between this new mood system and the general absence of subject-verb agreement in AAVE.

This brief discussion has touched on some of the ongoing changes that mark AAVE as an increasingly rich and vigorous dialect of English (Labov 1998). We now turn to the social conditions in which this dialect has flourished.

The Great Migration and Residential Segregation

Bailey (1993) argues that the development of modern AAVE is contemporaneous with the great migration of African Americans from the rural South to large cities, primarily in the North. The grammatical developments we have traced are essentially characteristics of these large urban speech communities where African Americans are heavily concentrated in homogeneous neighborhoods.

It is generally thought that residential segregation is a by-product of the initial movement of a population into a new city and that an immigrant group will follow a path of decreasing residential concentration over time as members obtain jobs, sometimes intermarry, and generally assimilate to American society. This has been the case for many immigrant groups, as shown in table 15.1, taken from Hershberg's studies of the history of Philadelphia (Hershberg et al. 1981). Irish, Germans, Italians, and Poles all show a regular decline in the *index of dominance,* which is the proportion of a person's census tract that consists of the same group. The trajectory of African Americans is just the reverse in these data. Starting in 1850, the index of dominance for African Americans steadily rises to its maximum in 1970, the last year reported on. This pattern is not peculiar to Philadelphia. Massey and Denton (1993) show a spectacular rise in residential segregation for all major American cities from 1930 to 1970. They argue that the high level of residential segregation is a root cause of the many other social problems that afflict the African American community, with a close interrelationship between poverty rate, residential segregation, crime rate rises, the percentage of female-headed families, and the percentage of high school students in the lowest fifteenth percentile.

Residential Segregation and the Core Speakers of AAVE

In the 1970s, we studied linguistic change and variation in the white community of Philadelphia (Labov 1980, 2001). All available evidence indicated that African Americans did not participate in the new and vigorous sound changes that characterized the

Table 15.1

Indices of Dominance for Five Ethnic Groups in Philadelphia from 1850 to 1970 (proportion of a person's census tract that consists of the same group)

	1850	1880	1930	1940	1950	1960	1970
Blacks	11	12	35	45	56	72	74
Irish		34	8			5	3
German	25	11			5	3	
Italian		38			23	21	
Polish		20			9	8	

Source: Hershberg et al. 1981, table 8.

Philadelphia vernacular: only a few older blacks and isolated youth showed any tendency to adopt these sound changes in progress. In the 1980s, we carried out research in North Philadelphia and found a linguistic segregation that matched the high level of residential segregation we have just seen (Labov and Harris 1986).

The majority members of the black community who consistently showed the defining features of AAVE were those who stayed within the black neighborhoods from one day to the other, worked only with blacks, lived with and talked with blacks, and rarely had face-to-face conversations with speakers of other dialects.[5] In the adult social networks of North Philadelphia we found a certain number of speakers who did not follow the AAVE grammatical pattern described earlier, but they were all people who, for one reason or another, had more extensive contact with whites. This second group sounded very much like the first on the surface and used the same vocabulary and phonetics, but they showed in their inflectional variables the influence of contact with white grammars.

We also studied two groups of white speakers of both middle and working-class backgrounds, one with extensive contacts with the African American community and one with very limited contact. Figure 15.4 shows the level of absence of three grammatical inflections for the four groups of speakers. The majority of blacks with minimal white contacts show a very high degree of inflectional absence of possessive and verbal {s}, while blacks with extensive contacts showed substantially lower levels of inflectional absence. Whites with extensive black contacts showed little tendency to shift their grammar in this direction.

The consistency of the core group reflects the general findings of Milroy (1980) that speakers engaged in dense multiplex social networks resist linguistic change from outside, while those with many weak ties to other social groups are subject to the influence of those groups. The other side of the coin is that within the core group of blacks, linguistic change has accelerated, in both the tense/mood/aspect system

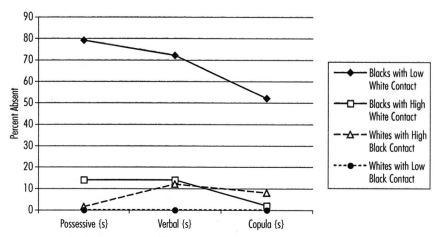

Figure 15.4 Percentage Absence of Three Morphological Features of Standard English by Race and Degree of Contact across Racial Groups in North Philadelphia

and the morphosyntactic reflections of grammatical categories. Dense and multiplex networks are, of course, a concomitant of residential segregation.

One might argue that the African American youth in these core areas are not isolated from other dialects, that they are exposed to more standard speech through the mass media or from their schoolteachers. But a great deal of evidence indicates that passive exposure of this type does not affect speech patterns or underlying grammars (Labov, Ash, and Boberg 2006). As far as we know, language changes occur in the course of verbal interaction among speakers who track each other's utterances for appropriate responses at possible sentence completion points (Sacks 1992). African American children in core areas do not have the opportunity to engage in such conversations with speakers of other dialects.

The Minority Gap in Reading

The first research on AAVE that we conducted in 1965–68 was supported by the Office of Education and was designed to find out if there was any connection between dialect differences and the minority gap in reading. In the yearly reports of the National Assessment of Educational Progress (NAEP) since 1971, the minority gap in reading proficiency levels has remained large and stable. In the most recent figures, only a small proportion of African American fourth graders, 13 percent, are rated as *proficient*—that is, able to use reading as a tool for further learning.

When we examine the situation at the local level in Philadelphia, a further relationship appears between poverty and low reading levels. Figure 15.5 is a scattergram of all Philadelphia schools at the time when we first began our efforts to raise reading levels. Each point registers on the vertical axis the percentage of students performing at the lowest quartile of the statewide Pennsylvania System of School

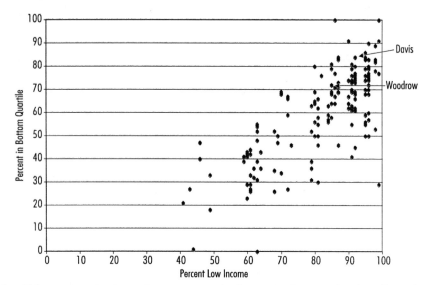

Figure 15.5 Percentage Readers in the Bottom Quartile of PSSA Reading Scores in the Fifth Grade of Philadelphia Schools (1997) by Percent of Low-Income Students

Assessment (PSSA) reading test, and on the horizontal axis, the percentage of students who qualify for free lunch because their family income falls below the poverty line. The symbol labeled "Davis" is the elementary school where we have worked most consistently in the period since 1997. It is evident that there is a direct relation between poverty and reading achievement.

The Relation between Speech and Reading

The data for figure 15.1 were drawn from an analysis of the spontaneous speech of 287 struggling readers in the second through fourth grades who were the subjects of our interventions in three regions of the United States. The same data can be used to examine the relationship between the use of AAVE variables in spontaneous speech and decoding success in oral reading. We can expect, of course, that there will be a correlation between the realization of each of these variables in speech and in oral reading. Table 15.2 shows a moderate but significant correlation between reading errors and features with high rates of simplification/absence in AAVE. The first column shows the correlation between the absence of each feature in spontaneous speech and absence in oral reading of a diagnostic text. The fact that there is such a correlation is not remarkable because the vernacular deletion of these inflections is in the first analysis indistinguishable from an oral reading error.[6] However, the third column of table 15.2 shows that the same degree of correlation exists between the AAVE speech variables and the mean error rate in decoding all orthographic aspects of onsets, nuclei, and codas.[7] This indicates a global relationship between the use of AAVE and decoding problems. The relationship is not necessarily a direct one, as there are many intervening factors that are likely to be responsible for a high use of AAVE and low performance in decoding. Before we explore these, we must consider an unexpected finding on regional differences.

Differences by Region

In the many studies of AAVE published so far, no major regional differences in the grammar have appeared (Baugh 1983; Labov et al. 1968; Rickford et al. 1991).[8] However, if we break down the data for African Americans in figure 15.1 into three regional groups, some surprising differences appear. Figure 15.6 shows that Atlanta and Philadelphia have the highest simplification of consonant clusters and absence of

Table 15.2

Pearson Correlations between Spontaneous Speech and Reading for Four AAVE Variables

	With Grammatical Variable in Oral Reading	With Mean Phonological Error Rate
Consonant clusters	.16*	.10*
Third singular {s}	.15*	.18**
Possessive {s}	.28***	.14*
Copula {s}	.15*	.21***

Note: $N = 287$; * $= p < .05$; ** $p < .01$; *** $p < .001$.

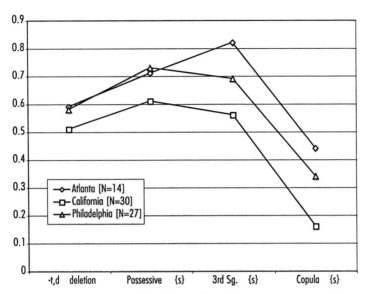

Figure 15.6 Four Morphosyntactic Variables of AAVE for African American Struggling Readers by Region

possessive attributive {s} and that Atlanta has even higher absence of third singular {s} and copula {s} than Philadelphia. Conversely, the California subjects are considerably lower than the other two regions for all four variables. If residential segregation were an essential component for the full development of the vernacular, we would expect to find a lesser degree of segregation in the West. However, Massey and Denton (1993) show that Los Angeles is not less segregated than any of the other large cities, and all schools were selected by the same socioeconomic criterion—the percentage of low-income families who qualify for the federal free lunch program. Why then should our California sample show a lower frequency of the defining AAVE features?

We examined the racial distribution of students for all the schools involved in California, Atlanta, and Philadelphia, including the relations of Latinos, whites, and blacks. Figure 15.7 displays the proportions of African Americans to Latinos on the horizontal axis, and the proportions of African Americans to Whites on the vertical axis. Each axis shows the log ratio of African Americans to the other group. The 0 rating on each axis is therefore the point at which there is an equal mixture of the two groups, that is, a ratio of 1:1. The schools with the most extreme segregation are at the upper right, where the numbers next to each symbol indicate the overall percentage of African Americans: 90 percent and 93 percent. No California schools show such a high concentration. The five schools in the lower left quadrant have relatively low ratios of African Americans to whites and Latinos: these California schools are quite isolated from all others. It appears then that the lower frequency of AAVE characteristics in the California schools is a direct reflection of the lower concentrations of black students.

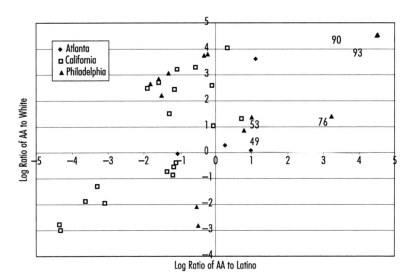

■ Figure 15.7 Concentration of African Americans in Schools in Atlanta, California, and Philadelphia in Which the Students of Figure 15.1 Were Interviewed

Note: Numbers next to Philadelphia schools in upper-right quadrant are percent African American in the student body.

The Development of AAVE in the Framework of Residential Segregation

Figure 15.8 models the development of AAVE within the framework of residential segregation, symbolized by the black rectangle. AAVE is shown as the product of its history, which begins outside of that framework, in plantations and small towns of the South (Bailey 1993, 2001) and in the earlier less segregated areas of northern cities. The twentieth-century developments of AAVE discussed in the first part of this chapter occurred in conjunction with the other social conditions outlined in figure 15.8. The first and overarching condition is the degree of poverty as indicated at upper left, with its interlocking relationships with other forms of social pathology. Unemployment is, of course, the primary cause of poverty: unemployment rates for young black men who have not graduated high school have recently been reported at 72 percent, as opposed to 19 percent for the corresponding population of Latino youth (Eckholm 2006). Unemployment, underemployment, and poverty jointly reduce or eliminate the economic base for the black family. Inability to participate in the formal, legal economy leads directly to participation in the informal, illegal economy, with a rapid increase in crime rates—the link shown at lower left. The incarceration rate of young black males has tripled in two decades, rising from 2 percent per year in 1981 to almost 6 percent in 2002 (Holzer, Offner, and Sorensen 2004). Coupled with increasing reinforcement of child support laws, young black males are removed from the formal economy during and after their prison terms. The economic base of the largely female-headed black family is then further eroded.

RESIDENTIAL SEGREGATION

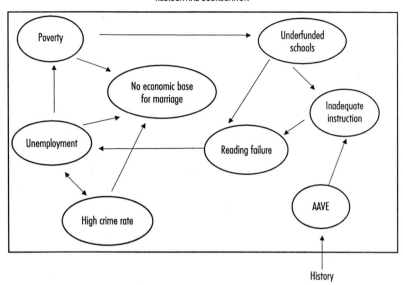

Figure 15.8 Model of the Development of AAVE in the Framework of Residential Segregation

Poverty in the inner city also affects the quality of schooling. Many of the schools we have worked in have a severe shortage of books, texts, art supplies, and most critical of all, teachers. One school we have worked with most closely in our intervention programs has lost four teachers this year through budget cuts, so that, in two classrooms, second and third grade students will be combined. Underfunding of schools plainly contributes to inadequate instruction and—no matter what instruction is used—to reading failure. The cycle closes as reading failure leads to further unemployment. Because the majority of children in the schools of figure 15.8 are reading below basic level in the fifth grade and cannot use reading to obtain information content in their other subjects, it is not likely that they will be able to graduate from high school without further intervention. Reading failure reinforces the cycle of poverty, unemployment, and crime.

A relationship of AAVE to inadequate instruction is indicated in figure 15.8. Since the Ann Arbor decision (Labov 1982; Smitherman 1981), it has generally been agreed that teachers need to know more about children's home language to be effective teachers of reading. How this can best be done is the major focus of our current research (Labov 2001, 2003). Whether our efforts will be effective enough to cut into the cycle of figure 15.8 is a question that will be resolved over time. This chapter has addressed a distinct but closely related question: What are the social conditions under which AAVE has developed, flourished, and become increasingly differentiated from other dialects of American English?

A major strategy of our intervention efforts is to respond in a meaningful way to the real-life situation of the children we are dealing with, who are all affected by the cycle represented in figure 15.8. Many of the narratives I have written for our

Individualized Reading Program deal with conflict between students and the school and the injustice that children see in the world around them. In contrast, most of the standard school reading materials deal with a happy, anodyne, and irrelevant world in which children take their sand buckets to the beach and dip their toes in the water. By the time they reach the fourth grade, most of our students are alienated from the reading process as they have known it and from the institution of education as a whole. Their rejection of the school as an institution is similar to the position of the adolescent Jets and Cobras of the 1960s, who saw the school system as a form of institutionalized racism (Labov et al. 1968). There is a generalized level of anger that may surface at any moment, expressed primarily in fighting with their fellow students rather than overt hostility to the teacher. Many of our most promising students were forced to drop out of our program when they were suspended for fighting.

It is therefore important to get a clear idea of the social condition that generates these powerful emotions. A study of one individual may be helpful.

An Angry Fourth Grader

Riana was a fourth grader when she entered the Individualized Reading Program. She scored in the thirty-fifth national percentile in the Woodcock-Johnson Word Attack subtest, in the thirteenth percentile in the Word Identification subtest, and in the sixteenth percentile on Passage Comprehension. On our analysis of decoding skills, she had more than 10 percent errors for twelve out of the twenty phoneme/grapheme relations, the benchmark we have adopted for remedial instruction. In addition to these reading tests, we recorded the spontaneous speech of all of our students in that year, using the sociolinguistic techniques that have been found to stimulate the flow of speech for children everywhere (e.g., asking such questions as "Did you ever get blamed for something you didn't do?" "Is there any place in your neighborhood that's really scary?" "Did you ever get into a fight with someone bigger than you?"). Riana talked very freely about the fights she had been in.

> I was in my old school and I was used to fightin' an' stuff. I only fought two times in this school. And I ain't never get in trouble but in the old school I got suspended three times. That's when I was a real fighter and I liked to fight a lot but I on't—I try not to fight a lot and I told this—I told one of the teachers I said I was gonna punch her in her face. . . . Uh—I say anything when I'm mad. When I get real real mad I just say anything. I don't be meaning it but I just say it. It then come out—anything comes out my mouth then but no curse words did. . . . Anything else I say I'm going to do something to somebody but it comes out my mouth only—only say that when I'm mad I don't—like— I don't mean to say it. It just come out my mouth when I'm real real angry at people.

This is what she said about scary places.

> TUTOR: Is there any place that you know about that's really scary? Some place
>   you wouldn't want to go?
>
> RIANA: Jail.

TUTOR: How come?

RIANA: 'Cause . . . it's a lot of people there that—that—a lot of *thiefs* there
and the police don't care what they do long as they stay in them jail.
As long as they stay in the bars they don't care what they do. And
then . . . long as they don't call the police in they don't care *what* they
do long as they ain't doing nothing to the police. And they might take
your food like if you there—you had to go there—they might—and
they have their own food—they own plate of food—they might—they
want yours and they snatch yours from you and they'll beat you up
there.

TUTOR: How do you know so much about jails?

RIANA: My—my dad is in jail.

The tutor had no intention of talking about jail; up to this point, she did not know
that Riana's dad was in jail. Without further reflection, she pursued the point.

TUTOR: Do you ever go and visit your dad?

RIANA: I never did . . . [sigh] I never saw him—the last time I saw my dad
was . . . I was in second grade and I was going on a trip. He—he
brought me money. That was the last time I saw him.

TUTOR: Do you know does he get out soon?

RIANA: I don't know.

TUTOR: You don't know.

RIANA: I don't think so. I—I've keep writing notes—I wrote my—I wrote—
uh—I wrote—we write to each other. . . . He say he gon give me a—
he say he gon give me a tape—he gon mail me a tape with him on
there reading cuz I suh—cuz at they jail I supposed to come there
every week so we could do like a parent—a father and daughter—
uh—reading.

Riana's sighs are quite audible. Her style is reflective and sad.

RIANA: So—and—he say he gon send me a tape with him readin' on it. It's
cuz instead—since I can't read then—since we can't see each other a
lot—I never saw my dad in there—for a long long time. I think I
saw—the last time I saw him was last year. My last birthday and it
wasn't—not on my June—not on this—the June twenty seven that
already came up. The one the buh—before that . . . And I didn't get—
that's the last time I saw him. And he came to my birthday party. . . .
[sighs]

Riana is not an exceptional case. The uncontrollable anger that she feels, which
will inevitably lead to her suspension from school, is the product of a despair that is
not known to children outside the ghetto but is commonplace within it. Mauer (1995)
reports that one in three black men between the ages of twenty and twenty-nine is either in jail or prison or on parole or probation: these are their children. The stories

that I write for them are quite remote from the happy tales that are written for suburban readers; they reflect—but only to a small degree—the grim reality of a world where the best we can do is to register a protest against the unfairness of it all. We made some progress with the children in Riana's class in 2001 and the four years that followed. But the size of the problem is staggering. Of the 156 schools in Philadelphia, 141 are in the bottom quintile on the state achievement test. So far, we have worked with only a dozen of them. Philadelphia is one of a long list of the hypersegregated speech communities: this is the norm for all large American cities. And the problem of reading failure is everywhere.

There are many ways in which what I have written here may be misunderstood, and I would like to be clear in the conclusion. I have shown that AAVE has developed its present form in the framework of the most extreme racial segregation that the world has ever known. In no way have I suggested that AAVE is a cause of the problems of African American people. On the contrary, it is their great resource, an elegant form of expression that they use when they reflect most thoughtfully on the oppression and misery of daily life.

If you love your enemy, they be done ate you alive in this society (Dayton 1996).

The great progress of the civil rights movement has given a large part of the black population access to education and jobs along with the means to move out of the inner city. There have been great gains. On the linguistic side, there has emerged a standard African American English in which the major features are phonological, such as the merger of *pin* and *pen* (Henderson 2001), or camouflaged grammatical markers such as the *come* of moral indignation (Spears 1982). If some forces in American society, perhaps led by Baugh's initiative on linguistic profiling (2000), were to make a major impact on residential segregation, then we would expect AAVE to shift some part of the distance toward other dialects, and we might then observe large-scale convergence instead of continuing divergence.

If the mixed populations of our Philadelphia schools should actually be integrated, we may even reach a time when young black children use elements of the white vernacular and take part in the radical sound changes that sweep over the white community. At that point, AAVE as a whole might be in danger of losing its own distinct and characteristic forms of speech. I am sure that many of us would regret the decline of the eloquent syntactic and semantic options that I have presented here. But we might also reflect at that time that the loss of a dialect is a lesser evil than the current condition of an endangered people.

NOTES

1. This chapter was originally given as a plenary address at GURT 2006 on March 5, 2006. It draws upon research on raising reading levels in low-income schools, supported by the National Science Foundation under contract 0115676 and the Spencer Foundation. I am indebted to Anita Henderson and Anne Charity for many thoughtful observations on the first draft, which are reflected in the current version.
2. Locative and adjectival environments are here combined, as in the original Harlem study (Labov et al. 1968), where these were found to be variable from one group to another. Cukor-Avila (1999) attributes this inconsistency to varying proportions of stative and nonstative adjectives.

3. In an earlier view, modern-day AAVE is the result of "decreolization," the gradual incorporation of standard inflectional elements into the grammar (Fasold 1976).

4. These figures are for plural and second and third singular (Bailey and Maynor 1987, figure 3). For the first-person singular, children used invariant *be* more than a third of the time, and the older speakers only 10 percent.

5. See also Baugh (1983) for a characterization of the vernacular on these dimensions.

6. See, however, Labov and Baker (2003), which resolves this problem.

7. These mean values are based on the error rates for twenty problematic relations of phonemes to graphemes in onsets, nuclei, and codas of a diagnostic reading.

8. Regional differences in pronunciation are not uncommon, principally in the degree of *r*-vocalization and moderate reflections of the Southern Shift (Labov, Ash, and Boberg 2006, chap. 22). See Myhill (1988) and Hinton and Pollock (2000) for regional differences in (r). The African American speech of East St. Louis is well known to have a centralized nucleus of /ehr/ in *there* and *where*.

REFERENCES

Ash, Sharon, and John Myhill. 1986. Linguistic correlates of inter-ethnic contact. In *Diversity and diachrony,* ed. David Sankoff, 33–44. Amsterdam: John Benjamins.

Bailey, Guy. 1993. A perspective on African-American English. In *American dialect research,* ed. Dennis Preston, 287–318. Philadelphia: John Benjamins.

———. 2001. The relationship between African-American Vernacular English and white vernaculars in the American South. In *African American English: State of the art,* ed. Sonja Lanehart, 53–92. Philadelphia: John Benjamins.

Bailey, Guy, and Patricia Cukor-Avila. 1991. *The emergence of Black English: Texts and commentaries.* Amsterdam: John Benjamins.

Bailey, Guy, and Natalie Maynor. 1985. The present tense of BE in Southern black folk speech. *American Speech* 60:195–213.

———. 1987. Decreolization? *Language in Society* 16:449–73.

Baugh, John. 1979. Linguistic style-shifting in Black English. PhD diss., University of Pennsylvania.

———. 1983. *Black street speech: Its history, structure and survival.* Austin: University of Texas Press.

———. 1984. Steady: Progressive aspect in Black English. *American Speech* 50:3–12.

———. 1999. *Out of the mouths of slaves: African American language and educational malpractice.* Austin: University of Texas Press.

———. 2000. *Beyond Ebonics: Linguistic pride and racial prejudice.* New York: Oxford University Press.

Cukor-Avila, Patricia. 1995. The evolution of AAVE in a rural Texas community: An ethnolinguistic study. PhD diss., University of Michigan.

———. 1999. Stativity and copula absence in AAVE: Grammatical constraints at the subcategorical level. *Journal of English Linguistics* 27:341–55.

Dayton, Elizabeth. 1996. Grammatical categories of the verb in African American vernacular English. PhD diss., University of Pennsylvania.

Eckholm, Erik. 2006. Plight deepens for black men, studies warn. *New York Times,* March 25.

Edwards, Walter F. 1992. Sociolinguistic behavior in a Detroit inner-city black neighborhood. *Language in Society* 21:93–115.

Fasold, R. W. 1972. *Tense marking in Black English.* Washington, DC: Center for Applied Linguistics.

———. 1976. One hundred years from syntax to phonology. Parasession on diachronic syntax at Chicago Linguistic Society, Chicago.

Gordon, Matthew J. 2000. Phonological correlates of ethnic identity: Evidence of divergence? *American Speech* 75:115–36.

Graff, David, William Labov, and Wendell Harris. 1986. Testing listeners' reactions to phonological markers. In *Diversity and diachrony,* ed. David Sankoff, 45–58. Philadelphia: John Benjamins.

Green, Lisa. 1994. *A unified account of auxiliaries in African American English.* Paper presented at Chicago Linguistic Society, Chicago.

Guy, Gregory. 1980. Variation in the group and the individual: The case of final stop deletion. In *Locating Language in Time and Space,* ed. William Labov, 1–36. New York: Academic Press.

Henderson, Anita. 2001. Is your money where your mouth is? Hiring managers' attitudes toward African-American Vernacular English. PhD diss., University of Pennsylvania.

Hershberg, Theodore, Alan N. Burstein, Eugene P. Ericksen, Stephanie Greenberg, and William L. Yancey. 1981. A tale of three cities: black, immigrants and opportunity in Philadelphia, 1850–1880, 1930, 1970. In *Philadelphia: Work, space, family and group experience in the nineteenth century,* ed. Theodore Hershberg, 461–95. New York: Oxford University Press.

Hinton, Linette, and Karen Pollock. 2000. Regional variations in the phonological characteristics of African-American Vernacular English. *Word Englishes* 19:59–71.

Holzer, Harry, Paul Offner, and Elaine Sorensen. 2004. *Declining employment among young black less-educated men: The role of incarceration and child support.* Institute for Research on Poverty Discussion Paper no. 1281. www.irp.wisc.edu/publications/dps/pdfs/dp128104.pdf.

Labov, William. 1966. *The social stratification of English in New York City.* Washington, DC: Center for Applied Linguistics.

———. 1969. Contraction, deletion, and inherent variability of the English copula. *Language* 45:715–62.

———. 1972. *Language in the inner city.* Philadelphia: University of Pennsylvania Press.

———. 1980. The social origins of sound change. In *Locating language in time and space,* ed. William Labov, 251–66. New York: Academic Press.

———. 1982. Objectivity and commitment in linguistic science: The case of the Black English trial in Ann Arbor. *Language in Society* 11:165–202.

———. 1994. *Principles of linguistic change.* Vol. 1: *Internal factors.* Oxford, UK: Basil Blackwell.

———. 1998. Co-existent systems in African American Vernacular English. In *The structure of African-American English: Structure, history and use,* ed. Salikoko Mufwene, John Rickford, Guy Bailey, and John Baugh, 110–53. New York: Routledge.

———. 2001. Applying our knowledge of African American English to the problem of raising reading levels in inner-city schools. In *African American English: State of the art,* ed. Sonja Lanehart, 299–318. Philadelphia: John Benjamins.

———. 2003. When ordinary children fail to read. *Reading Research Quarterly* 38:131–33.

Labov, William, Sharon Ash, and Charles Boberg. 2006. *Atlas of North American English: Phonetics, phonology and sound change.* Berlin: Mouton de Gruyter.

———. 2003. What is a reading error? www.ling.upenn.edu/~wlabov/Papers/WRE.html (accessed December 27, 2007).

Labov, William, Paul Cohen, Clarence Robins, and John Lewis. 1968. *A study of the non-standard English of Negro and Puerto Rican Speakers in New York City.* Cooperative Research Report 3288. Vols. 1 and 2. Philadelphia: U.S. Regional Survey (Linguistics Laboratory, University of Pennsylvania).

Labov, William, and Wendell A. Harris. 1986. De facto segregation of black and white vernaculars. In *Diversity and diachrony,* ed. David Sankoff, 1–24. Philadelphia: John Benjamins.

Legum, Stanley, Carol Pfaff, Gene Tinnie, and Michael Nicholas. 1972. *The speech of young black children in Los Angeles.* Technical Publication 33. Inglewood, CA: Southwest Regional Laboratory.

Massey, Douglas S., and Nancy A. Denton. 1993. *American apartheid: Segregation and the making of the underclass.* Cambridge, MA: Harvard University Press.

Mauer, Mark. 1995. *Young black Americans and the criminal justice system: Five years later.* Washington, DC: Sentencing Project.

Milroy, Leslie. 1980. *Language and social networks.* Oxford: Basil Blackwell.

Mitchell-Kernan, Claudia. 1969. *Language behavior in a black urban community.* Monographs of the Language-Behavior Research Laboratory, no. 2. Berkeley: University of California.

Myhill, John. 1988. Postvocalic /r/ as an index of integration into the BEV speech community. *American Speech* 63:203–13.

Poplack, Shana, and David Sankoff. 1987. The Philadelphia story in the Spanish Caribbean. *American Speech* 62:291–314.

Poplack, Shana, and Sali Tagliamonte. 1991/1993. African American English in the diaspora: Evidence from old-line Nova Scotians. *Language Variation and Change* 3:301–39. In *Focus on Canada,* ed. Sandra Clarke, repr., 109–50. Amsterdam: John Benjamins.

Rickford, John R. 1973. Carrying the new wave into syntax: The case of Black English bin. In *Analyzing variation in language,* ed. Ralph Fasold and Roger Shuy, 162–83. Washington, DC: Georgetown University Press.

Rickford, John R., Arnetha Ball, Renee Blake, Raina Jackson, and Nomi Martin. 1991. Rappin on the copula coffin: Theoretical and methodological issues in the analysis of copula variation in African-American Vernacular English. *Language Variation and Change* 3:103–32.

Rickford, John R., and Faye McNair-Knox. 1994. Addressee- and topic-influenced style shift: A quantitative sociolinguistic study. In *Sociolinguistic perspectives on register: Situating register variation within sociolinguistics,* ed. Douglas Biber and Edward Finegan, 235–76. Oxford, UK: Oxford University Press.

Sacks, Harvey. 1992. *Lectures on conversation,* vols. 1 and 2, ed. Gail Jefferson. Oxford, UK: Blackwell.

Satyanath, Shobha. 1991. Variation and change in the use of (daz) in urban Guyana. PhD diss., University of Pennsylvania.

Smitherman, Geneva, ed. 1981. *Black English and the education of black children and youth. Proceedings of the National Invitational Symposium on the KING decision.* Detroit: Center for Black Studies, Wayne State University.

Spears, Arthur. 1982. The Black English semi-auxiliary come. *Language* 58:850–72.

Weldon, Tracey 1994. Variability in negation in African American Vernacular English. *Language Variation and Change* 6:359–97.

Winford, Donald. 1993. Variability in the use of perfect have in Trinidadian English: A problem of categorical and semantic mismatch. *Language Variation and Change* 5:141–87.

Wolfram, Walt. 1969. *A sociolinguistic description of Detroit Negro speech.* Arlington, VA: Center for Applied Linguistics.

Wolfram, Walt, Erik Thomas, and Elaine Green. 2000. The regional context of earlier African American Speech: Reconstructing the development of African American Vernacular English. *Language in Society* 29:315–55.